CREATING

Fiction

CREATING

Fiction

Instruction and Insights

From Teachers of the

Associated Writing Programs

EDITED BY JULIE CHECKOWAY

STORY PRESS
CINCINNATI, OHIO

Creating Fiction. Copyright © 1999 by the Associated Writing Programs. Manufactured in the United States of America. All rights reserved. No part of this book may be reproduced in any form or by any electronic or mechanical means including information storage and retrieval systems without permission in writing from the publisher, except by a reviewer, who may quote brief passages in a review. Published by Story Press, an imprint of F&W Publications, Inc., 1507 Dana Avenue, Cincinnati, Ohio 45207. (800) 289-0963. First paperback edition 2001.

Other fine Story Press books are available from your local bookstore or direct from the publisher.

05   04   03   02   5   4   3   2

Library of Congress has catalogued hardcover edition as follows:

Creating fiction : instruction and insights from the teachers of Associated Writing
   Programs / edited by Julie Checkoway.
        p.   cm.
      Includes index.
      ISBN 1-884910-40-8 (hardcover)
      1. Fiction—Authorship. I. Checkoway, Julie. II. Associated Writing Programs.
PN3355.C73   1999
808.3—dc21   98-54596
ISBN 1-884910-51-3 (pbk. : alk. paper)
                                                                          CIP

Designed by Clare Finney
Front cover photo © Takeshi Nagao/Photonica

ACKNOWLEDGMENTS

When the idea for this book first arose, I had some idea that it was going to be an enormous undertaking to ringlead a group of talented but disparate and maverick writers into putting together a book that formed a cohesive, if mosaic, whole, but over the past year and a half I've been surprised again and again by the cooperation and generosity of those who've contributed. In addition to writing well and on time, all of the writers have donated the fruits of their efforts for no compensation at all, making it possible for proceeds from this book to go directly to the Associated Writing Programs to fund better services for writers at a time when public funding for the arts has all but disappeared. My thanks to all of them.

Particular thanks goes to Richard Russo, John Barth, Jane Smiley, George Garrett, and Charles Johnson, who signed on early and lent their good names and reputations to a project that Story Press and other writers couldn't pass up being a part of. I'm also deeply grateful to the people at Story Press, editor-in-chief Lois Rosenthal and editor Jack Heffron. My gratitude to the board of directors and the hard-working staff of the Associated Writing Programs—particularly to my predecessor Philip Gerard, whose initial queries to Story made the relationship between the AWP and F&W Publications possible—and to AWP's tireless executive director, D.W. Fenza, whose vision of what the AWP should and can be—a useful service to writers *and* the site of great intellectual ferment—is the guiding force behind this book. Finally, thanks to my undergraduate and graduate students at the University of Georgia, many of whom read and responded to drafts of these essays, and last but never least to Lee Thomsen, whose patented, good-natured, nurturing "husband test" always makes it possible for me to know whether what I've written is any good.

—*Julie Checkoway*

CONTENTS

INTRODUCTION

The romantic notion that good writing is developed only in a kind of tortured isolation has enjoyed some popularity through the ages. True, the *act* of writing—when individual talent confronts the material of the world—is necessarily practiced in solitude, but *being a writer* need not be as difficult or as lonely as writing itself, particularly when the good company of other writers is so proximate and so possible.

The Associated Writing Programs, a nonprofit organization which today includes nearly 300 creative writing programs, writers conferences, and festivals, and 16,000 writers, teachers, students, editors, and publishers, was founded in 1967 on the principle that, while writers must eventually retreat to their own garrets, they can take with them into their solitude the bounty of what they have learned about writing from others.

This book grew out of the reality that writing has been taught well in creative writing programs across this country for more than a generation. At Duke University, William Blackburn taught William Styron and Reynolds Price. Price, in turn, taught the novelists Josephine Humphries and Anne Tyler. At the University of California, Irvine, E.L. Doctorow taught Richard Ford. At Syracuse University, Donald Dike taught Joyce Carol Oates and she, in turn, now teaches undergraduate writers at Princeton. At Stanford, Wallace Stegner taught Robert Stone, Ken Kesey, Raymond Carver, and many others, and at Johns Hopkins, John Barth taught Michael Martone, Ralph Lombreglia, and Louise Erdrich. Today, writing programs are where much of literary life in America takes place.

The contributors to this volume—all of them members of the AWP, all of them accomplished novelists and short story writers—have devoted themselves not only to the production of their own work but to the proposition that teaching others how to write well is a worthwhile way to spend a life. These writers—among them winners of the Pulitzer Prize, the National Book Award, recipients of National Endowment for the Arts fellowships and the famed MacArthur "genius" grant—have staked their reputations on the notions that when it comes to writing, teaching is at least as important as talent, nurture at least as important as nature.

In twenty-three previously unpublished essays specially commissioned by the AWP, these writers share with you what they have shared with their own students over the years: their best-kept secrets about fiction writing. *What gives rise to a story in the first place? Should you write about what you know or what you don't know? What are the advantages and disadvantages of first-person point of view? How do you craft believable dialogue? How do you create and sustain dramatic tension? What is voice anyway? How do you structure a novel or a short story collection? What should you expect when you send your work out to be published?* The idea behind *Creating Fiction* is this: If you never have the chance to study in person with Charles Johnson, George Garrett, Richard Russo, John Barth, Jane Smiley, and the host of talented others who teach in creative writing workshops across this country, what have you been missing? *Creating Fiction* is designed to give writers both inside and outside the academy access to wisdom about the craft of fiction writing that they might otherwise have missed.

The book is not only as a collection of intelligently written and eminently readable essays by the best writers and teachers around but also a practical, instructional guide to craft for fiction writers of all levels. The book is addressed equally to students and teachers, and the essays cover issues around the act of writing as well as everything from plot development to magical realism to the construction of believable characters. Exercises at the end of each chapter direct writers to apply the insights of the chapter to their own work and can be used at home or in the classroom. Forty additional exercises, provided by writers as varied as Bret Lott, Michael Martone, R.A. Sasaki, Joe David Bellamy, and Dinty Moore, appear at the end of the book.

The purpose of *Creating Fiction* is to welcome writers everywhere into the lively, thriving national writing community and to give credence to the belief that finding community with other writers is as necessary and as important as cultivating writerly solitude in a room of one's own. "We do the work alone, as alone as can be," George Garrett writes in these pages. "But there is much we can tell each other and much to be gained by sharing our experiences. We must work together to be ready, one at a time, for the necessary angel to arrive on the scene and the mystery and magic of making to begin."
—*Julie Checkoway*
   President, AWP Board of Directors

I
Thinking About Fiction

Going to See the Elephant: Our Duty as Storytellers

GEORGE GARRETT

There is magic and mystery at the heart of it. Say anything you want about "the creative process," but what is clear and certain is that we don't really understand it. It breaks all the rules as fast as we can make them. Every generalization about it turns out to be at best incomplete or inadequate.

Yet the making, the discovery that becomes the first draft of your story or mine, is what we most want to think about, to talk about, to teach and to learn. We copy the rituals, the ways and means of the masters, hoping somehow to plug into the circuits of their mastery. Did Thornton Wilder sharpen dozens of pencils to begin his day's work? I'll try it. Did Hart Crane play classical music on his record player as he tried to compose *The Bridge*? Why not? Did Ernest Hemingway really stop writing each day only if and when he was absolutely certain what the next sentence would be? Did William Faulkner really write *As I Lay Dying* in six weeks flat, front to back, in longhand on the bottom of an upside-down wheelbarrow and never thereafter change a word? (Well, as we know now, not exactly. A bit of a stretch.) Did Truman Capote write his "dark" books in the wee hours of the night and his more cheerful works in the morning? Maybe that will work for you . . . or me.

Truth is, we don't know what will work for us until we take the breathless plunge, until we follow the original impulse to wherever it tries to take us. "Trust your original impulse," I tell my students. Your muse may fool you and tease you sometimes, lead you on merry chases; but you must nevertheless learn to trust the muse and take the risks. Without that trust and that risk—nothing. Nothing new or worthy or admirable or . . . *true*. With the blessing of the muse (speaking through the language of your original impulse, however vague and inchoate), you can sometimes do wonderful things.

Do you know the story of the first poet in the English language? It's a lovely story told in Bede's *Ecclesiastical History of the English People*, maybe a factually correct story and maybe not, but certainly true in the sense we are talking about. Caedmon was an illiterate cowherd who worked at a monastery. In the evening in the refectory, when the monks and workers sat down to supper, they would pass a stringed instrument, a harp that was a kind of precursor to the guitar, around the table. And everybody would pluck a few chords and sing or recite some verses. And, seeing the harp coming his way, Caedmon would always sneak off, tiptoeing out to the barn where he slept in the hay with the farm animals all around. Caedmon was all thumbs when it came to playing the harp, and he didn't know any verses.

One night he was sound asleep in the barn when an angel appeared out of the cloudy nowhere angels come from and woke him. Caedmon was dazed in humility and awe and fear.

"Caedmon," the angel said. "Sing for me."

As politely as possible, Caedmon reminded the angel of what the supernatural being must already know—that he couldn't sing a note and didn't know any verses and that was why he was here, alone in the barn, while the supper's evening festivities were still going on.

The angel wasn't having any. "Nevertheless you will sing for me."

"What shall I sing?"

"Sing me the story of the Creation."

And, as if by miracle, words came into Caedmon's head and he sang (or recited) a little poem about the creation of the world. Look it up sometime, the earliest known poem in the English language, therefore the earliest official poet in the English language.

The elements of the story are worth mentioning. The key, the trigger (see Debra Spark's essay for more on triggers), the source, of course, was the angel. No angel and no poem. Is that the same angel that Wallace Stevens had in mind (among many other things) when he called his book of essays about the art of poetry *The Necessary Angel*? Note that the first poem in our language, brief as it is, told a story. Storytellers are poets, also, even if they, mostly, don't tell their stories in verse. Bede tells us that Caedmon became a poet. The intellectual monks read him the Bible and other books, and he turned what he had learned from them and from his life into poetry (something none of them could do). Bede tells us Caedmon had a long life and a good one and died quietly.

We have to learn to wait for the angel to come to us. We have to be ready. The readiness is all. We have to believe in the magic and the mystery.

THE SHARED ADVENTURE OF CLASSES
AND WORKSHOPS

Classes and workshops can't teach us much about the mysteries of inspiration, only some of the ancient exercises and rituals that worked for others. The teacher is supposed to know them and to pass them on. But beyond that, once you have felt an undeniable impulse and made your first draft, be it ever so sketchy and clumsy, beyond the vision, then, we can share with each other, teach and learn some of the many kinds of revision that can allow an original vision to arrive at its full power and glory and clarity. The special thing about creative writing classes and workshops is that we're all in this together, students and teachers; we're all in the same boat. And that is the great pleasure of it for the teacher, for what I've been doing since my first teaching job in 1956. There are plenty of things to pass along, plain practical matters and personal experiences, the very things this book of essays is all about. But the teacher and the student are equally focused on the same problems, and there are no permanent answers. Nothing is unbreakable bronze or stone. Everything, the world, is up for grabs. I think this is what some of the great teachers of creative writing really mean when they say (as they do), "I love teaching. It keeps me young." The great poet William Butler Yeats put it another way: "I now can but share with a friend my thoughts and emotions, and there is a continual discovery of difference, but in those days, before I had found myself, we could share adventures." A good workshop is a shared adventure.

ELEPHANTS AND OUR DUTIES AS STORYTELLERS

I once met a man who had spent some years living with and among the Pygmies in what is now Uganda. They are a fascinating people who have managed to survive in a very hostile environment and under most difficult circumstances. They have a complex language, a *click* language mastered and known by only a very few people outside their group. The man I met had never fully mastered their language, but he could talk and listen. So I asked him, "What kinds of things do they talk about?"

"The usual things," he shrugged.

Myself, persistent: "Anything unusual? Special?"

"Well, yes," he said. "There is one thing I ought to mention." And he went on to tell me that from early childhood to old age, Pygmies are uniformly comedians, stand-up comics. They tell great jokes. They tell jokes about everything. It's possible, who knows, that he, the expert, was having a little joke at my expense. For sure, he couldn't remember any Pygmy jokes to tell me. But I like to believe, until proved otherwise, that he spoke the factual truth, that these people, living their lives far from the sound and fury of the rest of the world, deep in the camouflage and secrecy of a great rain forest, have come to terms with the absurdity of the human condition, which they fully share, by becoming a race of jokers, stand-up storytellers for whom laughter is the truly appropriate response to what the world has to offer them or to take away. (See David Bouchier's essay for more on humor writing.) Sometimes I allow myself to imagine that, come the apocalypse we still half-expect to arrive at any time, the Pygmies alone will survive to begin the human race all over again. Our proper elegy and requiem will turn out to be a joke in a *click* language.

We should be so lucky.

Meanwhile, though, I am thinking of the Pygmies as an emblem of us and for us, of our art and craft as storytellers. Years ago I saw a documentary film about the Pygmies. One of the things the film showed was a hunting party that had managed to kill an elephant, thus bringing home enough meat to last them for a long time. The occasion called for a feast, where there was a reenactment of the hunt. What was wonderful about this reenactment, something that confirmed the story the expert had told me, was that the hunters, now as actors playing themselves, introduced a good deal of comedy into the story. For the Pygmies, armed with spears and blowguns, an elephant is a formidable and dangerous prey. Most of the time the elephant wins at the expense of any number of hunters. And this particular time had evidently been a close call. The hunter-players showed that clearly enough, but through comedy. The imaginary elephant would lunge at them, and, to the laughter and amusement of the audience, hunters would throw away their weapons and hightail it to safety. The hunters were all heroes, but in performing the story they seemed to enjoy showing that at least some of them were heroes in spite of themselves. Perhaps if the hunt had ended in failure, the documentary would have shown us a Pygmy tragedy (if such a thing exists). But since the hunt went well (only one man had been slightly injured, and he played his part to laughter by exaggerating his injuries), it was an all's-well-that-ends-well comedy.

At the moment, sharing the double experience, the hunt and the reenactment with them, I understood something about our duty and function as storytellers. It is up to us to tell the story of the hunt (event, experience, quest) as honestly and as accurately as possible, thus to call up and to appeal to the emotions of our audience (one reader at a time). Whether the audience is moved to laughter or tears depends on how it came to pass, in success or in failure. That is our currency as hunter-players, the universal coinage of laughter and tears.

Seeing this film about the Pygmies I was reminded of something the novelist and historian Shelby Foote once told me. He said that, in the Civil War, veterans used to tell green recruits who were going into battle for the first time that they were "going to see the elephant." Bear in mind that few, if any, of these farm boys from the North and the South could have ever seen a living elephant in fact or in the flesh. The great traveling circuses came later in the century. It was a bad joke, whether any recruits believed it briefly or not. But it had a deep truth. Ever since Homer, storytellers trying to tell war stories have justly complained that the experience of combat is unimaginable to those who have not experienced it and thus, finally, no matter how accurately rendered, indescribable, incommunicable. Writing about the battles in Western Europe in November and December of 1944, Stephen E. Ambrose (in *Citizen Soldiers*) adds the stipulation that the experience of combat cannot be prepared for.

> Every rifle company coming on the line that November had a similar experience and drew the same conclusion: there was no way training could prepare a man for combat. Combat could only be experienced, not played at. Training was critical to getting the men into physical condition, to obey orders, to use their weapons, to work efficiently with hand signals and radios, and more. It could not teach men how to lie helpless under a shower of shrapnel in a field crisscrossed by machine-gun fire. They just

had to do it, and in doing it they joined a unique group of men
who have experienced what the rest of us cannot imagine.

Thus the Civil War metaphor—"going to see the elephant." You
are about to be introduced to something previously unimagined and
unimaginable. The experience will change you forever.

Both of the above elephants, the "real" one from the Pygmy drama,
the imaginary one from the Civil War, have something to do with what
we do, our ancient and honorable task as storytellers. So does the familiar story of the three blind men, each of whom touched and examined
part of an elephant and reported his finding. One touched the body of
the elephant and declared that it was a great wall. Another touched the
trunk and reported that it was a huge snake. The third touched the tail
and called it a piece of rope. All three were, of course, right. An elephant
is, indeed, all these things and more. It all depends—and every storyteller
knows this—on your point of view. And your point of view—Pygmy,
Civil War soldier, blind man—is always limited.

May I add one more brief, mildly irrelevant, personal elephant anecdote about which I can at least claim that it is true and it really happened to me?

Once when I was teaching at Bennington College in Vermont, I
received an invitation secondhand from the college telephone opera-
tor. She told me that the poet and professor at Brown University,
Michael Harper, had called and left a message for me, inviting me
to come to Brown and participate in an elephant festival there. I
prepared for the event by going to the library and reading up on
elephants and even learning a few elephant jokes. When I took the
Greyhound bus to Brown, I felt I was ready to be an active participant
in the festival. When I stepped off the bus, there was Michael Harper
standing by to greet me; and standing with him, smiling a welcome
was our mutual old friend, Ralph Ellison. *Ellison! Oh my God, it
was an Ellison festival . . . !*

There has got to be a moral for writers somewhere, earned and illus-
trated by that anecdote. Don't depend on secondhand information—
something like that. Somehow I managed to tell all the elephant jokes I
had learned before the weekend was over and done with (*waste not,
want not*). Other people must have thought I was obsessed with the
subject. I never asked.

A FEW GENERAL BELIEFS ABOUT WRITING

If we elders, veterans who have been to see the real-and-imaginary elephant, can't tell you much about the mystery and the magic, the secret initial (first draft) process of storytelling, what can we honestly and honorably tell you?

One of the first things I tell my students is a word or two about the literary past—how to live with it and how to use it. First of all, the past is simultaneous. That is, for the writer (for yourself as a writer, not as critic or reader), our literary past, our literary history, is not strictly chronological or evolutionary. Forms change and fashions come and go; habits are acquired and then are played out. But, for us writers, Homer and Virgil, Dante and Shakespeare and Hemingway are simultaneously past and can be, here and now, equally influential. They all have some lessons to teach us. Secondly, there is the related problem that none of us knows enough about our literary past or, indeed, about our time, the literary present. None of us, not you and not I, reads as much and knows as much as we ought to. I do not mean the weight of knowledge that could, if allowed, stifle or even silence us. Not by any means. Our studying, our reading of the past and the present, of the great ghosts and of each other, should liberate us. Unless we are willing to labor to know as much as we possibly can of our literary history and tradition, we are likely to be condemned to reinventing the wheel and the sail. (See Charles Johnson's essay on the literary apprenticeship and Jane Smiley's essay on the relationship of the literary past to the revision process.)

As to the present, in one sense that is even more important. Like it or not, the times they are a-changing all the time. We owe it to ourselves and to whatever gifts and talents we possess to appreciate and to try to understand the best that our contemporaries have already achieved. Judging by myself, and by my students, past and present, I conclude that we are all too often too ignorant for our own good. A primary generalization, then: Unless you love to read and unless you read as much as you are able to, frivolously as well as wisely and well, you will not amount to much as a writer.

It is the burden of all of us, here and now, to know (as best we can) what we are up to. *We have to be more self-conscious than we usually are.* I do not mean to encourage this kind of sophistication and self-consciousness in the process and act of creation, the first searching draft and vision. Remember (as I said before) that after vision comes revision. You need to feel that during revision you can fix anything, change things to suit yourself. Revision is really what we are talking about in all of our classes and workshops.

A general word or two about what we try to do in revision. We always try to tell the truth, but we deal with the ways and means of seeming. No good story is really inevitable, first word to last. It only seems to be so, and that seeming comes from your skill and your authority. Use your authority to make your story seem absolutely inevitable even though you are fully aware that what it is is a sequence of choices and compromises powered by an original impulse. Be true to that impulse. But also, in revision, be as sly, cunning, crafty as you need to be.

TWO GENERAL TRUTHS ABOUT CRAFT

And now a couple of practical suggestions about the craft of storytelling, truths that I came to realize slowly, the hard way. Therefore, I am eager to share them, obvious as they may well be.

Suspense and Engagement

The fuel of all good narrative is suspense. The goal is forward motion. (See John Barth's essay for more on plotting.) Coaches tell runners not to look back, because in a race you can lose a full step and more and break your running rhythm by trying to peek over your shoulder. A story is a run for it, a race without any serious interruption. Suspense is not merely a matter of what happens next; it is also a series of tantalizing questions. And it is not only a conflict between the ways of showing and the habits of telling. *Of course* we always want to dramatize as much as possible, to let the reader, engaged in the flow of imagined experience that is narrative, infer and discover. But we also have to find expeditious ways to *tell*. Show what you can and have to and tell what you must, but do so, in both cases, with suspense in mind. Let the reader hurry along to keep up with you. Don't tell any more than you have to, and don't tell anything until you have to. Exposition is the area of craft where beginners and amateurs, even gifted ones, are most likely to stumble. (See Julie Checkoway's essay for more on suspense and seduction.)

A little general rule worth considering is that when the story, by plot or the nature of its material, has built-in suspense, the less you have to impose suspense on it. And (maybe more important) vice versa.

If your story does not have a whole lot of inherent suspense, you can tell it the way the comics do when they tell a shaggy dog story: Divert attention with details.

All of the above suggestions add up to the real necessity, at some point, of discovering and knowing the essential nature of your story. It is urgently important that you should know the kinds of feelings your story will summon up from a receptive and sympathetic reader. You must be that reader even as you write.

If suspense is the fuel that all narrative runs on, then repetition and redundancy are the chief causes of breakdown. Make a point, only one time if that is possible, then move on to the next one. Don't repeat yourself if you can help it. If you discover, while rereading and revising, that you have made the same point more than once, this usually indicates you haven't yet found the place where the point belongs.

Writing is an art as well as a craft. What defines any art is that it is, first and foremost, a sensuous, affective experience. This means that what happens between you and your reader is the evocation and engagement of the senses. That engagement is just as important, maybe more so, as the details of plot, action, character, structure. You must first of all convince your reader that your story, whether it pretends to be "real" or professes to be the purest fantasy, is sensuously perceptive. Use all five senses as early and as often as possible. Somehow this sensory sleight of hand becomes part of the magic spell that makes everything else work.

Surprise

Another soapbox I like to stand on: Once you understand the story you are telling and what it seems to be about, try to go against the grain of it, in revision, as much as you can. For example, give a "bad" character some "good" traits. Similarly, give the good guys some bad habits. This won't change your story, or the point of it, but it will give your characters more dimension and complexity. (See Robin Hemley's essay for more on unsympathetic characters.)

Your greatest, deepest choice as a storyteller, once you understand your story, is whether or not to go with the grain of it, to follow the expectations that the subject raises or to take the reader in another direction—the direction John Keats advocated when he said that poetry should surprise us with a "fine excess." Surprise is almost as important as suspense in storytelling. You must recognize that, as an artist, your chief enemy is the easy stereotype. Any stereotype. To create something new and worthwhile, to surprise by "a fine excess," question all stereotypes, good ones and bad ones, and the shadow assumptions behind them. Turn the full force of your own doubts and skepticism against the commonplace assumptions of your age and most especially against your own personal certainties and assumptions.

DANGER AND DARING

It is, to be sure, a gamble, a real risk every time. Go back to those Pygmy hunters for a moment. When the meat runs out, they must go hunting, risking life and limb, again and again. And then, for the sake of their fellows and their tribe, they have to reenact the experience of the hunt. That is what we do, too. As storytellers we are reenactors. We are called to an ancient and honorable enterprise, at least as old and probably older than the paintings on the walls of caves where our ancestors (of all shapes and sizes and colors) painted pictures to illustrate their stories and rituals. Learn your craft, by any and all means, I tell the students in workshop. Then practice it with all the art and magic you can muster. Be worthy of your vocation, which is, after all is said and done, truly a career of danger and daring.

All that we can do, day by day, is share with each other, here and in the variety of essays that follow this one, some bits and pieces, fragments of guidance and understanding that we have managed to acquire. We do the work alone, as alone as can be. ("Nobody else can take a bath for you," as the existentialists used to say.) But there is much that we can tell each other and much to be gained by sharing our experiences. We must work together to be ready, one at a time, for the necessary angel to arrive on the scene and the mystery and magic of making to begin.

EXERCISES

1. Point of view: Choose a famous story or novel, and describe what happens when you tell it from a different point of view. For example, what happens to *Moby Dick* when you tell it from the point of view of the whale? ("Who *are* those guys?")

2. Characterization: It is said that Adolf Hitler, one of history's truly evil beings, loved music, including popular music by people like Cole Porter, and that he was a wonderful whistler. Pick a wicked figure (past or present), and try to find or create some sympathetic talent or good habit. What happens? By the same token, give some saint a bad habit.

3. Style, tone, and all of the above: Male or female, you have been offered a whole lot of money to pose in the nude for a popular magazine. You want that money and the fifteen minutes of fame or notoriety. Write four letters, one each to (1) the magazine, accepting the offer; (2) your girlfriend/boyfriend/spouse; (3) your parents; (4) your minister, priest, or rabbi. Explain, as best you can, why you are doing this. When you finish, notice how different you sound in each of the letters. Which one, if any, is the real you?

George Garrett is the author of twenty-eight books (poetry, fiction, biography, essays, and criticism) and editor or coeditor of nineteen others. One of the founders of the Associated Writing Programs in the 1960s, he has served as president of AWP and has edited five volumes of *Intro*. He teaches at the University of Virginia.

The Trigger:
What Gives Rise to a Story?

DEBRA SPARK

H ere is my mother, in the early seventies, with a group of Camp Fire Girls in Boston's Museum of Science. She is in a darkened (probably womblike) room with photographic displays of a developing fetus. As my mother tells it, and she does, often, in the years to come, the Camp Fire Girls are like so many kid ducks, waddling from photo to photo as she narrates the story of how babies are made. Other children, attracted by the explanation, wander over. An army of baby ducks! What my mother doesn't say, but what I remember, is that I am the laggard duck, ready to leave the exhibit. *The Miracle of Life*, I'm thinking. *Yeah, yeah.* Unlike the other girls, I've heard it all before. My mother is not uptight about the facts of life. For me, the cafeteria French fries, perfectly crisp and greasy, are the museum's greatest mystery. I'm wishing it were lunch. But we're still only three months into the wonder that is birth.

"Okay," Terry says, finally. She is my across-the-street neighbor whom I envy for years, for her early use of lipstick, her familiarity with boys and cigarettes. But today she is just a little girl. "Okay," she says again to my mother, "but what I still don't get, is how does the sperm get to the egg?"

Expectant faces. The Camp Fire Girls are now a different sort of baby bird. They are nestlings, necks craned upward, ready for a final worm of knowledge to be dropped into their open beaks. "Yeah," they might be chirping, "what about that?"

"Okay," my mother says, brightly, "Okay, everybody! Lunch!"

There is, after all, the moment of conception, and then there's the moment of conception, which no one wants to *explain*, good God, especially to children.

And so . . . with writing and the simple, yet hopelessly awkward question of where things start. Simple because there's an easy enough answer to, Where did *that* come from? And the answer is: Oh, an anecdote I heard, an image that came to me, a crazy article I started (but didn't really finish) in the newspaper. And hard because that's not the full story. It leaves out what my mother left out, and I don't mean the mechanics of sex but the whole messy issue of attraction.

FINDING THE TRIGGER

My habit, when writing about writing, is to proceed by a sort of benign plagiarism. I take the question at hand—in today's case "The Trigger: What Gives Rise to a Story?"—and get on the horn with my writer friends, make *them* answer. Once I've found a way to embroider their quotes together, I have my essay. Only when I pose the "What Gives Rise" question, half my friends answer with irritable "I dunno"'s. And who can blame them? Talking about the origin of a story is a bit like talking about the origin of a successful relationship. It only makes narrative sense in hindsight. ("At first, I thought he was such a jerk, but then . . .") Ideas for stories, until they prove themselves, are just another bad date, another fruitless notion flitting through the brain. ("At first, I thought nothing of the idea. The truth was . . .")

And there are other reasons we hesitate to talk about story origins. One is that it's not like talking about, say, point of view. It isn't an issue only of craft but of psychology. Ours. And we may want to keep that hidden. What's more, such talk seems presumptuous. Sure, John Updike can do it, but the rest of us—baby writers, all of us, we're all always baby writers—may feel like we're assuming too much when we talk about our process. We're assuming we're real writers, and as soon as we do that, we're bound to be punished for hubris. The punishment, naturally enough, will be that it will be taken away: Inspiration will flee. Permanently.

I went back to my old high school recently to sit on a panel with other writers. We were asked to talk about narrative, our individual narrative processes. I had a fuzzy hold on what this meant. I kept thinking, "My narrative process? You mean, how *I* became a story?" Then the youngest among us confessed that the question discomfited her, for she feared introspection would ruin everything, destroy the magic. And I thought, "Yes, *that's* why I can't make myself understand the question: because I don't want to answer."

Just because I don't want to tell, though, doesn't mean I don't want to hear. I'd have abandoned all thoughts of French fries if I thought my mother was going to answer Terry's question. The truth is: I *like* hearing how people got their story ideas, just as I like hearing about how people met. The same properties of attraction and repulsion, interest and doubt, seem to be at play. Then, there are the wrong turns and misperceptions along the path from there to *here*—here being the point at which the tale is finished, and the story of the story has its own narrative.

Not that this knowledge helps me, exactly, when I sit down to write. After all, anything can occasion a story: an overheard conversation, image, sentence, family story or book. Triggers are ubiquitous. They're also idiosyncratic; one person's method is never going to instruct another in how to go about "finding" a trigger.

Still, triggers have some common characteristics—not in content so much as form. And we can learn something by looking at these shared traits. Perhaps we can even discover markers that will give us a sense of whether our own seeds have the potential to grow and blossom.

TRIGGERS GIVE RISE TO QUESTIONS

John Fowles's *The French Lieutenant's Woman* started with a visual image: a woman standing at the end of a quay and staring out to sea. "That was all," Fowles writes in "Notes on an Unfinished Novel." "This image rose in my mind one morning when I was still in bed half asleep. It corresponded to no actual incident in my life (or in art) that I can recall." According to Henry James, Ivan Turgenev's fiction started with "the vision of some person or persons, who hovered before him, soliciting him." These were characters whom Turgenev imagined fully, in all their existential complexity. Similarly, Joan Didion's *Play It As It Lays* began with a "picture in the mind," an image of a woman in a white halter dress, walking across a Las Vegas casino to pick up a house phone. "Who is paging her?" Didion wonders aloud in her famous essay "Why I Write." "Why is she here to be paged? How exactly did she come to this?" Unlike Fowles's image, Didion's came from "real" life. One day, while sitting in a casino, Didion saw a vaguely familiar woman paged to a phone. Didion explains that "it was precisely this moment in Las Vegas that made *Play It As It Lays* begin to tell itself to me."

But plenty of curious images, real or imagined, don't trigger stories. Some good material becomes . . . nothing. For instance: Yesterday, my husband, two friends, and I walked by a deer's head in the bed of a pickup. The head was unmounted, severed from its body, staring pointlessly up at the sky. Last week, I had lunch with a friend, and the squirming legs of the ladybug she found in her salad looked like an animated false eyelash. I don't feel inclined to embroider these images with anything more than a simile.

But these two friends from yesterday—one is an old friend of my husband's, the other is the friend's lover of two years. They both have AIDS. The lover has a rather florid face. I don't know why he's so red: Perhaps it's just his complexion or maybe the drugs he's taking. His wife died four years ago; he'd infected her with the virus. Sometimes I think the red of his face is a form of combustion: He's aflame with grief and guilt. Both emotions—he doesn't need to say it; it's too clear—are consuming him. I wonder, I can't stop wondering, how it all worked out. The marriage, I mean. Was he always openly gay? Did they have an agreement? They were together for thirty years and had two children, whom he still sees on a weekly basis. Do they blame him for their mother's death? Or are they touched, as I am, by how the man speaks of how much he misses her? He mentions that in the end a Kaposi's sarcoma grew over her eye, so she couldn't quite open the lid. But I wait for him to volunteer all this. I don't ask much.

What I do ask is, "How did you become a graphic designer?"

His lover says, "Watch out. She's a writer, anything you tell her might go into a story."

The dirt on how he chose a profession? No. Though I *can* see plundering his life for fiction. I'd have only to answer the questions I'll never ask. So a generalization that *might* help: Triggers give rise to questions. They're triggers *because* they're incomplete, *because* they require elaboration. The red of that man's face leads me to the heart of what I most wonder about his marriage, and since I won't ask, it leads me to a mystery that only my imagination can resolve.

Melanie Rae Thon says that her story "Punishment" sprang from "a double mystery." While reading an article about slavery, Thon came across a line about a woman hanged for the murder of her master's son. Thon first wanted to know what the article didn't say: if the woman did it. Once Thon had pursued the fictional version of the slave's life long enough to realize she *had*, Thon wanted to know *why*. The answer seems easy to me. I'd say "hateful repression" and leave it at that. What's incomplete for one person isn't necessarily incomplete for another. Which is why the anecdote is a trigger for Thon and not for me. On hearing the basic facts, I don't ask a question. Of course, this doesn't mean I wouldn't want to read Thon's story, just that I don't have the curiosity necessary to write it.

FREEDOM FROM REALITY

Most people who have tried to write—and shared the fact, if not the product, of their efforts with others—have at one time had an acquaintance lean over a dinner table and confide, "Oh, I have a great story idea for you." This happened to me just last night. I was with a group of friends, most of them young Ph.D.s, talking about the academic job market. One friend—a hip, super-smart English professor, given to saying things like "Man, Thomas Hardy rocks my world"—encouraged another, a French instructor, about her job prospects: "You've got great publications, you've been teaching in a good school, and now you're going to run an overseas program." The French instructor smiled dismissively, in the way of those uneasy about receiving compliments. "I should be your agent," the English professor added.

"It's going to happen soon," the French instructor enthused, "agents for Ph.D.s!"

The English professor turned to me, "Debra, this is a *great* idea for a novel. This would make a *great* farce."

She wasn't truly serious, and it's just as well, for these ideas are invariably *not* great. Packaged up, unmysterious, they begin and end life as a dinner anecdote, unable to grow into fiction, because the work of comprehending the funny, queer, horrible, or touching moment has already been done by the teller.

Joyce Carol Oates's disturbing story "Where Are You Going, Where Have You Been?" was inspired by an article about a serial murderer named The Pied Piper of Tucson. When Oates's story became the movie *Smooth Talk*, she published a short essay in which she recalled purposely not reading the full account of the Pied Piper, since she didn't want to be "distracted by too much detail." Now, obviously, we need to have a decent grasp on the world to write well. At the same time, reality—at least at the moment of germination—*can* hamper the imagination. Presumably this realization is behind Virginia Woolf's claim that, for the writer, "There must be great freedom from reality."

People sometimes say that the problem with writing from life, with using autobiographical material, is the instinct for veracity; we can't stop ourselves from being true to the experience, even when that sort of truth is no good for the story. The problem may actually be that a true story provides too much material; it doesn't leave enough out. Henry James held this to be so. "Such," he wrote, "is the interesting truth about the stray suggestion, the wandering word, the vague echo, at touch of which the novelist's imagination winces as at the prick of some sharp point: its virtue is all in its needle-like quality, the power to penetrate as finely as possible." Anything more than this, and the effect is ruined, and if the suggestion is offered "designedly," as James puts it, "one is sure to be given too much."

SELECTING FROM THE CLATTER

In "Making Up Stories," Joan Didion reveals that Joseph Heller's most famous novel began as a line so mysterious that it had, like an algebra equation, an "X" for which the author needed to solve.

> Joseph Heller described the conception of *Catch-22* this way: "I was lying in bed when suddenly this line came to me: 'It was love at first sight. The first time he saw the chaplain X fell madly in love with him.'" The "X" turned out to be Yossarain, but Heller didn't have the name, didn't even know that this "X" was in the Army. "The chaplain wasn't necessarily an army chaplain," he said. "He could have been a prison chaplain. I don't understand the process of imagination though I know that I am very much at its mercy. The ideas come to me in the course of a controlled daydream, a directed reverie."

In her journal, George Eliot—just starting to write fiction and concerned about her ability to move beyond "mere" description to dramatic narrative—recalls, "One morning as I was thinking what should be the subject of my first story, my thoughts merged themselves into a dreamy doze, and I imagined myself writing a story, of which the title was 'The Sad Fortunes of the Reverend Amos Barton.' "

This notion of controlled daydream, directed reverie, or a waking doze is behind the "guided imagery" exercises that I sometimes use in my fiction-writing classes. Novelist Janet Beeler Shaw first introduced me to this technique. She learned it, in turn, from instructors at Illinois's Columbia College who rely heavily on this method. In one variation, a teacher asks students to close their eyes and imagine they're standing on the top stair to a basement they know well. Slowly, she guides them down the staircase, asking them, eventually, to open their eyes and say what they "see" in the basement. After everyone has answered, the teacher instructs the students to close their eyes and imagine descending the stairs again. This time, she tells them to picture a person in the room, a person doing something, and when they next open their eyes, she has them write, fast as they can, about what they see.

The exercise has endless permutations: A teacher asks students to imagine a long drive to an unfamiliar place, then to describe the first thing they see when they step out of the car; a teacher asks students to imagine themselves in a place of great darkness, then to describe the first light thing that strikes them; and so on.

What surprises me, each time I do these exercises, is the strength of the written responses and how favorably they compare to the pieces on which students spend time, the "at home" assignments.

The pedagogic notion of "guided imagery" is linked to what Joan Didion describes as the essential act of writing: "the process of thinking, of plugging into that electrical field of image and making an object out of the flash and the clatter."

And how do you plug in? How do you open yourself to worthwhile material and then select from it?

First, the clatter. It's not always easy to see, to be, as Henry James says, "one of the people on whom nothing is lost!" In fact, it may be harder for us than it was for our predecessors. There's more clatter around. Or so it seems: an MTV world, ready to assault us, even as we devise ways to retreat.

And for young people, media garbage may be the biggest obstacle to writing truly. At the small Maine college where I teach, I have a student whose life has been nothing short of astounding. He is cheerful, energetic, gay, born-again Christian, and black. His mother was an addict. I believe she beat him. A few years ago, in the Midwestern city he still calls home, his twin brother was murdered, on his way home from a card game. At first, whenever this student wrote for me, he wrote soap operas: Danielle Steel fantasies of treachery and big business, luxurious cars and perfectly attractive women.

"What do you do," people sometimes ask me, "with a student like that?" But it is only too obvious. I say: Tell your own story. This young man did, but only once, when he wrote about his brother, and then the story turned on the author's singing voice, a tenor which people tell me is achingly lovely.

I had this student in three consecutive classes. He wasn't shy about his life, and eventually his stories played themselves out in clubs or shared apartments or at drag pageants, but they retained that sense of a story borrowed from the media, of a tale as yet unmediated by life.

And why? Because the "public," or prevailing, notion of story overwhelmed the private notion. Notions of entertainment got in the way of felt truth. When "guided imagery" exercises work, it's because students are thinking about life instead of art, what they've experienced instead of what they've read or "viewed." For some, this means abandoning the idea of Rambo as fiction, but even sophisticated students let their notions of story overwhelm them.

I had lunch recently with two women whom I'd met at a writing retreat. They're both quite accomplished and intelligent: One is a literature professor, the other a public relations specialist. Over the course of the weekend, both had written wonderful short exercises for me. In talking about why they'd written so little in the months since then, the literature professor said, "Oh, I have plenty of ideas. I just don't know how to make them into stories." The public relations specialist nodded her head: That was exactly *her* problem; she had characters and situations but nothing else. There was a silence, then she said to the professor, "I always remember that exercise *you* wrote, about the woman walking across the street." I smiled. I remembered it, too. It had been a striking piece, about a young woman hurrying across a Paris boulevard to go . . . somewhere. The piece never got that far. "But what am I to do with it?" the professor said. We'd all become friends, so I felt strange playing teacher; still, I felt I should offer something. What I came up with sounded insufficient, obnoxiously breezy, but it was my honest answer: "Just have her go somewhere the next street over, and when she gets there, have something happen."

I think in this regard of Jane Smiley, who said that her short story "Lily" came about when she imagined what would happen if some friends of hers—a couple and a woman who didn't know each other—were to meet. Though I don't know how Smiley composed "Lily," I can guess at her process. She already had her characters, so she didn't need to start with that. Instead, she had to imagine an occasion for bringing the couple and the woman together. The three could have met at a restaurant or on a ship or in an adult ed class, but as Smiley set it up, the couple ended up being guests in the house of a woman named Lily. And, then, of course, there needed to be a reason why the couple was visiting Lily, a reason they knew her, a reason they were coming to say hello; there needed to be a history and a current situation.

To think of all this isn't to think about story so much as character and situation, the very thing that the professor and public relations specialist already knew how to do. To develop their stories, my former students had only to do what Turgenev did with his hovering visions; they had only, in Henry James's words, "to imagine, to invent and select and piece together the situations most useful and favorable to the sense of the creatures themselves, the complications they would be most likely to produce and feel." They had only to do what they were already doing . . . and forget about story.

I'm making it sound easier than it is. Still, there are ways to help oneself. Short story author Patricia Henley asks her students to take long walks before they write. The idea, she says, is to get them in a contemplative mood, to let motion induce thought, to get "junk stories" out of their heads so their own stories can emerge.

Others have less healthy methods of making this happen. There's a reason alcohol is an occupational hazard for writers. It's a way—among ways—to access material. But it's probably less true that drugs "give" one material than that they release inhibitions, allowing (some) writers to ignore the part of themselves that dismisses a trigger before it has a chance to develop. Back to my professor friend: If she had allowed her character to finish crossing the street, and if she had abandoned the question of whether her piece did or did not have a strong narrative, her imagination might have taken care of the rest. The painter Philip Guston once said, "If the artist starts evaluating himself, it's an enormous block, isn't it?" And, of course, it is. At the very least, to "plug into the electrical field of image," one needs to shut one's censor down, to give the creative self a chance.

Of course, "plugging in" is only the first problem. Plugging in may open us to something like Turgenev's "hovering visions," but it leaves us where my professor friend was left: with the problem of selection. Once we've plugged in, what will we pick to address? What will we make happen? In "The Death of Justina," John Cheever writes:

> Fiction is art and art is the triumph over chaos (no less) and we can accomplish this only by the most vigilant exercise of choice, but in a world that changes more swiftly than we can perceive there is always the danger that our powers of selection will be mistaken and that the vision we serve will come to nothing.

This notion of choice has its parallels in the other arts: You choose to paint the peaches and not the landscape. You sculpt the bust and not the torso. You can't do the whole world; you can't do all your perceptions; you have to pick. But what should your criteria for selection be? Cheever complains, directly or obliquely, in almost all the stories in his *Some People, Places, and Things That Will Not Appear in My Next Novel*, about the mutability of values that makes it so hard to decide what we *should* write about. How, he wants to know, would Gogol or Thackeray write about a suburban bomb shelter decorated with composition gnomes?

There's a famous story about Chekhov telling a visitor that one could write a story about anything. "Do you know how I write my stories? Here's how!" He picked up an ashtray lying nearby—presumably it was the first object he saw—then said, "If you want it, you'll have a story tomorrow. It will be called 'The Ashtray.' "

And what, I wonder, would Chekhov do if he were sitting in my chair? The first object he'd see would be a Trophy Treat, a plastic Michael Jordan head filled with gumballs. What's with that? The problem here isn't junk stories borrowed from the media, but junk, the junk of life. In contemporary society, so much that is worthless claims our attention. And then we don't always know how to evaluate what we do see. Perhaps our confusion is the best we can do. Perhaps our confusion will have to be our subject.

TRUSTING THE UNKNOWN

In his essay "Getting Started," John Irving writes, "Here is a useful rule for beginning: Know the story—as much of the story as you can possibly know, if not the whole story—before you commit yourself to the first paragraph." Irving has written far more novels than I. Clearly he knows what works for himself in a way that I don't always for myself, but this seems to me terrible advice. I'm more inclined to E.L. Doctorow's wisdom. He once wrote that writing a novel is like driving at night: You don't need to see the whole road, just the bit of illuminated blacktop before you.

It's true you wouldn't tell a story at a party unless you knew the whole story start to finish. Presumably, only children and hopeless bores say, "Oh, listen to this," and then ramble until something comes to them. But that doesn't mean Irving's advice is good. There are more parallels between party anecdotes and publishing, the final stage of writing, than with the beginning stages of writing. That's why we don't publish our first drafts, why we wait a long time before we say, "Oh, listen to this."

William Faulkner didn't know his whole story before he put pen to paper. "The stories with me," he said in an interview, "begin with an anecdote or a sentence or an expression, and I'll start from there, and sometimes I write the thing backwards—I myself don't know exactly where any story is going."

Even if you decide, with Irving, that you must know the road before you travel, you may not end up where you intended. That's why writers say that writing is discovery. And mean it. And that's why a trigger can be buried in a story or so transformed that no one, save the author, could ever guess at a story's source.

Joan Didion writes that the woman in the white halter dress, the one who inspired *Play It as It Lays*, "appears in the novel, only obliquely, in a chapter which begins: 'Maria made a list of things she would never do. She would never: walk through the Sands or Caesar's alone after midnight. She would never: ball at a party, do S-M unless she wanted to, borrow furs from Ben Lipsey, deal.' "

Another example: When writer Amy Godine's close friend's father came out of the closet, he was vilified in his community. But the daughter, Godine's friend, decided to return home from college to say that *she* accepted who he was. Only, when she returned home, she found two young men smoking pot in front of the living room TV. Instead of embracing her father, Godine's friend sat down and got high with the visitors. Godine says, "I never got over the image of coming home to say, 'Dad, I love you,' and there were these street toughs . . . it was so heartbreaking and funny."

Heartbreaking and funny. Fiction fodder. Godine decided to tell the story as she knew it: from her friend's point of view. But that didn't work. In the end, the story Godine *did* write—"The Gardener," which appeared in *The North American Review*—was told from the point of view of one of the father's lovers, a man who, in fictional garb, became the house gardener.

For both Godine and Didion, the trigger anecdotes (about the friend returning home or the woman walking across the casino) have a point: a certain emotional resonance, about disappointed expectations or dissipated glamour. Both stories, though, ended up lying elsewhere: in the unknown aspects of the anecdote, in the questions that party guests might ask (if they dared) after the telling. "Okay, okay, but what I still don't get . . ."

EXPERIENCE AND INVENTION

If most fiction is a mixture of experience and invention, then one way to trigger a story may be to self-consciously lead yourself to invention through experience. To get her students writing, author Elizabeth Searle asks them to start a page with the words "I remember." She instructs them to write for as long as possible, and when they can think of nothing else to say, they write "I remember" again. Short story writer Lisa Ruffolo has her students do "memory maps." They draw the floor plans of the houses or apartments they grew up in, then put a memory in each room—not a description, but a specific memory of something that took place there. A more sophisticated variant of this is in Pamela Painter and Anne Bernays's helpful book, *What If? Writing Exercises for Fiction Writers*. In "Family Stories, Family Myths," an exercise from Katharine Haake, student writers start by selecting an oft-told family story. Assuming the persona of one of the participants in the story, the student writer composes a letter to another family member, explaining the "truth" of what happened. Then the students trade letters and respond by taking the persona of the addressee of the original letter. (I can almost imagine Eudora Welty's famous story "Why I Live at the P.O." as a response to this assignment.)

The purpose of all these exercises is to help identify what matters to you and, in the process, to stumble across a story idea. Good exercises don't ask you to be clever or go hunting for the meaningful. After all, if you *begin* thinking in terms of what is and isn't important to write about, the "emotionally and intellectually significant" (which, John Gardner held, you *must* address), you'll undoubtedly veer off track. It's probably best to look for triggers in what genuinely interests you . . . and trust the universality of your particular concerns.

F. Scott Fitzgerald used to advise young writers "to sell your heart, your strongest reactions, not the little minor things that only touch you lightly, the little experience that you might tell at dinner." Note: His emphasis isn't on what's important, but what's important to *you*, what attracts or compels *you*. Your problems with food? Your father's death? You could be Jenefer Shute and write *Life-Size* or James Agee and write *A Death in the Family*. You could exploit your anxiety about environmental disaster or your general feelings of failure. (Think of Don DeLillo's *White Noise* or Saul Bellow's *Seize the Day*.)

It needn't be personal history, though. Your "strongest reaction" could come from song lyrics. (One of my favorite student stories was inspired by a Tom Waits line.) It could come from an overheard bit of conversation. (Eavesdropping: a time-honored literary tool.) It could come from a peculiar experience. (Jill McCorkle was just starting a new novel when she happened to dig up a high-top sneaker in her garden. The find unnerved her. *What if*, she thought, *there's a foot attached*? And so, in the novel *Carolina Moon*, a woman gets a delivery of topsoil, and there *is* a body in it.) It could come from a story you heard years ago. (Paging through a worn volume from a secondhand shop, Joseph Conrad stumbled across an anecdote about a silver thief. He'd originally heard the story, decades earlier, when he was sailing in the Gulf of Mexico. The anecdote itself didn't spark his imagination—there was nothing much to it—but the recollection did, for it made him reminisce about his seafaring youth when, as he writes in "Preface to *Nostromo*," "everything was so fresh, so surprising, so venturesome, so interesting; bits of strange coasts under the stars, shadows of hills in the sunshine, men's passions in the dusk, gossip half forgotten, faces grown dim." And all this made him feel that, "Perhaps, perhaps, there still was in the world something to write about.")

And finally, though I've hardly exhausted the alternatives, your strongest reaction could come from a dispiriting outing. What's bad for life, after all, is often good for fiction.

I went once with Lorrie Moore and a group of other fiction writers to the Cave of the Mounds, a rather tacky tourist spot in Wisconsin. We were a group of women that day, either single and unhappily so or toting a boyfriend whom we would dump within the year. There were exceptions. Lorrie may have been an exception. There may have even been a happily married couple along, but my sense of that day—and it may be a projection of my own situation at the time—was of a shameful female irritation that there weren't any good guys around. I don't remember much about the cave, save that the walls were creepily veined, and that the tour guide turned off the lights so we could experience the complete darkness of the cave, and that when the lights were flicked on there was Lorrie, taking notes. *Notes*! I thought. *What could she find here*?

I do remember some other things about the day: some rock-shaped candies that I bought in the gift shop, but mostly the ride home. A doe ran out of the woods and darted up a highway embankment. Two others followed. This seemed strange, seeing so many deer, up close, then I realized: They were terrified. We passed by a suburban house with a deer up in a tree, blood draining onto the front lawn, and everything snapped into place. Orange vests started appearing. It was the first day of hunting season.

Two years later, I opened up *The New Yorker* and read Lorrie Moore's funny, sorrowful story "The Jewish Hunter," which takes place partially at the fictitious Cave of the Many Mounds in Minneapolis. I felt excited, the way one does when one's a party to another's romance or sees a setup working at a dinner. Why, I had been there! Had seen the initial sparks! And I felt something else, too: jealousy. Sure, we'd all met the guy, but only one of us had the skill to fall in love.

EXERCISES

1. Begin a story with the line "I never told this to anybody but . . ." (For a model, read Stuart Dybek's "I Never Told This to Anyone" in Susan Stamberg's anthology *The Wedding Cake in the Middle of the Road: 23 Variations on a Theme.*)

2. Save the next five postcards you receive. Choose the card with the most puzzling image, then tell the story of what's going on in the card. For example, pick the photograph of the woman dressed up as a butterfly over a "Wish You Were Here" card from Hawaii.

3. Tell the story of a large or small act of rebellion that took place in your hometown. (For models, read John Cheever's "The Death of Justina," T. Coraghessan Boyle's "Greasy Lake," or William Maxwell's short novel/memoir, *So Long, See You Tomorrow.*)

Debra Spark is the author of the novel *Coconuts for the Saint*. She teaches at Colby College and Warren Wilson College.

Other Bodies, Ourselves:
The Mask of Fiction

JOHN GREGORY BROWN

Fiction writers are, by their very nature, middle children. They are searchers, doubters, malcontents. They believe themselves somehow abandoned, uncoddled, unloved. They deserve more, understand more, desire more. They are voyeurs, con artists, liars. They are fallen angels, gold-hearted whores. They are confirmed cowards who, when push comes to shove, know their courage will be—*must be*—restored.

I am the fifth of eight children, the quintessential middle child. I possess neither the certainty and ambition and energy of my elder siblings nor the contentment and security and faith of the younger.

A doctor, two lawyers, a college basketball coach, a financial advisor, a public policy specialist, a social worker. By the remarkable ardor and skill of my seven siblings, broken bones are repaired, disputes are resolved, life savings are secured, young men are steered toward excellence, the poor are offered a measure of solace.

And then there's me, the misfit, the metaphorical orphan, the searcher, the doubter, the malcontent. A writer.

And not merely a writer—a writer of fiction, one whose days are measured solely by the marks left on the page. But what exactly is the significance of the fiction writer's *mark*, of the scribbled or typed or word-processed lines that spiral down the page with the simplest, most ancient of goals: to tell a story, to fabricate a tale, to pretend that what *is not* has been, to burnish the false until it bears the priceless luster of truth?

The fiction writer's aim, of course, is not merely fabrication; it is fabrication whose aim is to enlighten, to lay bare the soul and spirit, to declare the supple and subtle complexities of our existence. It is as bloody an enterprise as the anatomist's, as darkly mysterious as the monastic's.

And if it's done well, it's as tricky an endeavor as the pickpocket's, for every writer of fiction must be, first and foremost, a liar—a liar with a noble aim, of course, but a liar nonetheless. And the aim of the liar, his one true guiding light, is deception.

SECRETS AND LIES

In my novels, a father steals his children from their stepmother, the world's longest bridge collapses, a black child is left on the doorstep of a wealthy white family, a child falls from a tree and is crippled and orphaned, a man pretends to be a blind artist to acquire tourists' spare change.

All lies, of course—the typical stuff from the fiction writer's bag. And with only a few exceptions, all the characters who appear in my books and all the events that transpire are utterly and completely invented. They are out-and-out lies.

And yet for all the lies I've now told in my work, an awful suspicion has been growing within me that I am giving away more secrets than I ever intended. And the more outrageous my lies, the more I seem to reveal. Though there's hardly a lick of true autobiography in my work, I somehow seem to have painted as complete and revealing a portrait of my life as I could ever hope to divulge—more honest and complete, frankly, than I'm comfortable having divulged.

The conventional notion of autobiographical fiction, of course, is of a work where the author exploits the characters and events of his own life, where the story he tells is, in essence, his own life's story or some portion thereof—the characters and circumstances perhaps altered somewhat from the truth but only enough to keep the story rolling along, to keep it interesting, or to invoke with some measure of clarity the author's message.

But I'd like to explore here a different notion of autobiographical fiction, one that I've come to a bit reluctantly, somewhat hesitantly, but one that has been of invaluable guidance as I sort out the worth of my own work, the value to me of all those marks I've left on the page— and the far greater value of all those other marks that other fiction writers have left, the marks that have guided me through my life.

My fiction is, of course, flawed. There are sentences and paragraphs and scenes I'd like to take back. One day, I suspect, there will be entire novels about which I'll feel the same. But it's no small thing, I've learned, for a writer to figure out why he does what he does. It is, in fact, a moment of pure grace.

WRITING BLIND

Usually, when I am preparing to read to an audience an excerpt from one of my books, I say a few words about what I was trying to accomplish, what themes the book addresses, why I set about telling such a story in a particular way. What I don't say is that I was two-thirds of the way through writing these books before I had a clue what was going on, before I figured out this information that I so confidently and wisely declare has been my grand aim all along. Prior to my discovery of what the hell I'm up to, I write the way one walks through a dark and unfamiliar hallway or alley—blindly, hesitantly, fearfully.

Here, though, is an actual bit of autobiography. I began my first novel under extreme and difficult circumstances. My wife, Carrie, had spent nine weeks of a pregnancy lying in a hospital bed. Our daughter Molly was born prematurely, weighing two pounds, eleven ounces. Her twin sister lived for only sixteen hours. For two months, Molly remained in the hospital, an hour's drive from our home. Three days after she was born, two days after our daughter Frances died, I threw away the novel I had been working on and began what was to become *Decorations in a Ruined Cemetery*. I woke at five in the morning and wrote until eight, at which point Carrie and I made the hour's drive to the hospital to see Molly.

During those drives, Carrie read whatever I'd written that day, and we discussed the story. She offered advice—kind, generous, and perceptive advice. She encouraged me to keep going. Two months later, when Molly came home, I was more than a third of the way through the novel.

Even then, though, I was writing blind.

I thought when I began *Decorations* that I was writing a novel about race in New Orleans and about the damage that can occur in families when they can't speak about their lives, their history. It was only later, once I was nearly finished with the book, that I realized I'd written a novel about grief and regret, about the terrible pain and sadness that can overtake a life, about the ways we struggle to overcome the sadness by telling our story to someone who will listen, someone who will listen the way my wife, as she read my pages, listened to the words I had to say about my own grief and sadness. I had disguised those feelings, of course. I had given them the mask of fiction. I had assigned them to other characters whose lives looked nothing like my own, but they were my feelings nevertheless. Their lives were, in some shadowy and indecipherable way, my own life. My own grief, my own regret, had enabled me to imagine those *terrible* emotions in others, to create a world where those one loves are irretrievably lost.

I didn't know then, of course, and neither did Carrie, that she would one day write her own novel about grief and loss. Conrad Morrisey, the seventy-year-old widower of Carrie's novel, is a gilder who keeps homing pigeons; a man who one evening sees an angel in his garden. Like me, Carrie created a character wholly unlike herself, circumstances wholly unlike her own, and yet, *Carrie's* life, her soul and spirit, are there in that book.

Both Carrie and I had come to see our own faces through the mask of fiction.

THE MASK OF FICTION

The writer's recognition of the autobiographical nature of his work would not be particularly meaningful, of course, if it had no relevance to the reader. But the process of discovery, of transformation, is the reader's as well. It is where the power of literature resides. We read of lives and circumstances and events that seem to bear no relation to our own, and yet, in the process of reading, we discover, as if by some miracle, that here indeed are our own lives. Here are the complicated issues we face. Here is our own sense of loss and grief. Here is our struggle for understanding. Here are our own small but precious triumphs.

When a fiction writer recognizes that this is his obligation—not merely to tell a good lie but to tell a lie so good that it has the very ring of truth, the taste and touch and smell of truth—he begins to see that his own life, his own notion of right and wrong, of how we are meant to live our lives, must always be there in his work.

It is a peculiar paradox, perhaps, that I have found myself most able to explore such territory by writing of lives that do not seem at all like my own. When I have attempted to write directly from my own experiences, it has been as though I could not step back far enough from the characters to sort out who they are, why they behave as they do. But making the leap to characters who bear little resemblance to me has charged not simply my imagination but my moral compass, as it were.

Writing teachers frequently exhort students to write what they know. What we know, though, is not all there is to us. We are also, in a way, what we *don't know*. It's not just writers, after all, who are searchers, who long for companionship and affection, who wish each day to make something more of their lives. Not in a million years *would* I claim the philosopher's wisdom, but it seems to me that young writers might be well served—both in pursuit of their craft and in pursuit of their lives—if they attempt to write beyond what they know. Whether we write toward or away from our own experiences, though, we are nevertheless setting off on the grandest and most grueling imaginative adventure. John Barth has suggested that "the first and the final question that a storywriter puts to his or her memory, regardless of the subject and kind of story in progress, is not, as we usually take it to be, the question 'What happened?' but rather the essential question of identity—the personal, professional, cultural, even species-specific '*Who* am I?'" Barth goes on to add that "the question 'Who am I?' is what ultimately motivates the reader or hearer of fiction as well as its writer/teller."

Who am I? How different, really, is that question from, What is the meaning of fiction?

Both reading and writing are, then, acts of supreme faith. They are both, in essence, a call to grace, a belief in the miraculous—that we might come to see through stories what we had not previously seen, that we might come to understand what had, before that moment, remained uncertain, undefined. The mask of fiction, of writing and reading stories, does not, in the end, disguise our faces but instead reveals who we really are. In the end, I think, stories acknowledge life's difficulty and sadness but insist that we go on anyway, that we always hold to our faith, to our belief in grace.

It is both a great privilege and a terrible struggle for fiction writers to offer so much in their work, to concoct stories that attempt to inch their way toward an answer to that difficult question of why we do what we do, what it is exactly that we hope to offer the world.

What is the meaning of fiction?

The best I can offer is this humble reply. The meaning of fiction is, I believe, the grand and glorious leap we make, both as we speak and as we listen, from our own lives to those of others. The meaning of fiction is our empathy, our ability to recognize ourselves in others, others in ourselves. The teller of stories, the writer of fiction, wears a mask that possesses, if the writer has done his job well, the remarkable power to reveal the writer's true face, the writer's truest features. And the listener, the reader of fiction, wears his own mask, a mask that the story strips away to reveal what is nothing less than a startling and miraculous transformation: for the face beneath that mask has become the face of human tragedy and struggle and triumph and grace. It is a face, lo and behold, much like that of fiction's characters, a face precisely like that of the writer's. It is the face of empathy, a face always ready to be reshaped, reconfigured, and ultimately transformed.

EXERCISES

1. Make a thorough list of those events in your life that have marked major turning points in your thinking and your ways of being.

2. From the above list, choose one event to write about truthfully, making the details of one particular scene as specific and as realistic as possible.

3. Now think of a parallel situation—one that has all the same emotional impact as your real circumstance but that is not what happened to you. Posit a character to whom it could happen, and recraft the scene so that it is entirely fictional, so that it takes place in a different time and setting and is removed as much as possible from the original scene that inspired it.

John Gregory Brown is the author of the novels *Decorations in a Ruined Cemetery* and *The Wrecked, Blessed Body of Shelton Lafleur*, both published by Houghton Mifflin. He has received a Lyndhurst Prize, the 1994 Lillian Smith Award, the 1996 Steinbeck Award, and a Horward Foundation Fellowship. He was named a regional winner in *Granta*'s Best Young American Novelists competition and holds the Julia Jackson Nichols Chair in English and Creative Writing at Sweet Briar College. He has three children and is married to the novelist Carrie Brown.

Creative Adventures: The Fiction Writer's Apprenticeship

CHARLES JOHNSON

To be perfectly honest with you, I don't know what a writer should be. And I always wince when I call myself a writer, despite the fact that I've been publishing stories since I was seventeen. My formal training was not in a writing program, although I've taught now for twenty-two years at the University of Washington alongside splendid colleagues like David Wagoner, the late Nelson Bentley and William Matthews, Heather McHugh, Sharon Bryan, Shawn Wong, Colleen McElroy, Maya Sonenberg, David Bosworth, and David Shields. They are real writers to me, and when I'm in their company, I sometimes feel like a fraud.

I feel that way because when I was a teenager my great and only passion was to be a professional cartoonist, which I was for seven terrific years. Then, when I was in my late teens, philosophy became my second passion, and I did my graduate work in that area. I came to writing not because I wanted to be a writer but because when I was twenty-two years old the idea for a philosophical novel came to me and would not leave me alone. I couldn't sleep at night for thinking about the characters and their possibilities. So I wrote that book over the summer of 1970, and it was predictably awful.

But I did learn from that experience how to organize 250 pages of something, which I'd never done before. And I found the experience— the process of discovery—to be as seductive and rewarding as the work I was doing in philosophy. So I wrote another book. Then a third one.

And a fourth. At the end of two years, I had six. I was so thrilled by the process I trained myself to write ten pages a day. All six of those novels went through three drafts. Because I wasn't in a writing program, I didn't have anyone to tell me that what I was doing was outrageous. The school I attended used the quarter system. I was used to taking a class and finishing it within ten weeks. And I didn't see any reason why you couldn't do that with a novel. So I did, one book a quarter for two years until I started the seventh book and decided maybe I needed some help.

MAINTAINING DISCIPLINE AND A BEGINNER'S MIND

Help arrived in the incredible person of the late John Gardner, who was then a young professor in the English Department at Southern Illinois University. Most of you know something about Gardner's work, but I would like to testify that, as his former student, he provided me with an astonishing example of what an artist and scholar could be. Gardner knew twelve languages, ancient and modern. He was a Chaucer scholar. Gardner so loved the poet Homer that at age forty-five he taught himself Greek in order to do his own translation of *The Iliad* for his students, whose work Gardner published at his own expense in a magazine he started in the 1950s. He translated Japanese authors whose work he admired and published over thirty of his own books—novels, short stories, and poetry.

He wrote librettos, screenplays, book reviews, everything possible in the English language, and on top of all that he played the French horn. In short, Gardner was a writer—a teacher of writing—on whom nothing of importance in the world around him (or the literature of the past) was lost. Since he was the first "serious," literary writer I met, I just assumed his indefatigable energy, passion, love of great storytelling, originality, and productivity were characteristics that he expected all his apprentice writers to develop.

With him looking over my shoulder, I wrote the seventh book, *Faith and the Good Thing*, in nine months, which I—at age twenty-four—thought was a terribly long period to devote to a novel or to anything else. Gardner brought me into the book world, where I was a complete innocent, although I had published two books of drawings and created an early PBS how-to-draw series before I met Gardner. But I was an artistic Grendel among the literary Danes. I didn't know the subculture of "serious" writers, or why—as Gardner's friend and literary executor Nicholas Delbanco once put it—they all talked in a kind of clipped, elliptical shorthand, which I'm still working to perfect.

I was *tabula rasa*, without any rigid preconceptions about literature, what it should be, or how writers should think or behave, or what were appropriate or inappropriate subjects to explore. In fact, as a phenomenologist—that was my grad school specialty—I was inclined to "bracket" or set aside all assumptions about the world (or as many as I could) whenever I examined phenomenon. To this day, when I sit down to write a story, I don't ask myself what a story is or what the rules should be; I just try to listen to the characters, try to see clearly and vividly what they're going to do next, and chase down any thought, any image, or any impression that arises during the creative process, even if it contradicts my most cherished ideas and beliefs.

With each new story or novel or essay or screenplay or item of literary criticism, I've always returned to what Buddhists call "beginner's mind." Each new story shows me what a story can be. All my early models were from philosophy—where authors like George Santayana, Miguel de Unamuno, Jean-Paul Sartre, and William Gass worked on fiction one day, then wrestled with an essay on epistemology the next. I never developed the ability to perform a kind of apartheid on creativity; I never learned how to segregate my interests in fiction, philosophy, history, the visual arts, and the martial arts because they all struck me as forms of expression, means for interpretation, and ways of getting at the truth.

And I'll reveal to you something even stranger.

WHAT SHOULD ONE WRITE ABOUT?

When I first began writing, I was never interested in writing about myself. I saw my own daily life as pretty ordinary and boring and predictable, and I still like it that way. I much preferred to tell imaginative stories. In fact, rather than dwell on myself in my writing, I was more fascinated and intrigued, for example, by the dilemma of Descartes when I read the following in a book by Bertrand Russell.

> In 1649, Queen Christina of Sweden became interested in Descartes' work, and prevailed upon him to come to Stockholm. This Scandinavian sovereign was a true renaissance character. Strong-willed and vigorous, she insisted that Descartes should teach her philosophy at five in the morning. This unphilosophic hour of rising at dead of night in a Swedish winter was more than Descartes could endure. He took ill and died in February 1650.

Rather than autobiography or memoir, it was a tale such as Descartes' that sparked my imagination. And I was powerfully intrigued by the real-life stories I heard in the black world, stories about the ex-cowboy Charlie Smith who at 137 years old was the oldest living American in 1978, stories about the struggles of the young Booker T. Washington, or stories about how the all-black town of Allensworth was founded in California around the turn of the century. When I was young, these stories never appeared in my high school and college textbooks, and they were not in our fiction any more than the life and legacy of Martin Luther King Jr. has been explored in our imaginative literature.

THE WRITER AS MIDWIFE

So, naturally, when I began to teach at the University of Washington in 1976, I was hopeful that perhaps my students would turn in stories that filled in the gaps in our cultural and intellectual history. I'm very happy to report that one of my former students from the late 1970s, David Guterson, did just that with his award-winning novel, *Snow Falling on Cedars*, which by now has probably sold over a billion copies. I watched him from the time he was twenty years old. He was dedicated. He was determined to write well and not about himself. He would take pages of a story he was working on, paste them into a college notebook, then carry that notebook around so he could revise his fiction all day long as he rode the bus to work or went to the baseball game of one of his children. And if you've read *Snow Falling on Cedars*, or if you've seen the movie, you'll know this book is not about Guterson. Rather, it is a gift. It is the lives of Japanese-Americans in the Northwest that he is writing about. He is simply the midwife for their story. And when a midwife is finished delivering a beautiful baby, the last thing she does is jump in front of the baby and wave her hands and shout, "Look what *I* did!" No, the midwife gets out of the way and moves on to the next delivery and the next and the next.

By the way, Guterson stopped by my house in Seattle the day after Christmas last year. He came to pick up the present I had set aside for him. And when he went back to his car, he opened the trunk and showed me the research materials he'd picked up earlier that day at the University of Washington library for the new novel he was working on. He had lots of books. I saw a dissertation on the state of nursing in the 1940s, and he was very excited about the process of discovery he found himself in with the characters, their "world," and the themes in his new novel. Indeed, the process is the alpha and omega for Guterson.

Unfortunately, the vast majority of my former students at UW during the last two decades were not like Dave Guterson. Most of them would probably agree with what one intermediate short story writing student told me in the mid-1980s. I had just finished lecturing on some aspect of fiction and I gave my students a photocopy of what I call "A Theory for This Course," printed here in its entirety. Please don't laugh as you read it. I was a much younger, fire-breathing professor on his first teaching job and eager to take on the world when I wrote these words.

Real writers—journeymen writers—are technicians. They do not cringe fearfully before a creative writing chore, but regard it with healthy contempt. It is merely a task and, as technicians, the real writers know that they have at their disposal several ways of executing it successfully.

If you are a writer who regards literary creation as, not merely a possible profession, but as a passion, there is always something to do. If you are not writing fresh material, you are revising; if you are not revising, you are reading—literature, philosophy, mythology, the sciences—everything that employs the word. If you're not researching, you are relaxing over a meal, or with a book, or a film, but only truly with a portion of your mind—the rest of your thoughts are mindful of how the film or book is constructed, and even at the dinner table (yes, even here) as you sip a glass of wine (if you drink wine) you are—or should be—focusing on the particular taste, smell, and feel of things so you won't draw a blank when you sit down at the typewriter. [The word "typewriter" tells you how old this document is.] And so a first principle emerges for your writing: observe. It is the world itself that is your subject. Not necessarily an objective, pre-established world where meaning has been worked out, but one that requires your voice and vision to make it more intelligible.

It is incumbent upon the creative writer to find, cultivate, and sustain his or her own individual voice and vision, and this is the project of a lifetime. Regardless of the work and sacrifice, regardless of the years of apprenticeship required, there is no other goal worthy of an apprentice writer. You must learn the craft of your predecessors thoroughly and, when the happy moment comes, contribute your own work in such a way that it is continuous with the past of your discipline yet projects into the future. If these goals sound lofty, they are meant to be because we live at a time when the competition for publication is severe. Therefore, it is crucial that your fictions should be complete in every respect. For this course, they must present (1) A story with logically plotted sequences; (2) Three-dimensional characters, that is, real people with real problems; (3) Sensuous description, or a complete "world" to which the senses of the reader can imaginatively respond; (4) Dialogue with the authenticity of real speech; (5) A strong narrative voice; (6) Rhythm, musicality, and control of the cadences in your fiction; (7) And, finally, originality in theme and execution. Lacking these elements, there is surely no reason why readers, who are already tight-fisted about their time, should spend half an hour with your story when they could be playing with their children, working out, or enjoying an evening with friends.

And that brings me to the heart of this essay, the single point that underlies the endless study of craft, why one creates fiction in the first place instead of, say, selling dictionaries from door to door, and how such work—constant writing and rewriting—is bearable. The writer is not a leader. He or she is not, as some 19th century poets may have believed, always the best seer. The writer, when he is most authentic, is a servant who, seeing what others perhaps have missed, gently and persuasively informs them of a meaning by making them feel its presence in the theatre of a fiction. Such an author writes about people for people, and it is surely a fact that no writer should put on paper anything he or she could not say to someone's face.

After I was finished huffing and puffing, a young woman sitting in the classroom raised her hand, and she said, "You know, I'm glad you told us that." I asked her why. She said, "Because now I understand that I don't want to be a great writer. I just want to write a few stories and maybe get some of them published, and that's all."

And I said, "Okay. That is fair. I will do everything possible to help you reach that goal," and I did. I would say after teaching thousands of young writers in workshops that 98 percent of my students enroll for precisely the reasons this young woman did. No doubt they can learn to be better readers of fiction. And some of them will go on to publish well, like my former student Gary Hawkes (a contemporary of Guterson), who is now chair of the English Department at Lycoming College and had two novels, *Semaphore* and *Surveyor*, published simultaneously in the summer of 1998. What I'm saying is that much of my job is to serve young writers who have strictly commercial ambitions or simply want to tell stories about their first sexual experiences.

THAT SAME PROF'S ADVICE TWENTY YEARS LATER

However, my mission here is to reiterate the obvious, and with all humility, by saying that if writing teachers do not present students with the finest literary work from the past and present as models for the future, models that they draw from all disciplines—history, painting, biography, philosophy, the sciences, the cultures of the so-called Third World—they will not produce the David Gutersons of tomorrow. Our best teachers teach students how to write in numerous forms, Western and Eastern, because these forms are their global inheritance. Good teachers make you think about why James Alan McPherson says whenever he writes a story, he feels the duty, the moral obligation, to include some datum of black American history—which is American history—in that story because the lives of people of color, who shaped this country's evolution from the year 1619, have been marginalized and are hardly known. Good teachers tell you that if you want to be a good midwife, and not just a narcissistic writer, you must devote a lifetime to craft. And after saying that, they tell you what Gichin Funakoshi, the founder of Goju-Ryu karate, said about the martial arts also works for writing: Spirit first, technique second. (Then tell you it's okay to sometimes contradict yourself, as I just did.)

Good teachers convey to students the thoughts of Ernest Hemingway, who said, "What a writer in our time has to do is write what hasn't been written or beat dead men at what they have done." They tell you it takes fifteen years for a fiction writer to become "established" after he or she first publishes. They tell you that you must master all the exercises at the end of John Gardner's *The Art of Fiction*, as I made David Guterson and Gary Hawkes do. They tell you that you must be interdisciplinary, be able to solve any writing problem three different ways, and find the perfect painting, sculpture, and piece of music or work of philosophy that complements your fiction. They tell you that you must be prolific as a writer, if only to survive, and especially prolific if you are a black, brown, or Asian writer. They tell you to research a literary form not used for a major work in the last hundred years—some literary dinosaur once popular in the West or the East, then pushed aside by the course of fiction's evolution—and then have you plot a new story using its conventions, updating them for a late-twentieth-century audience as I did in my second novel, *Oxherding Tale*. They tell you that writing well is the same damned thing as thinking well. Not just being clever, but thinking critically and independently. They tell you what Nobel laureate Saul Bellow wrote in an essay called "Culture Now" in the 1970s.

> This society, like decadent Rome, is an amusement society. That is the grim fact. Art cannot and should not compete with amusement. It has business at the heart of humanity. The artist, as Collingwood tells us, must be a prophet, "not in the sense that he foretells things to come, but that he tells the audience, at the risk of their displeasure, the secrets of their own hearts." That is why he exists. He is a spokesman for his community. This account of the artist's business is old, much older than Collingwood, very old, but in modern times this truth, which we all feel, is seldom expressed. . . . No community altogether knows its own heart; and by failing in this knowledge a community deceives itself on the one subject concerning which ignorance means death. . . . The remedy is art itself. Art is the community's medicine for the worst disease of the mind, the corruption of consciousness.

THE FOUR RULES

And, finally, to shore up their students for the lifelong creative adventures that await them, good teachers recite August Wilson's four rules of playwriting. These, of course, apply to all creative work. Wilson's Rules for Writing are as follows:

1. There are no rules.
2. The first rule is wrong, so pay attention.
3. You can't write for an audience; the writer's first job is to survive.
4. You can make no mistakes, but anything you write can be made better.

EXERCISES

1. Make an exhaustive list of historical events or figures who have long intrigued you.

2. Choose five of the above list and write for five minutes on each of them, exploring their metaphorical possibilities in a work of fiction.

3. Do some research and then write a short story that centers in full or in part on one of the events or figures.

Charles Johnson is a 1998 MacArthur fellow and received the National Book Award for his novel *Middle Passage*. A literary critic, short story and screenwriter, philosopher and cartoonist, he is the S. Wilson and Grace M. Pollock Endowed Professor of Creative Writing at the University of Washington. His most recent novel is *Dreamer*.

II
Characterization

Icebergs, Glaciers, and Arctic Dreams: Developing Characters

KIM EDWARDS

Shortly after I moved to Japan, I found myself studying a soda machine in a train station late at night, trying to decipher katakana, which is the Japanese alphabet devoted primarily to foreign words. It was pretty basic stuff, but enthralling, too; I'd study a string of symbols, spelling out the monosyllables *Gu-Re-Pa-Fu-Ru-To*, feeling a surge of pure excitement as meaning flashed—*grapefruit*. I was intent, absorbed, thinking that I must have felt like this when I first learned to read, a rush of sudden magic as a new layer of the world was revealed.

I didn't notice the man until he was beside me. The fine dark suit, the white shirt, the polished shoes, the leather briefcase—at first glance, he was hardly distinguishable from the dozens of other businessmen I saw each day. When he bowed slightly and asked if he could be of any help to me, it was all too easy to dismiss him as yet another *sa-lu-ri-ma-nu* out to practice English.

But there was an urgency to this man, who introduced himself in English as Mr. Ide, a kind of intentness that seemed unusual. So instead of smiling politely and walking away, I tried instead to explain the thrill I felt when the randomness of katakana characters gave way to meaning. Mr. Ide nodded, enthused, and pushed his glasses back on his nose. He felt the same, he said, learning English.

We talked easily in the warm summer night, and when the train came, he took a seat across from me, leaning forward with his elbows on his knees and his large hands clasped loosely between them. His face was nearly unlined, but pale. He had a wonderful laugh, deep and resonant, and though the ride to my stop was not long, by the time we parted, I knew that Mr. Ide had three grown children, that he translated German poetry in his spare time, just for pleasure, and that not a day went by without his mourning an American friend, a very good friend, who had recently died of cancer. He pulled bits of paper from his pockets to show me his translations. "And then Joseph said goodnight," he read aloud, one blunt finger running under a line of characters.

It's been years since I stepped off that train, but I can still see Mr. Ide waving good-bye with one broad, expressive hand, pushing at his glasses with the other, an expression of both pleasure and sadness on his face.

THE ICEBERG THEORY

I frequently tell this story when I teach classes in creative writing, for I think the experience illustrates well what we must do as authors: Take our characters from their sketchy, shadowy beginnings and make them come alive. For a character to be convincing, what's on the page must somehow evoke knowledge that extends beyond what's strictly visible. Readers must feel a certain empathy so that a character's actions seem both unique and understandable. Even if this character doesn't cause a car accident or lose a parent or leave a spouse, the author must have a clear sense of what he or she would do in such situations—and readers must, as well. When we close the book or put down the story, we should be able to imagine these people going on with their lives, just as we might imagine a sister, an uncle, an acquaintance on a train, moving through the world when we're not there. In a story, what's invisible must hulk like a shadow, informing the visible, supporting it. In some true sense, allowing it to be.

This is sometimes called the iceberg theory of character, the idea being that what's unstated must nonetheless exist clearly in the author's mind for a character to have sufficient depth. Much of what readers know about any given character is never stated explicitly but is rather submerged in the way a character speaks and moves and thinks—and all of this, in turn, is shaped by the author's knowledge of each character. The iceberg is a metaphor made common because it works, contains a truth that's slippery, hard to grasp, harder to convey. Characterization causes frequent problems, whether the writers are beginners, sliding dangerously close to stereotypes of the sort I initially inflicted on Mr. Ide, or more advanced, creating characters who have unique concerns and visions, yet who somehow fail to coalesce convincingly. In workshops we talk about these people-on-the-page, what impressions they make, what contradictions leap out, ways in which they are believable or fail to convince. We look for places where the author might make a deeper exploration. And then I send my students off to try again.

Still, I'm always conscious of the ways these discussions fail to answer a basic and essential question: Hidden ice, all right, but *how*? During my own years as a graduate student, and during my early years of apprenticeship as a writer, I, too, struggled to make my characters come alive on the page, to make them real, convincing. It was no news to me when people would hand back my rough drafts saying that the characters seemed thin, too two-dimensional. Like all beginning writers, I was struggling with many aspects of storytelling—shape and structure, pacing and plot—but creating convincing characters seemed both the most important and also the most elusive problem. If it's true, as John Gardner claimed, that characters are the first reason a reader reads a book, then it was clearly vital that I get them right. But if my characters were shadowy, "cardboard," as the criticism often went, how could I learn more about them, what glimpses could I give to make them alive and three-dimensional on the page?

THE IMPORTANCE OF TRUTH

Fiction writers, though they spin stories, are really in the business of getting at the truth. Not a single, final, absolute truth, but rather the multiple and varied truths of how we live, what shapes our lives. Good fiction reveals worlds previously unknown, or sheds new light on the familiar.

Not surprisingly, then, one way for writers to get inside their characters is to begin with the truth—the true experience, the true scene witnessed or overheard, the true emotion. In his *Paris Review* interview, Gabriel García Márquez talks about his own progression as a writer. García Márquez began as a journalist, and he characterizes his early attempts at fiction as being "totally intellectual short stories because I was writing them on the basis of my literary experience and had not yet found the link between literature and life." Gradually, through reading and through his own daily experiences, Márquez began to recognize the gap between his fiction and the reality of life all around him, and this recognition turned him away from intellectualized fiction and back to the world, back to his own life and childhood.

There he found his true sources, and his characters began to come alive. Interestingly, though García Márquez is known for the vividness of his imagination, he claims that "there's not a single line in all my work that does not have a basis in reality." For García Márquez, the key to understanding his characters was a close, perceptive study of the world around him.

Similarly, Raymond Carver talks in his *Paris Review* interview about using something said to him, or something he witnessed or overheard, as the starting place for a story, saying, "The fiction I'm most interested in has lines of reference to the real world. None of my stories really *happened*, of course. But there's always something, some element, something said to me or that I witnessed, that may be the starting place."

When Carver goes on to say that "everything we write is, in some way, autobiographical," he doesn't mean that authors stay close to true events when they write—indeed, to do so can actually rob a character of the freedom to react in a natural and individual way—but rather that there's a clear relationship between the events of the world and the events of a story. Art doesn't imitate life but grows directly from it.

The essays by John Gregory Brown and Debra Spark, which you can find earlier in this book, develop this link more fully in relation to finding one's material. Since our focus here is on character, let's follow that course.

Perhaps the most important truth to begin with is the authentic transfer of emotion from author to character. Even when an author has not experienced what her character is experiencing, she can find parallel events and emotions in her own life on which to draw. While writing my story "Sky Juice," for instance, in which a young Asian woman is forced into prostitution and then later flees to England via an arranged marriage, I drew on my experience of moving across the world into cultures and landscapes that held no emotional resonance for me. As someone raised in upstate New York, to me the feathery leaves of early spring always have joyous connotations. However, because I've lived in places where the land was always lush, I was able to imagine how these new leaves might seem to someone from another culture. Not beautiful or full of restrained hope, but sparse and rather ugly, like "half-plucked chickens." My character's experience is not mine, yet I was able to find within my own life emotions and reactions that gave me insight into hers, that made it possible for me to understand her in a deeper, more complex way. In this aspect, authors are not unlike actors, needing to dig into the depths of their own experiences to understand the emotions their characters might feel. It's a vital step, and a powerful one, for as long as a character's emotions are consistent and convincing, the character will be believable, even to the point where a writer can stretch the limits of the known. Remedios the Beauty can ascend with the sheets, Gregor Sampson can wake up one morning as a giant cockroach, and the reader will read on, drawn by the desire to see not just what will happen next but *how* these particular people will respond. Writers leap from the particular experiences of their own lives to the universal emotions and states of mind those experiences reflect. From there they can particularize the experience once again, into the life of the imagined character.

HISTORICAL INSPIRATION

Sometimes authors take this idea of using a true fact or a true line one step further, and use an actual historical character as the inspiration for a fictional one. For example, in her story "Concerning Mold Upon the Skin, Etc.," Joanna Scott began with the Dutch naturalist Antonie van Leeuwenhoek, who invented the microscope. He was a real person, and the story has historical origins, yet it is not simply a reiteration of history. The characters come alive on their own terms, placed within the framework of history yet also independent of its constraints; their actions, though fictional, ring deeply and humanly true. According to Scott, in her commentary for the story in *The Best American Short Stories*, the key was the naturalist's daughter, who "floats silently in the background of her father's biography . . . she became the center of the narrative, the presence that enabled me to reshape history into fiction."

Scott began with facts—Leeuwenhoek's "fierce secrecy," his position outside the mainstream scientific circles, his microscope—but it's the power of Scott's imagination that let her put this sketchy character in a very human situation. In her narrative, the scientist, determined to examine every aspect of life underneath his microscope, approaches his daughter, whom he has neglected for many years. He hugs her, weeping, and for a moment she believes he has changed, has finally recognized his selfishness and is filled with remorse. Quickly, though, she realizes that this is not the case. He wants something from her—a tear, to examine under his microscope. She tries to push him away, but he kisses her,

> . . . not as a father should kiss a daughter, but like the devil kisses . . . It was Marie who understood first. She did not move, only closed her eyes so she would not have to see him. And for a moment her father understood, too. Looking at Marie he couldn't help but understand and was ashamed. But his shame flickered and went out when he saw—oh, gracious Marie!— the thing he most desired: a large, milky tear that seeped from between her eyelids and slid down her cheek.

He cannot help himself; he does not even try. Instead, he captures the tear and takes it to the microscope to study, composing all the time the letter he will write to the Royal Academy in London describing the "incredible number of little animals of various sorts which move very prettily, which tumble about and sideways, this way and that. . . ."

Scott's story turns on the human dilemma she imagines for her character, a man so consumed with the pursuit of microscopic life that he ignores, and even abuses, the central relationships of his own life. His passions are compelling, his weaknesses human. Historical facts inspired the story and lend legitimacy to it, but it's through the power of Scott's imagination that it comes alive.

FOLLOWING VOICE

The choice of voice is crucial to establishing character, both for the reader and in the author's mind. Voice reveals perspective and personality traits; moreover, what a character is apt to do is imbedded in the voice through which that character speaks. It's been my experience that a story will often not take shape until I've been able to get the voice of the main character right. Once I have this voice, however, a deeper intuitive understanding of my main character follows, and the narrative tends to unfold, not predictably, but in ways that make sense for this particular character. In other words, voice is a key to personality, and through personality to plot. Once I know how someone speaks, it's easier to understand who that person is.

The effect of voice on character is perhaps easiest to see in first-person narration, where word choice, syntax, pacing, and emphasis all establish the speaker's character. In Mary Ann Taylor-Hall's striking first novel, *Come and Go, Molly Snow*, the narrator is Carrie

Marie Mullins, a tough young woman determined to become a blue-grass fiddler. She opens the book with these lines.

> The day after I graduated from high school, I cut out. Left my mama weeping in the carport. "I'll be back, honey, don't cry," I yelled out the window of my inheritance, Daddy's old Riviera. But she knew what I meant: back for Christmas, back for the Shorter family reunion. In all other respects, goodbye flat dirt and frozen-out orange groves, hello I-75. If you want to play the fiddle in a bluegrass band, that's one of the roads you'll *be* on.

The story's begun; there's movement, momentum. Vital aspects of Carrie Marie's character are immediately clear: her determination, her impatience, her willingness to take risks and fly in the face of the expected. She's direct, focused, headstrong, and she believes in her own talent, qualities that carry her through the difficult early years of establishing herself as a musician and becoming a single mother.

But when her beloved daughter, Molly, just five years old, dies in an accident, Carrie Marie is stopped in her tracks, forced into stillness. Just getting through each day becomes an extraordinary effort; the early speed and jazzy energy are gone, yet the lyricism of her fiddle playing settles into the prose, and the toughness, the determination so evident in those first lines are still very much alive. The book reads like a song, a melding of music and grief, as Carrie Marie struggles to accept her loss and determine her future. Still, given who she is in the first paragraph of this novel, the question that truly shapes the book is not *whether* she will do it but *how*. She herself doubts that she can make it through, but anyone tuned to her voice knows better; her gritty determination, her passion, and her humor all indicate that she'll come through. Changed, yes, saddened, certainly, but a survivor nonetheless.

LETTING CHARACTERS SURPRISE

One of the paradoxes writers face is creating characters who behave in consistent ways without becoming predictable. Like their real-life counterparts, fictional characters have habits, personality traits, and a framework of beliefs, all of which determine their reactions to situations. When a character responds as we expect she will, we find the reaction convincing; we say she is responding "in character." Yet it's also true that human beings are quirky, never completely predictable, and our characters must be able to move within a range of reactions, as well. There is no single way for each character to behave. Just as we sometimes astonish ourselves, our characters, too, must have the capacity to take us by surprise.

A close examination of convincing characters reveals the way the expected and unexpected work together, bringing depth to the person on the page. I'm thinking in particular of an Alice Munro story called "Prue." This story focuses on the relationship between the title character, who is presented as being "unintense . . . civilized . . . bright and thoughtful, a cheerful spectator," and Gordon, with whom Prue has been involved for years, off and on. During the course of this brief story, their pleasant dinner is interrupted by an angry young woman who turns out to be Gordon's lover. Prue's reaction seems at first to be very much in character, very much what we have come to expect from her. She doesn't scream or yell, or even laugh when Gordon reveals that he'd like to marry her, in a few years' time, once he gets over being in love with this young woman. Instead, she seems amused, a distant observer, one who can find the humor in the grander scope of events without taking them to heart. This is also the tone she adopts when telling the story to others.

However, at this point in the narrative, Munro explores the inner side of Prue, reveals her secret.

> She doesn't mention that the next morning she picked up one of Gordon's cufflinks from his dresser. The cufflinks are made of amber and he bought them in Russia, on the holiday he and his wife took when they got back together again. They look like squares of candy, golden, translucent, and this one warms quickly in her hand. She drops it into the pocket of her jacket. Taking one is not a real theft. It could be a reminder, an intimate prank, a piece of nonsense.

Prue takes the cufflink home and drops it in a tobacco tin, which holds several other items from Gordon's house, "all small things, not of great value, but not worthless, either."

Thus this story changes, turning not on the infidelity but rather on Prue's thefts and what they reveal about her character. That is, the thefts fall into the story like a shaft of light, forcing us to reconsider Prue. On one hand, this action is consistent with what we know about her: a quiet protest against betrayal, so subtle that it's likely to go unnoticed. Yet at the same time, this small theft reveals a new dimension. She's no longer the spectator that others see, that she herself presents to the world. It's suddenly clear that her passions run much deeper than we've been led to believe, and because of this, everything we know about Prue is called into question—her lightness, her humor in the face of disappointment and betrayal. She may forget about the items in the tobacco tin, but we cannot. Indeed, Prue has startled and surprised us. She is not who she seems to be, and this wonderful frission forms the heart of Munro's story.

LIVING IN THE WORLD

Writers, of course, don't live in a vacuum, and neither do our characters. Just as our interactions with the events of the world keep us in a continual state of discovery about our own hidden selves, so, too, our characters reveal themselves through their exchanges with others. Thus, the question of creating believable characters, whose secret lives surface in brief glimpses, like clues, becomes even more complex. You have not one character to consider, but many, and the ways they interact will lead the author in new directions and alter a reader's perception in subtle ways.

William Trevor's story "Widows" in *After Rain* is worth studying for the way conflicting relationships sharpen and clarify character. Waking on an October morning, Catherine finds that her husband, Matthew, has died in his sleep. Theirs was a good marriage, and her grief is deep; through the condolences that are offered, it quickly becomes clear that Matthew was well respected, known as a man of his word. Initially, the narrative focuses on the small tasks with which Catherine and her sister, Alicia, busy themselves in the wake of Catherine's loss. However, six weeks after the funeral, a workman named Tom Leary appears at the house, claiming he has not been paid for painting done the previous summer. Trevor's description of Leary is precise and revealing. He is depicted as unappealing, a person careless in his work and personal habits, a man who inspires a fleeting, furtive impression in the minds of others. This description contrasts what we know of Matthew, and the clear differences between these two men further establish the characters of both. We know right away that Leary will behave badly, and he does; likewise, Matthew's integrity is reinforced through Leary's actions.

However, the heart of this story does not lie in the surface conflict over the payment, but rather in the very different reactions of the two sisters to this conflict. Alicia, the elder, wants to go to the police, to the priest. She wants to have the matter stopped by outside forces. Catherine, however, after some internal struggle, decides to simply pay the bill, though she knows Leary's claim is false. She does this to ensure that Matthew's memory is not accidently tarnished by the gossip and speculation that would accompany any investigation. The sisters argue over this, harshly, but despite the reason of Alicia's argument, and the force of their shared past, which would have Alicia resume her childhood role as the leader, Catherine follows her own mind. Her years of happy marriage have changed her in ways she hadn't understood until this moment. Trevor uses a shifting point of view to illuminate this change. Though the story is primarily Catherine's, he moves into Alicia's mind to clarify what's happening.

> A disappointment rose in Alicia, bewildering and muddled. The death of her own husband had brought an end, and her expectation had been that widowhood for her sister would be the same. Her expectation had been that in their shared state they would be as once they were, now that marriage was over, packed away with their similar mourning clothes. Yet almost palpable in the kitchen was Catherine's resolve that what still remained for her should not be damaged by a fuss of protest over a confidence trick . . . . knowing her sister well, Alicia knew that this resolve would become more stubborn as more time passed. It would mark and influence her sister; it would breed new eccentricities in her. If Leary had not come that day there would have been something else.

Clearly, Trevor understands Catherine's motivations, the changes she has undergone, in ways that Catherine herself perhaps intuits but does not articulate. He knows her better than she knows herself, in other words, and this knowledge reaches the reader both through Catherine's conversations with Alicia and through Alicia's own perceptions. Likewise, through the interactions of these two characters, we're allowed a glimpse into the sadness at the center of Alicia's life. What's visible in this narrative is supported by the hidden depths of character that Trevor knows and reveals, sparely, powerfully, through the relationship between these two sisters.

GLACIERS

Perhaps the most vital step in gaining insight into characters is the process of revision. It's true that in a finished story each character is rather like an iceberg, suggested by insightful dialogue, action, and interior thought, strokes of language that imply what's hidden as much as they reveal what's visible. Yet it's also true that the process of realizing such characters is often slow, often incremental, something added here, something scraped away there. The iceberg might be a good-enough metaphor for the characters in a finished story, but a glacier, in my view, comes closer to capturing the process of making that character come alive.

You can't know a person from a single meeting, and so, too, characters gain depth and originality over time, through familiarity. This is frequently a slow process, one that requires patience and persistence. Seldom do characters rush out fully formed, and often it's necessary to write, and then discard, whole paragraphs, scenes, pages, just to discover a few essential facts about a given character. For instance, in one of my stories, "Spring, Mountain, Sea," the narrator remembers trying to teach his Korean wife how to pronounce the English consonant *r*. His recollection in the published version is only two sentences long, but it's informed by half-a-dozen pages, written and infinitely revised and finally thrown out, where I tried, unsuccessfully, to make that scene come alive. It was discouraging to realize that this scene, which I struggled with so mightily, didn't belong in the story after all. Nonetheless, what I learned about my characters' persistence and resistance is present in the story. The effort wasn't wasted, though it seemed so at the time. Instead it was part of the necessary process of discovery, creating the invisible to support what would readily be seen.

BREAKING THROUGH THE ICE

Characters are the beating heart of any story. Who people are defines what they do, how they respond to a given situation. Like the varied and unpredictable human lives they grow out of and reflect, successful fictional characters are sometimes consistent, sometimes surprising, always full of quirks and complexities. There are no easy answers about how to create such characters, but the seeds for every character who comes alive are all around us, in the world: in the true fact, the true experience, the true emotion. All writers, even the greatest, have struggled to make their characters believable. Certainly one of the reasons I keep writing is that each story teaches me something new about human complexities and motivations, deepens my instinct about how to transfer life onto the page. I'm not sure it gets easier, exactly, but the rewards do get richer, as characters take on lives of their own. No longer frozen on the page, preserved intact, in stasis, but stepping instead out of that icy region between the known and the imagined, melting through barriers and emerging into the world, vibrant and radiant and alive.

EXERCISES

1. Remember someone you met briefly but who made a strong impression. Write everything you can about that person and that encounter, from the way this person dressed and spoke to the time and place where the meeting happened. What was the weather like? What scent was in the air? What about this person made the discussion so memorable? Now, imagine that person standing up from your meeting and walking away. Where did he go? What did he think about? Who was the next person he encountered, and what happened in that meeting? Let yourself go. Write quickly without stopping. When you can't write any more, pause to examine where you've gone. How does the character you developed differ from the real-life person who inspired him? How did your observations from the original meeting shift and blossom in your imagination? What clues have you left yourself to take this sketch further?

2. Remember a situation when you reacted in a way that was unlike you. Write everything you can remember about the event. What led up to it? What inspired you, finally, to take this action? Had you ever done anything like this before? How did this action deepen your knowledge of yourself? Now, take a closer look at what happened. Instead of focusing on how this action surprised you, look for ways in which it's consistent with your character. For instance, perhaps you are a problem solver; even if the action itself surprised you, it might be consistent with your desire to find a solution to a given situation. Consult your friends—they may see connections or departures that you yourself miss. Then imagine yourself in a similar situation in the future. How do you think you would react next time?

3. When you've completed exercise two, go through your journals and rough drafts and find a character whom you think you know rather well. Start writing, putting that character into an unusual situation. This shouldn't be high drama: No need to conjure a mugging or a car wreck. Instead, have your character face a situation that's annoying but not obviously life changing. An incessantly barking dog, perhaps, or a lost billfold, or a teenager who's learning how to drive. Let your character respond as you'd expect him to, given what you know about him. Once you've finished, go back and write the scene again. This time, however, give your character a little more freedom. What might he do if he was under a particular amount of stress that day? How might he surprise you, and himself? What actions might he take that would be unusual, yet consistent with his overall character? Draw on your own experiences to open up the possibilities.

Kim Edwards is the author of *The Secrets of a Fire King*, a short story collection that was an alternate for the 1998 PEN/Hemingway award. Her fiction has been widely published and has been anthologized in *The Best American Short Stories* and in Pushcart Prize collections. She has been awarded grants from the National Endowment for the Arts, the Pennsylvania Arts Council, and the YMCA National Writer's Voice, and has taught writing for many years, both in the United States and overseas, most recently in the writing programs at Carnegie Mellon University and Washington University. She lives in Lexington, Kentucky, with her husband and two daughters.

Extras, Chorus, Supernumeraries, and Walk-Ons: Bringing Minor Characters to Life

W.D. WETHERELL

An opera house would seem to be the last place an aspiring young fiction writer would frequent for inspiration. Opera—that melodramatic, old-fashioned, and sentimental art—has always gone to fiction for inspiration, seldom the other way around. And yet there was a time when I was younger, living in New York, that I went every chance I got, finding in the full-throated passion, the swelling crescendos, the no-holds-barred melodrama a welcome catharsis from the tighter, leaner emotions I was spending my mornings trying to pin down on the page.

The downside of all this was that I had bad luck with the leading voices; on the nights I could afford to go, Luciano Pavarotti was always sick, or Beverly Sills had to cancel, and I ended up watching the second-string cast. To keep myself interested, I began focusing more and more on the chorus, the supernumeraries, the minor characters, finding they were done perfectly and often brought the performances to life. Opera is rich in these: the chorus in *Boris Godunov*, representing the entire Russian people; Ping, Pang, and Pong in *Turandot*, those jeering mockers; Coline in *La Boheme*, going out to sell his overcoat to buy medicine for the dying Mimi. Done well, they give opera a charming verisimilitude—a depth and variety and richness that the main characters alone can not always provide. Conversely, one lazy spear carrier in *Aida*, slouching, mugging at the audience, can ruin an entire production.

This was the literary lesson I took from all those performances—the potential that resides in minor characters in fiction, what they can bring to a story or novel, especially if they're done with imagination and verve. Moving the plot along, bolstering the main theme, touching upon other themes, adding a second, metaphoric level of suggestion, injecting shots of veracity, even, in lucky circumstances, bringing in a dose of profundity. These are a few of the aesthetic benefits minor characters can bring to the page. Nathaniel Hawthorne can have his young Goodman Brown see "the slender form of a veild female, led between Goody Cloyse, that pious teacher of the catechism, and Martha Carrier, who had received the devil's promise to be queen of hell," and they jump off the page at us, come alive in all their evil hideousness, though they're mentioned nowhere else in the entire story.

And while I'm not one to play the "real life" card in the teaching of writing, it's important to remember our lives are filled with minor characters, and they're important for their own sake, as fellow members of the swarming pageant of humanity. Just today, I came upon a whole repertory company of walk-ons. There was the Brazilian butcher wearing a Tottenham Hotspur soccer cap; the oil delivery man who complained his wife was running out on him as he angrily shoved his nozzle into our pipe; the screaming fifth-grade basketball coach who obviously patterned herself on Bobby Knight; the man I saw in the distance picking up trash by the side of the road, smelling it, sticking it into his pocket. All these coming to me on a day when, the family gone off on errands, I didn't see a single one of the main characters in my life at all.

Successfully translating these into fiction is one of the hallmarks of a good writer. Anton Chekhov, Charles Dickens, Eudora Welty, Saul Bellow. Any character who appears in their writing is vivid, believable, and memorable, even if the character only appears for the flash of a single line. One of the reasons we read fiction in the first place is for the delight of good characterization, and it can be done in minor ways just as in major. How much poorer would literature be if it didn't include not only the major Madam Lefarge of *A Tale of Two Cities* but the minor Mr. Cruncher, the affable grave robber of Temple Bar, who likes to describe his occupation as being "a tradesman in Scientific Goods; something of a Resurrection Man."

Minor characters not only add color to a story but can reflect something about the central action in a story, serving as a counterpoint to what is going on in the foreground. Sometimes minor characters can also be reflections of parts or characteristics of major characters— fragments of the self whom the major characters meet along the way. Pure selfishness, vanity, saintliness, for example, in a minor character can be a mirror of selfishness in a major character. It's important not to let the opportunity to make full use of a minor character slip by.

THE BASICS

Just as so many vivid minor characters swarm into our life every day, so do many drab and anonymous ones, those whom we hardly notice, or notice only as types. The temptation in writing fiction is to brush these off with the quickest fable we can find—a soldier, a waiter, a baby—and move on without a second glance. This is a pity and can be worse than that—the sign of sloppy writing that simply doesn't give a damn about the characters who are only passing through. Writing minor characters well involves the same kind of attention that comes into play when writing major characters. They must be fully fleshed and believable, motivated well, interesting in their own right, cliché-free, credible—all these things, and yet *briefly* so, bit players who must take maximum advantage of their brief moments in the reader's attention. This is where the craft comes in, the challenge and the delight—in characterizing in miniature.

Often, focus alone is enough to make a difference. I'm going to take a simple walk-on character, one who will only appear in our imaginary story once, and show some alternate ways of describing her.

Something passed by on the street.

A nothing line, the only purpose being to shift the reader's attention out the window. The character, the *something* on the street, has hardly been noticed by the writer, and will not be noticed at all by the reader.

Someone passed by on the street.

The *something* is personified and immediately becomes vaguely interesting. It awakens in the reader that first glimmer of voyeuristic interest, if nothing more than this. An advance on our first line, but not by much.

A woman passed by on the street.

Gender is added, which helps a little; at least we have *one* particular to go on now, and yet how many women are there in this world for the reader to guess which one is she?

An Arab woman passed by on the street.

Okay, nationality. The reader's curiosity has been piqued, especially if our story takes place in a Midwest city where Arab women are not an everyday occurrence.

An Arab woman with luxurious black hair passed by on the street.

This is the first sentence in which we actually *see* her—a big improvement now over the previous four, thanks to that bit of descriptive detail.

An Arab woman with luxurious black hair and a purple shawl passed by on the street.

Added details equal added interest; the purple shawl is just the kind of particularization that helps make her visible.

An Arab woman with luxurious black hair and a purple shawl passed by on the street, rolling a plastic hoop.

We've added action, which adds a fluid quality, curiosity, oddness, even suspense—uh, rolling *what?* Details one chooses should not merely be random.

An Arab woman with luxurious black hair and a purple shawl passed by on the bomb-shattered street, her hands over her eyes, crying.

Lots going on now, a suggestion of tragedy, a whole political/historical element, big stuff indeed, at least compared with the generic first line we started with. This is a walk-on who *matters.*

Once you've got the details of a minor character, it's helpful to think about what function that character may have in a scene (you may also want to do this before you add the minor character), what her relevance will be. Is, for example, the Arab woman meant to reflect a sadness that the main character, watching her, cannot feel at his own losses? Is she meant to underscore some unbearably happy event from a previous scene? It's important to take every opportunity in a short story to make details that are happening in the background reflect or refract on something that is happening in the foreground.

And this, in a nutshell, is what good minor characterization is about: taking a throwaway character and making her or him into much more. It's accomplished by treating minor characters with care, keeping an eye out for their potential, refusing to let them merely disappear into anonymity. These basics taken care of, there's room to take them a further step, make them accomplish a whole range of fictional tasks.

A MASTER OF MINOR

So important are these basics, and so easy to overlook, that the use of minor characters forms a convenient, all but infallible litmus test in coming to a shorthand evaluation of a person's writing talent. Good writers always use minor characters well; bad writers use them hardly at all, or settle for stereotypes, a quick dose of satiric venom. This last is a real danger; as George Orwell points out in his essay on George Gissing: "any novel will inevitably contain minor characters who are mere grotesques or observed in a hostile spirit." The conceited poet, the miserly rich person, the complacent yuppie. How tempting it is, when scanning humanity, to let it go at that, a quick snicker with your reader, then on to finer things. Since every good fiction writer does minor characters well, it's not hard to find good examples of the art.

Dylan Thomas, more famous as a poet, wrote some funny and poignant short stories that are largely forgotten today. Perhaps because of his poet's eye, he seems to see his minor characters with clarity and depth.

Here's a quick, simple use of minor characters taken from "The Peaches," wherein a boy accompanies his father on a pub crawl.

> I could see into half of a smoky, secret room, where four men were playing cards. One man was huge and swarthy, with a handlebar mustache and a love-curl on his forehead; seated by his side was a thin, bald, pale old man with his cheeks in his mouth; the faces of the other two were in shadow. They all drank out of brown pint tankards and never spoke, laying the cards down with a smack, scraping at their matchboxes, puffing at their pipes, swallowing unhappily, ringing the brass bell, ordering more, by a sign of their fingers, from a sour woman with a flowered blouse and a man's cap.

A crowd scene, a small one, and yet how vividly these characters come to life, with the man with his cheeks in his mouth and a sour barmaid with a man's cap. Important for their own sake, they're harnessed to a subtle, but important point: How they're described helps characterize the point-of-view character, the boy, as someone who has the all-important gift of standing back from his environment and really *seeing* it—someone who is cut out for a destiny that will take him far from provincial pubs.

In "One Warm Saturday," Thomas expands the crowd scene, describes the sunbathers on a Welsh beach, picking details that emphasize the loneliness of the young man watching.

The young man, in his wilderness, saw the holiday Saturday set down before him, false and pretty, as a flat picture under the vulgar sun; the disporting families with paper bags, buckets and spades, parasols and bottles, the happy, hot and aching girls with sunburn liniments in their bags, the bronzed young men with chests, and the envious, white young men in waistcoats, the thin, pale, hairy, pathetic legs of the husbands silently walking through the water, the plump and curly, shavenheaded and bowed-backed children up to no sense with unrepeatable delight in the dirty sand, moved him, he thought dramatically in his isolation, to an old shame and pity.

In "Who Do You Wish Was With Us," two boys play a wishing game, giving Thomas a chance to demonstrate his ability with minor characters, not in a crowd scene this time but individually and unforgettably distinct.

George Gray is the most curious man I ever met, queerer than Oscar Thomas, and I thought nobody could ever be queerer than that. George Gray wears glasses, but there's no glass in them, only the frames. You wouldn't know until you came near him. He does all sorts of things. He's a cat's doctor and he goes to somewhere in Sketty every morning to help a woman put her clothes on. She's an old widow, he said, and she can't dress by herself. He's only been in town a month. He's a B.A. too. The things he's got in his pockets! Pinchers and scissors for cats and lots of old diaries. He reads me some of his diaries, about the jobs he did in London. He used to go to bed with a policewoman and she used to pay him. She used to go to bed in her uniform. I've never met such a queer man. I wish he was here now. Who do you wish was with us, Ray?

A small masterpiece, one that, in its full length, could make a fine short-short on its own, illustrating two important points of the minor character art: one, that you can easily do minor characters via dialogue alone; two, that doing them this well, you risk having them steal the show entirely from your main characters, and so you better be sure they're causing you to elevate your art with your leading players so your leading players are keeping up with them.

MAJOR MINOR CONSIDERATIONS

There are many other examples worth considering for the way they illustrate the tactically important function minor characters can have. In John Cheever's "Goodbye, My Brother," the family cook serves a vital purpose, even though only a few lines are devoted to her. She partakes of certain universal qualities that suggest *all* good cooks everywhere—her love of food, her judging people's character by what they do or don't eat—and yet she escapes being a mere stereotype by such details as her passionate love for the New York Giants. She's a shrewd judge of character—and early in the story, she does judge, being the first one to see through to the essential darkness of the brother's bitter nature, being repelled by it, quite literally, off the island.

In "Babylon Revisited," F. Scott Fitzgerald's bittersweet farewell to the jazz age in Paris, a short list of names begins the story, the habitués of a bar who, we come to understand, will never return to Paris. The names alone suggest all the *temps perdu* quality; it's a technique Fitzgerald also uses to even greater effect in *The Great Gatsby*, where we find a list of people who were invited to one of Gatsby's parties— a roll call that not only helps convince us of the reality of all this having happened but that gives a biblical cadence to the passage, helping raise the novel to a mythic and monumental level.

It's tempting to say that the only difference between minor characters in stories and minor characters in novels is the size of their minordom. Obviously, in novels a walk-on can have an entire chapter devoted to him or her and still be considered minor. The chief tactical difference seems to be that in novels the minor characters tend to be *running* characters, appearing at regular intervals. Marcel Proust, in his masterpiece *Remembrance of Things Past*, has a lot of fun with the reappearing character of the hotel manager at Balbec, an inveterate snob who mispronounces every multisyllabic word, always picking the most pretentious of the various possibilities. "I hope," he says, apologizing yet again for a less than satisfactory room, "that you will not interpolate this as a want of discourtesy, but I did it in connection with the noise, because in that room you will not have anyone above your head to disturb your trapanum."

We saw in Thomas the danger of having minor characters steal the show; it's clear that many major characters were originally intended to be minor characters but then struck the writer's imagination so forcibly, had so much potential, that they then became the chief focus of interest.

63

(I think here of Sam Weller in Dickens' *The Pickwick Papers*, who, like so many servants before him, is much more interesting than the master he serves.) It can work the other way around as well. Herman Melville, outlining *Moby Dick*, apparently didn't intend to make Ahab the central character, nor Ishmael, but instead, a lonelier, sparer figure, the one who occupies the whole of tiny chapter twenty-three, and is only mentioned elsewhere once.

> Some chapters back, one Bulkington was spoken of, a tall, new-landed mariner, encountered in New Bedford at the inn. When on that shivering winter's night, the Pequod thrust her vindictive bows into the cold malicious waves, who should I see standing at her helm but Bulkington! I look with sympathetic awe and fearfulness upon the man, who in midwinter just landed from a four years' dangerous voyage, could so unrestingly push off again for still another tempestuous term. The land seemed scorching to his feet. Wonderfullest things are ever the unmentionable; deep memories yield no epitaphs; this six-inch chapter is the stoneless grave of Bulkington.

A grave? Not quite that, since having had Bulkington loom so large in his original conception, Melville is not ready to abandon him as a minor character without his contributing his injection of metaphorical profundity and weight.

> But as in landlessness alone resides the highest truth, shoreless, indefinite as God—so, better is it to perish in that howling infinite, than be ingloriously dashed upon the lee, even if that were safety. . . . Take heart, take heart, O Bulkington! Bear thee grimly, demigod! Up from the spray of thy ocean-perishing-straight up, leaps thy apotheosis!

A HUMBLE END

I've saved my favorite minor character for last. Gordon Weaver's *The Eight Corners of the World*, in the ten years since it was first published, has gained a much-deserved reputation as one of the comic masterpieces of World War II. It tells the story of one Yoshinori Yamaguchi, better known simply as "Gooch," a young Japanese boy who grows up in love with everything American—jazz, Hollywood flicks, baseball, hipster slang—and goes on to epitomize in his life everything that's ironic, bitter, and comic in the long love-hate relationship between the United States and Japan.

Early in the novel, Gooch is enlisted by the visiting New York Yankees to help translate. The Yankees are taken to meet the emperor, and a bigger cannon than Gooch is needed to translate the baseball chatter into the proper high-court formulations.

> Ambassador Joe Clark Grew's interpreter (prep-schoolish W. D. Wetherell, reet?) steps forward, renders fair-to-middling full fifty-degree kowtow from waist, delivers riposte (natch!) in incompetent High Court, eyes downcast (natch!) to avoid straight look at Son of Heaven etcetera blah. To wit: "On behalf of all worthy personages gathered in the presence of God's sunshine, in the mouth of Franklin Roosevelt, and in the mouths of Ambassador Grew and the American League warriors of repute here, I extend my congratulations to your heavenly majesty. I now demand to speak the names at the legends who reside in our midst."

Wetherell introduces Babe Ruth, Moe Berg, and continues on in the same incompetent fashion.

> Grew's interpreter Wetherell: "I honor your divine scrutiny with the visage of Connie Mack, whose fabled exploits of execution and delight create a legend rivaled only by his famed brother John McGraw whose twin symbols inspire the worship of youth's ambition in our grand landscape."

Wetherell drones on, making a fool of himself, doing it memorably, personifying, as Gooch does himself, all the mutual incomprehension that, even with the best of intentions, divides the Japanese and American cultures. A great minor character—and not just because author Weaver likes to have fun with his friends, inject them into his fictions, especially a friend who is somewhat famous for bringing out malapropisms of his own. And maybe that's the humbling, chastening conclusion to our survey of this neglected but important aspect of the writer's art, the one lesson we need to keep in mind when we're searching for just the right perspective: That while we are all each one of us major characters in our own lives, to the rest of the world we're strictly minor characters *all* the way.

EXERCISES

1. Buy a sketchbook and a pen. Keep it with you on your daily rounds for a week, jotting a list of all the passersby, the extras, the bit players that flash quickly in your life and just as quickly out of it again, trying to identify the one (or at most two) characteristic that brings them vividly and immediately to life on the page.

2. Try creating three minor characters who come alive via dialogue between two main characters, keeping in mind that those talked about will not appear in the story again. The dialogue should accomplish two goals simultaneously, not only describing the minor characters well, but, by the *way* they're described, revealing much about your two protagonists, their attitudes toward life and toward each other.

3. Write a story with no main characters, only minor ones, none of whom is mentioned more than twice. For setting, take a beach on an out-of-season Sunday afternoon. For theme, the unbridgeable isolation of the human soul.

W. D. Wetherell's books include *Chekhov's Sister*, the story collection *Wherever That Great Heart May Be*, his personal narrative *North of Now*, and eight others. In 1998 he was named the recipient of the Strauss Living Award from the American Academy of Arts and Letters, a fellowship designed to allow a writer to concentrate on his writing for a period of five years.

Location, Location, Location: Depicting Character Through Place

RICHARD RUSSO

My first novel, *Mohawk*, as it was eventually published, was a kind of ensemble novel with a dozen or so important characters and employing numerous points of view. Put all the stories together and you had at their center a portrait of a place, a small fictional town in upstate New York, and in the center of that town a dive called the Mohawk Grill. The town and the grill proved so compelling, at least to me, that I set another novel there. But the first completed draft of the novel that was published as *Mohawk*, you may be surprised to learn, was set in Tucson, Arizona, where I happened to be living when I wrote it. The book was about an elderly woman named Anne Grouse, who began the book bitter and ended up more bitter still, not an emotional trajectory I particularly recommend, though it describes a fair number of contemporary novels.

Beyond these few facts, I don't really remember much about this early draft. I gave it to a friend and mentor who read it and told me what I suspected and maybe even knew but certainly didn't want to hear—that the book wasn't very good, that being in the company of a bitter person in a long work of fiction isn't much more fun than being in the company of a bitter person in real life. Also, my writing betrayed a tourist's knowledge of the Southwest, where I had spent the last six years in a study carrel at the University of Arizona library. On the slender plus side, my friend noted that Anne was a much more interesting person when she was younger, when she still had hopes and dreams and hadn't managed to mess up her life. About the only scenes that really lived were set in the upstate New York town where Anne was raised—one in a glove shop where Anne's father worked and the other at a down-at-the-heels amusement park on the lake.

Also, he told me, the minor characters were far more interesting than the major ones.

Well, this brutal honesty pretty much squared with my own sense of the book. The minor characters, mere functionaries I'd thought, people who grew out of the place and the necessity of the place, were far more interesting than my major characters. The glove shop where Anne's father worked was the one my grandfather had spent his entire adult life toiling in, and the dying amusement park, along its shabby midway, was where both my mother in the thirties and I in the fifties had learned to dream among the fluttering lights and the rigged games of chance. I was no tourist on that midway, but there was a problem: I *wanted* to be a tourist there. I'd left my hometown of Gloversville, New York, when I was eighteen, enrolled in a university twice the size of that town, and by the end of my first week there, learned my first lesson: that I'd do well to hide where I was from. For the next ten years, first as an undergraduate, then as a graduate student, I'd walk backward, erasing my tracks with that wonderful switch we call education. I'd learn how to read carefully and talk to smart people and work from the outside in when confronted at a table with more than one fork. In becoming a writer, I had intended to make use of lessons I'd learned, and for this reason, I was not pleased to learn that the only things I'd managed to bring to life in my first novel were the things I'd hoped—Judas that I was—to deny.

DISCOVERING YOUR PLACE

Intellectually, of course, I already knew that place *was* character. That's Intro Fiction 101. I could illustrate the point with numerous examples from my reading. I knew that London was a character in Dickens, and that it spawned Mr. McCawber, and Crook, and Scrooge. And I could tell what happened to Dickens when he ventured too far from the place that gave him the majority of his people. There's only one reason people read and teach *Hard Times* (the only Dickens novel not set—at least partly—in London) when the rest of the Dickens canon is available: It's short.

And there were plenty of contemporary examples. I could see Larry McMurtry's characters growing directly out of the west Texas soil, its windswept small towns, and saw what happened when he tried to set a novel in Las Vegas. I'm sure McMurtry spent serious time in Vegas, and not in a study carrel either, but still.

Yes, I knew that place was character, but I knew it without, somehow, believing it. Otherwise, how to explain the sense of wonder I felt in the rewriting, the reimagining, of the book I eventually published as *Mohawk*? How else to explain the surprise I felt when, having created the Mohawk Grill from the memory of the half dozen greasy spoons I frequented with my father, I discovered enough vivid characters to occupy every stool at the Formica counter?

INTERIOR PLACE

There's a distinction that's often made in discussions of place—that is, the difference between *interior* and *exterior* setting. Interior setting has come to mean, basically, an indoor place. The setting of *The Glass Menagerie* is primarily an interior one—Amanda Wingfield's apartment. We never leave it, never venture out of doors. We're told the action takes place in St. Louis, but it could be any city. Usually the play is staged in such a way that we glimpse an urban view from the windows of the Wingfield apartment—close brick walls and dark fire escapes and neighboring windows with tattered shades. The Wingfield apartment also has a fire escape, where Tom retreats to smoke, but the play makes clear that the fire escape is an illusion. There's no real escape for the characters, and none for viewers while we watch.

Most beginning writers do a pretty good job of interior setting because they understand that the objects people own comment on them, at times even define them. Anyone who needs convincing might take a look at Mary Gordon's "The Important Houses," included in *The Best American Short Stories 1993*. In the back matter of the book, Gordon admits that the story isn't really a story at all, but rather an excerpt from a long memoir that happens to read like fiction, despite its lack of anything like a plot or chronology or scene. What's amazing is that we get a marvelous sense of character despite the fact that we never meet any of the people, either directly or dramatically, who live in the houses she describes. The grandmother's house, its very contents, offers us a portrait of the woman who owns it—honorable, harsh, judgmental, daunting, repressed, dark. The narrator describes the house.

> . . . every object in her house belonged to the Old World. Nothing was easy; everything required maintenance of a complicated and

specialized sort. . . . each object's rightness of placement made me feel honored to be among them.

The other important house is the residence of the narrator's aunt, whose husband owns a liquor store.

> The house was full of new or newish objects: the plastic holders for playing cards, like shells or fans, the nut dishes in the shape of peanuts, the corn dishes in the shape of ears of corn, the hair dryer like a rocket, the make-up mirror framed by light bulbs, the bottles of nail polish, the ice bucket, the cocktail shaker, the deep freeze.

Though an apprentice writer's descriptions may not be as lush as Gordon's, even beginners understand and accept the basic principles of interior setting—that a person who owns an ice bucket and silver cocktail shaker is different from someone who owns a claw-footed tub for bathing.

EXTERIOR PLACE

The relationship between character and exterior setting is more mysterious. We don't own a landscape, a street, a neighborhood, or a river in the same sense that we own a cocktail shaker or a claw-footed tub, nor can they be said to own us, in the way Thoreau meant when he observed in *Walden* that the things we own can own us in return. True, exterior landscapes can "run through us," in the sense that the river runs through the two brothers in Norman Maclean's memoir. But because the relationship is more tenuous, less sharply defined, it is more likely to be ignored, either in whole or in part, by apprentice writers. I'm forever asking my undergraduates very literal-minded questions about their stories, and the thinly veiled irritation with which these questions are often answered is suggestive.

Where does this story take place? I'll ask innocently, especially when it doesn't seem to have taken place anywhere. Well, I'll be told, it's really more about the people. In a story with a vague urban setting, I'll ask, Which city are we in here? It doesn't really matter, I'll be informed. Well, okay, but I need to know.

In fact, the need to know is not universally conceded. There are examples of great works of literature where the external setting is not specified, the city is not named, the landscape more symbolic or moral than real. My more sophisticated students will dredge up the ghost of

Kafka. Where is the penal colony? We don't know. We don't need to know. Okay, I concede the point, but only after sharing an anecdote and some speculative theorizing.

Some years ago, I was making small talk with an influential New York editor, and I asked him what books he was excited to be bringing out on his spring list. He named and described half a dozen. I don't remember any of the books he wanted to recommend, but I do remember the way he talked about them. The first thing he'd say about each one was where it took place, a fact I remarked upon, because it's often the way I begin talking about books I like, and the way people often begin talking about my own books. I hadn't really given the matter much thought beyond the fairly obvious fact that the "where" of a book is an easy starting place, certainly easier to describe than the "who." But for this editor, it went much deeper, and it turned out my small talk had opened, or reopened, a vein. All the books he published and wanted to publish, he informed me, were ones with a strong sense of place. He said he had little faith in the vision of writers who didn't see clearly and vividly the world their characters inhabited. His most powerful need as a reader, he claimed, was to feel oriented. We agreed that we could do that anywhere, on a street in Calcutta, in the middle of an Iowa cornfield, on a boat in the ocean (that is to say, one place was probably as good as another), but that we couldn't feel oriented either nowhere or anywhere.

We discovered, too, that we had similar habits. We often didn't read very far into books that were set in places we'd never been before putting the book down long enough to consult an atlas. And we also agreed that we didn't care whether the place in question was fictional or real; we still wanted to know where it was located geographically. We'd both consulted maps of Minnesota to locate Jon Hassler's Staggerford, and I explained to him that my Mohawk was located north of the New York State Thruway in the foothills of the Adirondacks.

UNIVERSALITY IN A SMALL TOWN

In some graduate student writers I've taught, the prejudice against rich, detailed, vivid exterior settings was also rooted in the fear that the more specific the setting, the more regional, the less "universal" the story's appeal. Nobody wants to be labeled a regional writer. At one point in his career, McMurtry announced his intention to leave Texas and never return in his fiction, and he had his reasons, among them, I suspect, a desire to be more a citizen of the world than of Texas. If so, who can blame him?

But a moment's reflection will suggest the truth of the matter, and that is that there's no reason to fear the regional label. The American writer of the twentieth century who is the most universal in his concerns is probably William Faulkner, who is also the most regional, having seldom strayed imaginatively outside a single county. The real fear of being labeled regional—in the sense of, say, Hamlin Garland or Sarah Orne Jewett—is its unstated implication. These writers weren't more regional than Mark Twain and Faulkner; they, I believe, were less talented, less visionary, less true. It's *this* kinship with them that we fear, and it's not a fear that's rooted in geography. Writers have to recognize and accept an essential artistic paradox—that the more specific and individual things become, the more universal they feel.

The clearest expression of this that I can share with you is in the form of the two most consistent compliments from people who have read my work. "Boy, you really know those small upstate New York towns," they tell me. Often they explain how they know I know. "Hell, I've lived up there all my life," they say, or, "I've got relatives in Utica and we visit them every year. It's like visiting a Richard Russo novel up there." The second group of people pay me what appears to be on the surface a contradictory compliment. "I thought that was my hometown you were writing about," they'll say about my Mohawk or North Bath, then they'll tell me about their hometown in Georgia or Oregon. Even in England I get this. My advice? Don't try to resolve the paradox of things that are vividly differentiated seeming more universal and familiar as a result. There's neither mathematical nor scientific logic to this. Just take advantage of it.

DESTINY IN A PLACE

In the end, the only compelling reason to pay more attention to place, to exterior setting, is the belief, the faith, that place and its people are intertwined, that place is character, and that to know the rhythms, the textures, the feel of a place is to know more deeply and truly its people. Such faith is not easy to come by or to sustain in this historical period.

Most people, in any historical period, seem able to focus on only one or two ideas at a time. In the matter of human destiny, an issue of some concern to fiction writers, the question of how people become what they become, why they do what they do, has been settled. In our time, the two great determiners of destiny are race and gender. It was not always this way, of course. There was a time in the not too distant past when social class was thought to have been a determining factor in human destiny. Remember the great proletarian novels of the thirties and forties? They seem dated now, in part because the idea of seeing human destiny as determined by class seems not to have survived the Second World War and the GI Bill, this despite the fact that in the last two decades the gap between the haves and the have-nots has widened.

For my mother and many others of her generation, the issue is time. Since his death, my mother and I have spent many hours talking about my grandfather, a man who played a central role in our lives. Her devotion to his memory requires fierce loyalty, which in turn makes it difficult for her to admit her father's frailties. When she's able to do so, it's always with the same proviso. "Well," she says, "I guess he was a product of his time." She never lets it go at that either. She fixes me with a motherly gaze. We're *all* products of our time, she reminds me.

The truth, of course, is that we're products of a lot of things—race, gender, sexual orientation, time, genetics, and chance among them— and we're under no obligation to rank these larger forces. What's interesting to me is that just about the only people I know who seem to believe that place is crucial to human destiny and the formation of human personality are fiction writers. Admittedly, I intuit this from their work, but I think it's true.

Take E. Annie Proulx. *The Shipping News* is, at one level, the story of a man who manages to conquer a gesture. Her protagonist, Quoyle, has a huge jutting chin, courtesy of his Newfoundland genes, and we find him at the beginning of the book self-consciously covering his chin with his hand. Returning to Newfoundland, he finds a place where his movements, clumsy and awkward in New York, feel natural and graceful, a place where he can live without apology, without undue self-consciousness.

Ivan Doig seems to believe in place as a determiner of behavior. Like many western novelists, he suggests that the physical landscape of the West is responsible, at least in part, for philosophical, emotional, political, and spiritual differences between East Coast and West Coast mentalities. Danish author Peter Høeg is also a believer. No work of fiction I've read in recent years is so dominated by a sense of place, where landscapes, interior and exterior, loom so powerfully over character, as in *Smilla's Sense of Snow*. Race, gender, and social class are also powerful forces in the novel, but in the end, it is literally Smilla's sense of snow—of the properties of snow, as well as her ability to navigate in a blizzard that is both physical and moral—that saves her, that provides her with the answers she's been looking for from the beginning.

WHERE HAVE ALL THE PLACES GONE?

Running contrary to such wisdom is our entire cultural climate, which minimizes the importance of place. Witness all those IBM commercials advertising "Solutions for a small planet." In these ads, we listen to people in other cultures speaking in foreign languages. Only the clever running subtitles reveal that the people are talking about their computers, their computer needs, which, it turns out, are the same as ours. We all yearn for more megabytes. It doesn't matter where we live. This message—it is a small world, it doesn't matter much where you are—is being reinforced by both perception and reality. As James Howard Kunstler points out in *The Geography of Nowhere*, the interstate system of highways that allows us to travel five hundred miles a day in about half the time it would have taken thirty years ago has also had the unintended effect of making it seem, when we get to our final destination, that we haven't really gone anywhere. The exit where we get off the interstate is a dead ringer for the one where we got on, their being fifteen hundred miles apart notwithstanding. Interstate travel (even more than air travel, I suspect) also suggests that the places we bypass aren't worth pausing at, a conclusion difficult to reconcile with the growing sameness of our major destinations.

A few years ago, I was invited to attend the Nashville Book Fair. I'd driven through, or rather around, Nashville many times, but I'd never stopped, never visited. I was put up in the Hilton, which was a lot like other Hiltons I'd stayed at, except you could get grits. The cable TV offerings were identical to those offered by our local cable company in Maine, including the Nashville Network. The first of the conference sessions I attended was one on contemporary Southern writing, in which several writers I'd long admired tried to identify what made Southern writing Southern and to offer suggestions for how to preserve it. I have to say it was one of the stranger discussions

I've ever listened to, and not just because I was a Yankee. There was little talk of landscape, or the rhythms of daily life, or architecture, or occupations. Members of the audience wanted to discuss the scent of magnolias and the redness of the earth, and a couple of members of the panel nervously admitted to having relocated to places like Massachusetts. I came away with the distinct impression that even to articulate people who cared about it, our sense of place and what place means is rapidly eroding and that even our vocabulary for discussing place may be gone with the wind. One of the ideas I kept hoping would crop up was the question of how writers should handle the Wal-Mart sameness that is creeping into our cultural life regardless of where we happen to be located. If what made Southern fiction distinctly Southern was being subtly eroded, couldn't the same be said for the notion of place in general? There may be a Burger King in every small town in America, but does that mean they should be similarly ubiquitous in our fiction?

I am of two minds on this subject. Personally, I avoid Burger Kings in fiction as I do in life, and for the same reasons. To me, they are neither nourishing nor enjoyable. I am suspicious of the fact that all you have to do is name such places and the reader is located, a kind of cultural shorthand. I prefer places that require and reward lots of description. This may explain why I'm occasionally accused of harboring a nostalgic view of America. It's true that I become more curmudgeonly every year, and what's needed may be younger eyes. I still remember chortling with glee reading Sam Hodges novel of the new South, *B-Four*, several scenes of which are set in a local IHOP, where the pancake syrup containers are so stuck to the lazy Susans that grown men have all they can do to liberate them. On the other hand, the simple truth may be that there's no place in the world, and no object either, that can't be brought dancing to life when seen by the right eyes. Whether or not Burger Kings deserve a prominent place in our literature is less the issue than whether place itself, which is under siege both in reality and in metaphor, can be rescued from the endangered species list of important concepts.

ADVICE

If I have convinced you that place is an important resource for fiction writers, consider the following practical tips on how to handle place in your fiction.

Describe Selectively

The relative importance of place to any given story is independent of the amount of description given it. The best examples I can think of are John Cheever's Shady Hill stories. They are, in my opinion, the best stories in the Cheever canon. I've read and reread them and taught many of them, and so when one of my students wanted to write a critical essay on the importance of setting in fiction, I suggested the Shady Hill stories, remembering the vivid sense of life's rhythms that Cheever had created through what I remembered as lush descriptions.

The problem was that when my student read those stories herself, she found very little description. She couldn't, she told me, find a single sustained passage of description in any of them. Preposterous. "You've read 'O Youth and Beauty'?" I asked her. " 'The House-breaker of Shady Hill'?" She had. Closely. Which forced me to go back to the stories myself, and of course she was right. There were very few descriptive details, and these were woven so skillfully into the stories' drama, in such seemingly subordinate ways, that they were difficult to extract, like molars in the back of the mouth, unseen but with the deepest roots imaginable. What kind of furniture does Cash Bentley hurtle in his friends' living rooms before his wife shoots him in midair? What's the architecture of the houses that Johnny Hake burgles? I'd had the impression that such information was offered in these stories.

By comparison, the later Cheever stories, many of which take place in Italy, are much more descriptive, but there's a touristy feel to them, as if the author feels compelled to give us what filmmakers call "estab-lishing shots." The film takes place in New Orleans? Then you open with a shot of the bridge over Lake Pontchartrain, Cajun music in the background, then obligatory shots of the French Quarter. By contrast, the deep sense of place that emerges from the Shady Hill stories has more to do with life's rhythms, where things are in relation to other things, whether the characters can walk there and how long that will take, whether they'll drive or take the train. We won't be told that the cocktail shaker is pure silver; we'll be told that it's sweating in the lazy Sunday mid-morning sun. Rendering such passive details active makes us insiders, not tourists. We become giddy, well-heeled drinkers trying to banish hangovers, not sober, anthropological observers of curious behavior.

See Clearly From the Start

Something to guard against: My own experience of writing, which may be different from yours, is that even when I acknowledge the importance of the physical world, even when I make mental notes and scribble reminders, I still have to guard against the temptation to believe that I'll be able to add onto a scene later, flesh it out after I've attended to other matters. If the scene is talky (too reliant on dialogue), or if it's too interior (too reliant on a character's thoughts at the expense of the physical world), I'm often tempted to let it go, move on to the next scene, promising to return later with a bucketful of descriptive details.

I know I'm not alone in this. When I complain to my students that their scenes are vague, that the dialogue seems to be coming out of thin air, as if the scene were wired in such a way that we had to choose between the audio and the video, they frequently tell me not to worry, that they'll go back and add the details of the physical world later. What they want to know is whether the characters are doing and saying the right things. Such an attitude not only ranks the various tasks of the fiction writer, subordinating the objective world, but it suggests something about the process that I've never found to be true. When I'm writing badly, I'm almost always in a kind of fast-forward, taking shorthand notes on what the characters are doing and saying. The edges of the picture are fuzzy and blurred by speed. Later, when I realize the scene isn't working, when I go back and try to "fill in the details," what I find is that the details I fill in often invalidate what the characters have said and done. Better and more efficient to slow down and see clearly to begin with. If character can grow out of place, as I've suggested, it follows that place cannot be the thing that's "grafted on" late in the process.

Create Distance

My own experience has been that the place I'm living is probably not the place I'm writing about. Now that I've lived in Maine for several years, I'm often asked by people who consider me a Maine writer by virtue of my address when I'll be writing a novel set in Maine. They don't realize what they're probably asking is when I plan to leave the state. The simple truth of the matter is I've never written effectively about any place I was currently residing. I not only need to leave but actually need to have been gone for some time for my imagination to kick in, to begin the process of necessary tempering of knowledge.

It may be different for you, but the ability to look out my window and see what I'm describing in a story is not an advantage. If what I'm describing is really there, I'm too respectful of and dependent upon the senses, and the thing described, as a result, will often not have the inner life I want it to have. I'd rather make a mistake, get something physically wrong, put the button on the wrong side of the sleeve, than be dictated to by literal reality, than place intuition and imagination in a straitjacket. Maybe this is just a feeble justification for the many things I get wrong as a result, but I don't think so.

Use Research Selectively

Just as the importance and vividness of place is independent of the amount of description given it, there is also no direct correlation between the vividness of your setting and comprehensive, factual knowledge. Granted, throughout this essay, I've been insisting on the essential relationship between place and character, but I'm not particularly advocating Micheneresque research. An intimate understanding of place can lead to character breakthroughs, but that's not the same as to say that encyclopedic knowledge of the facts of place will yield interesting characters.

Often, the exact opposite will happen. Too much knowledge of the literal can stifle the metaphorical. Many best-sellers give the impression of having been written *by* tourists *for* tourists, and such books, for all their insistence upon location, somehow locate me in a world that's halfway between a library and a good travel agency, and the difference between the places in these novels and the places in reality is the difference between the place itself and the picture of it on a color brochure.

A PRODUCT OF PLACE

Finally, even those among you who are convinced by the argument I've been articulating about the importance of place and the link between place and character may not end up as place-oriented in your fiction as I am in mine. The writers I've discussed above are, as I'm sure you've noticed, like-minded. If I'd chosen different writers to draw examples from, my conclusions might have been different.

I can only give you my sense of how profoundly important place has been to my own life and my life as an artist. If I were black or gay or a woman, chances are my life as a person and as an artist would have been shaped more dramatically by race or gender or sexual orientation. But insofar as I'm a "product" of anything, to borrow my mother's term, I feel I'm a product of place, of places, and insofar as my fiction has been a product of anything, since the moment I realized that my first novel could not be set in Arizona, it has been a product of places that have, in turn, offered up people by the dozens.

Some years ago, at an East Coast writers residency, C.J. Hribal and Michael Martone and I were referred to by some as "the corn boys," the result, I suppose, of our teaching in Midwestern universities. It was odd for me to be referred to this way and I tried to conceal my annoyance lest it be considered geographical snobbery. I don't, believe me, consider the small, shabby town in upstate New York where I grew up to be superior to other places, and if I'd grown up in Iowa, I doubt I would have minded much being referred to as a "corn boy." I simply felt mislabeled, and therefore misunderstood, in much the same way I feel now when I'm referred to as a "Maine writer."

I may not be "the product" of upstate New York either, but the link is there, and I feel it profoundly. How else would I explain the strange dreams I'm subject to for days before I visit my remaining relatives in my hometown? How would I explain the irrational fears that descend upon me when I return, primary among them the fear that I will be killed in an auto accident during one of these quick visits? This was my grandfather's fear for me. We lived one house down from one of the worst intersections in town, where local drivers routinely ignored a stop sign in plain view, bashing into each other, narrowly missing small children who were crossing the intersection on errands to the corner market.

My grandfather feared I'd be run down in sight of the front porch before I could make my mark on the world, and now, forty years later, I have inherited his fear. How else would I explain the fact that when I pass the open door of the worst dive in town I sense that the empty barstool farthest from the light is really mine, that it's being saved for me, that perhaps in some alternate universe I'm already occupying it, that when the phone rings, I no longer even have to remind the bartender that I'm not there. What these irrational fears have in common is the sense that this place has a claim on me, a claim that may be presented at any time, a claim that seems less perilous to acknowledge than to ignore.

EXERCISES

1. Write a first-person narrative in which you develop another character by describing that second character's house or room (or his gym locker or the trunk of her car—anything that belongs to the character). To insure focus, don't let the second character enter the narrative.

2. Describe a landscape (urban, rural, suburban) in such a way that it might help to explain the behavior of the people who live there. (For example, a description of a huge, empty, closed-down factory with broken windows might help to explain why so many of the people who live in that place congregate idly in the parking lot of a convenience store a couple blocks away.)

3. Write about a public place from your childhood (a movie theater? ballpark? town dump?) that still inspires powerful emotions.

Richard Russo is the author of the novels *Straight Man*, *Nobody's Fool*, *Mohawk*, and *The Risk Pool*. He has taught writing at a variety of colleges and universities, including Colby College in Maine and Warren Wilson College.

Sympathy for the Devil: What to Do About Difficult Characters

ROBIN HEMLEY

I've heard people say about one story or another that there's no one who is sympathetic in it, no one who is likable, and they offer this as a reason why the story is no good. I know of people who only read stories with likable characters with whom they identify. I once had a student from North Carolina who told me he only read stories set in North Carolina and written by North Carolina writers. I was dumbfounded. A friend of mine once received a rejection from a highly respected magazine that read: "We do not know these characters," and this didn't seem to be a lack on the author's part, but more an admission that the editors had not met any of these characters at a party.

I've found that I can be intrigued with characters without necessarily liking them. And it's certainly not important for me to identify with them. But I *must* feel sympathy for a character, and here I'm using the word "sympathy" not merely as a synonym for "like," but more in terms of "understanding." If we as writers understand our characters, even the unlikable ones, if we understand their motivations, and convey this understanding to the reader, then perhaps we will come to understand something more about the mysteries of human behavior and aspiration, not the givens we already grasp, not the people and borders we know well.

A few years ago, writers talked a lot about feeling compassion toward one's characters, as though a story were a kind of charity ball put on by the author to get all these likable folks together, the characters and the readers. I suppose that sounds cynical, but I don't mean it that way. One can, after all, go too far in the other direction and lose all reader sympathy.

NEVER KILL YOUR MICE

When I was in graduate school, I wrote a story called "The Mouse Town," a first-person, semiautobiographical piece about two boys whose fathers have died, and who test the boundaries of love and death with their twenty-six pet mice. In plainer language, you might say they torture these poor mice. My own father had died when I was seven, and I had twenty-six pet mice that a friend and I kept in an aquarium at school. One day, a girl in our class made a gift of a cardboard mouse town for my mice, with a mouse market, a mouse house, a mouse ice-cream parlor. When I tired of the mouse town, little pyromaniac that I was, I burned it. These were the bare facts of my personal experience, and I put them together in a first-person story. The fictional boys far exceed my own misadventures with the real mice. They swing the mice around in pillowcases, nearly drown them, and finally burn the mouse town with several of their mice inside.

Now here's where the problem of sympathy gets tricky. If I had allowed the mice to die, if I had focused on their charred bodies and rendered the scene grotesquely, that would have become the story—it would have overwhelmed the characters and certainly any care the reader might have for them. All we would think of, quite rightly, would be "Those poor mice!"

An editor was visiting our workshop the day my story was critiqued, and she liked the story but told me to get rid of the first paragraph in which I had explained everything. I wrote, in part, "We were two sociopathic brats, but much to our credit our mice never were hurt."

Of course the reason the editor told me to take out that paragraph was that it telegraphed the entire story and undercut the tension of the narrative. I had written that sentence in part, too, because I didn't want people to identify me too closely with the narrator and think I was a bad person. As Alyce Miller alludes to in her essay in this book, I wanted to be liked, which is always a bad impulse when writing a first-person story. The writer, like the reader, should not confuse the main character with him- or herself. If you want to be liked, give gifts, don't write stories.

Next, the editor told me to extend the scene in which the boys burn down the mouse town. In the original version, the burning takes all of two paragraphs and then the mice are saved. In the final version, the burning takes two-and-a-half pages, the reader uncertain until the end whether or not the mice will live. In a story, one wants to create tension, not dissipate it, and at the climactic scene especially. If the reader was going to think my main characters were brats for those two-and-a-half pages while the kids frantically tried to save their mice, then so be it.

But the mice don't die in the story. And here, the visiting editor gave me a valuable pointer. She said, "I'm glad the mice didn't die. If they had, you would have lost me as a reader. Never kill the mice."

And that seems like a valuable axiom to me. Never kill your mice, though even this simple admonition I hesitate to write because there are undoubtedly stories in which the mice need to die. But in my story, the characters would have tipped from understandable (we see them trying to come to terms with their fathers' deaths) to characters who make us want to say, "I don't care to understand them."

A CRACK IN THE ARMOR

Writers have always been drawn to difficult subjects, characters, and points of view. Like everything else, it's a matter of how you approach the subject and whether your goals are simple or complex.

After Medgar Evers was assassinated in Mississippi in the early sixties, Eudora Welty decided to write a story, "Where Is the Voice Coming From?" from the point of view of his then-unidentified assassin. I venture to say that it was not her intention to show this man as a soulless monster, but instead, she was showing exactly what made this assassin human, what made him too much like us, not so different that we could say, simply, "How horrible," as we do when we pass a car wreck on the interstate. As Hannah Arendt said about the Nazis, it's dangerous for us to think of them as monsters. If we do, then they become apart from us. Evil, as she said, is banal, not extraordinary. What's extraordinary is the natural human inclination to look away from it, not to understand it in ourselves. The point here is that Welty, also a Mississippian, knew any number of people who could have murdered Evers, and she felt that she could, to borrow a phrase from the writer Grace Paley, get under "the rock of his reasons." I'm not entirely sure if this is apocryphal, but I've heard a number of times that when Welty's story was published, the FBI contacted her and used it as a profile to help catch the murderer.

It's tempting sometimes to make characters either too good or too evil, to give them, as in old westerns, black hats or white hats. But most people are neither all good nor all bad, and even the best are capable of small and large betrayals. This is certainly not news, but writers need to constantly remind themselves of it.

Mixing Good and Evil

Flannery O'Connor's "A Good Man Is Hard to Find" starts off innocuously enough: "The grandmother didn't want to go to Florida." She and her son Bailey, with whom she lives, his wife, and two children, John Wesley and June Star, are off for a family vacation, but the grandmother selfishly doesn't want to go to Florida, because she'd rather visit some relations in east Tennessee. But instead of admitting this, she points to the newspaper and tells Bailey that there's a murderer loose who calls himself the Misfit, and he's loose in the direction they're headed.

The grandmother is portrayed as selfish and conniving, wanting to bring her cat, Pitty Sing, with her because she's afraid he might accidentally asphyxiate himself on the stove's gas burners and also because he might miss her too much. She is full of simple pieties and polite chitchat that disguise her racism, elitism, and solipsistic view of the world. When she and her family do, in fact, run headlong into the Misfit, she stays on her selfish path. She tells the Misfit to "Pray, pray," begging him not to "shoot a lady," while her family, in pairs, is being led off into the woods and shot. Her behavior is understandable under the circumstances—she's afraid for her life. But it's this behavior that's brought her to this crossroads, so to speak, in the first place. She keeps telling the Misfit that he's a good man, she just knows it. He doesn't have common blood at all, she tells him. She can tell by looking at him. And, in fact, the Misfit, by her superficial standards, is a good man. He takes off his hat in front of the ladies. He makes chitchat about the weather. He's respectful and polite to everyone as each is led off to the woods to die.

The Misfit is definitely evil, but O'Connor does not make the mistake of turning him into a monster. He's spectacled and almost distinguished looking. His face has a vulnerable quality. And most importantly, O'Connor understands his motivations. She has created a history for him, and even a warped but genuinely held philosophy, "No pleasure but meanness," is his motto. And what set him off on his crime spree is the fact that he was accused of a crime he says he did not commit—the murder of his own father. He claims to the grandmother that he did no such thing, that

> a head doctor said what I did was kill Daddy, but I known that for a lie. My daddy died of the epidemic flu in 19 ought 19, and he's buried in the Mount Hopewell Baptist Church yard and you can go there and see for yourself if you don't believe me.

This is, of course, a classic case of someone protesting too much. We come to understand that he has blocked out his horrific crime. But the point is that he believes that he didn't murder his daddy, and so he says, everything was thrown off balance, and that's why he calls himself the Misfit, and now whenever he commits a crime or some other meanness, he signs his name to it so in the end he can put all the crimes he's done against all the punishment he's suffered and see if they match up.

As I said, he's warped but believable. And he's more sincere than the grandmother, who, with all her religious pieties, is pretty much a hypocrite. When they start talking about Jesus, she does so simply to save her skin, but the Misfit is really upset and captivated by the notion of Jesus, saying that Jesus, too, threw everything off balance by being punished for crimes he didn't commit.

Toward the end of the story the grandmother sinks to the ground, delirious with fright, as the Misfit bends furiously over her. He's wearing a yellow shirt with bright blue parrots that belonged until a few minutes before to her now-murdered son. Confusing the Misfit for her son, both physically and spiritually, she reaches to touch him and says with true compassion, "Why, you're one of my babies. You're one of my own children." The Misfit reacts to her compassion with horror, so conditioned is he to the world's vilification. He shoots her three times in the chest, prompting his remark to his henchmen, Hiram and Bobby Lee, that, "She would have been a good woman if it had been someone there to shoot her every minute of her life."

Not that I'm happy to see anyone die, but it's lucky for us that the grandmother wasn't all that good. In fact, no one in the story is good: certainly not the Misfit or Hiram and Bobby Lee; not the grandmother's son Bailey; not Red Sammy Butts, the owner of The Tower Barbecue; definitely not the wonderful brats of the story, June Star and John Wesley. There's also a baby in the story, the cat, Pitty Sing, and the children's mother, whose face is "as broad and innocent as a cabbage."

These characters are incidental to the story and are not so much good as innocent. Goodness requires some choice, some volition, and the cat has no will, nor the baby, and not, in this instance, Bailey's wife. It's the grandmother's volition, her will, that leads her to make the selfish choices that result in the deaths of the family.

Imagine if the grandmother had been a good person, if she had been worthy of the reader's unadulterated love and admiration. My reaction to the story would be, "How horrible," and little more, the same reaction I have when I read a newspaper account of a distant and regrettable tragedy. It's O'Connor's genius to make the grandmother fallible and believable and too much like ourselves for us to conveniently ignore or pity.

Making the Reader Care

In the end, we feel a kind of sympathy for the grandmother *and* the Misfit, because both have been fundamentally changed by the other. The grandmother, of course, has been killed, but she's also become compassionate for once. The Misfit, too, has been led to the brink of compassion and is left unsure of his own mean-spirited credo, and we see him without his glasses, his eyes "red-rimmed and vulnerable."

This is perhaps the most important point to remember if you want to make us care about characters who are otherwise bad, immoral, selfish, mean, or obnoxious: You must make us care about them. You must make them capable of change, whether they, in fact, *do* change, or at least you should intimate that they were not always as low-down as they appear now. The way I always put it to my classes is this: Show us the crack in their armor. Sometimes it takes a whole story or even a novel to get to that crack, and you don't want it to seem forced or too easy as in, "Sam hadn't always been so skunklike, but when his mama died and his daddy run off with the preacher's daughter and his big brother whupped him for stealing his baseball cards, a heinous crime, but one he had *not* committed, Sam decided 'what the heck,' and became Desperado Sam."

There's not a whole lot of difference between my Desperado Sam and O'Connor's Misfit in terms of what has made them outcasts, *except* that the Misfit is believable and Desperado Sam ain't. We're talking here about character-based, traditional fiction. If you want to write a satire about Desperado Sam, then all bets are off. Don't show us the crack in the armor; exaggerate the violence, satirize our gun-crazed, TV-addled culture. In this case, you're after effect rather than revelation, or the revelation is of a different sort. Instead of giving us a more complicated understanding of the human psyche, you're exploring a theme, an issue, a single idea or word, and twisting it until it becomes strange and hilarious. T. Coraghessan Boyle does this exquisitely in his short story "The Hit Man." In Boyle's story, we see the hit man in a variety of situations from grade school to old age, leading a fairly normal existence except for his penchant for mob-style hits and the stylish black hood he's worn since birth.

AN UPHILL BATTLE

Another way to make your unsympathetic character more sympathetic is to give him an uphill battle to fight. Usually these uphill battles are of the character's own devising—because of his own shortcomings or mistakes, the character must now suffer, and the skilled writer will make her characters suffer greatly. The suffering, of course, is not an end in itself. The uphill battle has a goal. This all sounds very high-handed and moralistic, and in a sense it is, but it does not have to appear so to the writer or reader. The outcome of this uphill battle should not seem preordained to the writer or reader. The outcome should always seem in doubt—there should always be the hope of happiness, of tragedy averted, or, conversely, the suspicion that the character's happiness and dreams are short-lived and that real sorrow lurks around the corner.

Why give a bad character an uphill battle to fight? Why not a story about a good person fighting an uphill battle? Sure, the latter can work, too, but to me, it's much more interesting, complex, and ambitious to make us care about a character who, for example, has alienated all those who truly love him.

King Lear is an example. It's Lear's willfulness and foolish pride that make us almost hate him for succumbing to the empty flattery of Goneril and Regan while punishing Cordelia. By the end of the play, not only have we seen a crack in his armor, he's basically walking around in his underwear. And he has suffered greatly: evicted by his false daughters, made to wander mad around the stormy heath, and finally imprisoned and sentenced to die.

By the end of the play, as we see Lear caged with Cordelia, only the most callous of us would shrug our shoulders and say, "Big deal, he deserves it." By this time, he's fought an uphill battle with himself and won, even though the price is his own life and the life of Cordelia. And while we see he's foolish, he does, too, and in a sense has earned back our sympathy.

THE FATAL FLAW

As a writer and a reader, I think it's always important to question constantly motives and portrayals. While fiction certainly deals with conflict, it's also about seeing into the true nature of people, uncovering falsehoods and half-truths. Most people (and by extension, most characters) have fatal flaws.

If I were to write about Charles Lindbergh, I wouldn't treat him as the simple gawky hero of 1927. I would certainly deal with his cruel sense of humor, his practical jokes, his racist views, and his pro-Nazi leanings. I'd make him real. I might use, for instance, his real words that I obtained through the Freedom of Information Act from an internal FBI memo to J. Edgar Hoover, in which Lindbergh is quoted in 1941 as saying,

> There is only one danger in the world—that is the yellow danger. China and Japan are really bound together against the white race. There could only have been one effective weapon against this alliance, underneath the surface, Germany itself could have been the weapon. . . . But instead the British and the fools in Washington had to interfere. The British envied the Germans and wanted to rule the world forever.

That's certainly not the two-dimensional view of Lindbergh portrayed in *The Spirit of St. Louis*, starring Jimmy Stewart. Can you imagine Stewart reciting a speech such as that? I can't, and I'd hate to change the movie. But a more complicated view of Lindbergh in, let's say, a novel, would not only be more accurate but also, I think, ultimately more intriguing.

If I were to write about Amelia Earhart, someone I *do* admire, I still would show her faults. I would deal with the fact that she wasn't that great a pilot. In fact, she often cracked up her planes and invariably blamed these crack-ups on mechanical failure. There were many women pilots of the time who were much better than she, but they did not have access to the publicity machine of Earhart's promoter husband, G.P. Putnam. Her fatal flaw—and in her case, it really was fatal—was her belief in the hype G.P. built around her. One of her biggest mistakes before she took off on that final leg of her journey from New Guinea was that she opted not to take along certain equipment that would have helped to locate her.

None of this makes Earhart bad or even less admirable—simply complex, and a perfect subject for fiction.

THE COMPLEXITIES OF HUMAN BEHAVIOR

The serious writer of fiction, I believe, is interested in the complexities of human behavior. For this reason, some of the best stories deal with actions that would seem to us at first glance to be reprehensible and beyond our ken. The murder of a child, for instance. Who could possibly make a child murderer sympathetic? Toni Morrison does in *Beloved*. I understand and completely sympathize with the character who kills her child to protect her from the institution of slavery. Who could possibly make us sympathize with someone who covers up the evidence of a hit-and-run accident in which someone dies? Andre Dubus does in "A Father's Story," in which a man covers for his daughter who kills a man on the side of a highway while she's driving home from a party. Encapsulated, as synopsis, this still seems horrific and completely unsympathetic, but that's why it takes a whole story for Dubus to reveal the characters' motivations; we might as well ask a poet to give us in a pithy phrase the gist of his or her poem. Dubus also writes a story in which a man kills the killer of his son. The man does this because he's frustrated that his son's killer will not be punished, and so he does it himself. Even now, I'm horrified as I say this, that I could feel sympathy for such a vigilante by the end of Dubus' story.

I'm using the word "sympathy" again not simply as a synonym for "like," though I do, in fact, like all of these characters who have done things we might normally consider unsympathetic. If we understand why someone feels she has to kill her child, why someone feels he has to protect his daughter, why someone feels he has to kill the killer of his son, we might not say, "Bravo!" but we might be brought to a place of genuine compassion and understanding that would hardly seem possible without the prose writer's magical ability to make us recognize our deepest selves, the ones we try daily to bury.

This is what fiction does sometimes. It makes you the outlaw. It makes you question your assumptions about yourself. It makes you question your boundaries and tests what you might and might not do, your pieties, your hypocrisies, your simple repetition of phrases that make you feel safe and good, in the moral know, in the political know. People are full of contradictions. That, to me, is the central truth we learn our whole lives long. Bad people do good things. Good people do bad things. If you want to fuel the plots of your stories, to make your characters believable and intriguing, make them contradictory. Reveal who they think they aren't. Show us their fatal flaws.

THE GUN IN THE HANDBAG

Sometimes a writer will choose a character who, even by the end of the story, is completely reprehensible, more so than the grandmother in "A Good Man Is Hard to Find," but a character who retains his humanity nonetheless. Here, I'm thinking of John Cheever's, "The Five-Forty-Eight," about a cold and solipsistic businessman named Blake, who is stalked and made to beg for his life by a mentally unstable woman, Miss Dent, with whom he has slept and then fired from her post as secretary at the firm where he works. There's nothing likable about Blake, no cracks in his armor at all. He does one reprehensible act after another. When Miss Dent gives him roses at work, he throws them in the wastebasket. When his wife fixes his dinner late, he stops talking to her. He goes so far as to circle a date on the calendar two weeks from that day to let her know when he'll speak with her again. He's so self-unaware that he verges on parody.

Why would a writer focus on such an unsympathetic character? Because he's *the most interesting* character. In the end, Miss Dent tries to show him some things about himself by holding a gun to his head, much as the Misfit holds a gun to the grandmother's head in O'Connor's story.

Miss Dent's motive seems self-explanatory, though she's a complex character as well. But it's Blake's self-deceptions and rationalizations that have fueled Miss Dent's violence in the first place. Perhaps, Cheever wanted to see if Blake, like the grandmother, could be a good person when confronted by his mortality. He couldn't. Blake wouldn't be a good person even if there was someone to shoot him every minute of his life.

In "The Train," Raymond Carver, as a kind of homage to Cheever, continues the story where Cheever left off, but from a different point of view: Miss Dent's. In Carver's continuation, we see Miss Dent waiting in the station for the return train to the city, perhaps twenty minutes or so after her confrontation with Blake. By this point, she's no longer concerned with Blake. She's accomplished her mission. Here's how the story opens.

> The woman was called Miss Dent, and earlier that evening she'd held a gun on a man. She'd made him get down in the dirt and plead for his life. While the man's eyes welled with tears and his fingers picked at leaves, she pointed the revolver at him and told him things about himself.

After a paragraph of background, Miss Dent is finished with Blake forever. Shortly, two strangers join her in the waiting room. These two, an older barefoot man and a middle-aged woman, have come from a party, and what do they make of Miss Dent sitting there primly and quietly? Not much. These two characters are fairly obnoxious, and here, too, is another strategy worth considering: One way to write about unsympathetic characters is from the point of view of someone who *is* sympathetic. But you have to be careful that your characters don't come across as the sympathetic ones versus the unsympathetic ones. Miss Dent, after all, is a little cracked, and the couple who barge in on her reverie, while obnoxious, seem relatively harmless, unlike Blake. And unlike Miss Dent, whom they *think* is harmless.

They don't know about the revolver in her handbag.

That, too, is something worth remembering. Your characters, in a sense, should always have revolvers in their handbags. Not that they should use them. In fact, Miss Dent doesn't. It's enough for Carver that we know she's already used it once this evening. It's enough for him that the other characters *don't* know this about her.

There's an old saw that goes, "If you have a gun in a story, it has to go off." I'm saying it doesn't.

I once tutored a former CEO of a major bank. He didn't like being a student. He didn't like following someone else's suggestions. And the strangest thing was that he didn't want anyone besides me and the chair of my English department to know he was being tutored in fiction writing. Might give him a bad name, I suppose. So every week he'd arrive in dark glasses after hours at my office and I'd go over the fairly mediocre and dry novel he was writing about a barge captain who gets caught in a hurricane. The story was technically perfect. Everything you ever wanted to know about piloting a barge was in that text, but the only tests the captain had to face were tests of the elements, nothing darker than a darkened sky. One time, we were discussing stories and I told him about "The Lottery," Shirley Jackson's story about the gentle folk of a town who wind up stoning to death one of their own in an annual spring ritual. After about five minutes, this man's face grew white and he said he remembered this story. In fact, he'd read it when it first came out in the forties in *The New Yorker*, and the story had so horrified him that he'd canceled his subscription. And then the CEO stopped coming to his meetings. He couldn't deal with someone who liked a story about such nice people doing something so completely horrific and impossible. I wonder what horrified him so, what made him cancel his subscription in the first place, this person who went on to fund the bulldozing of an inner-city neighborhood in Charlotte, North Carolina, in the name of urban renewal.

Oh well. The person who became CEO after him was even worse, though I never tutored the second guy in fiction. But people who know the new CEO of this bank have told me of one of this man's endearing habits. At board meetings, he tosses a disarmed grenade from palm to palm, and when the meeting is over, what does he do? He pulls the pin, of course.

Now who can't love such an unsympathetic character as that?

EXERCISES

1. Find a published story with an unsympathetic character in it, and like Carver did with Cheever's story, continue it from a different point of view. If it's told from the point of view of a more sympathetic character, use the less sympathetic character's point of view, or vice versa. Try at all times to retain your character's essential credibility. This exercise is not about satire but about understanding the different ways in which we can approach human behavior.

2. Write a satire using an unsympathetic character in the way that T. Coraghessan Boyle has written "The Hit Man." Maybe you'll write "The Dictator" or "The Senator." Exaggeration is the key here.

3. Sketch a character who has a basic blind spot. Either she's selfish and petty like the grandmother in "A Good Man Is Hard to Find" or foolishly prideful like Lear or dominating and egotistical like Blake in Cheever's story. Or whatever else you can think of. Give the character a fatal flaw or at least one that will engineer his own downfall. Now set that fatal flaw in motion. In other words, make the person act on that flaw. Don't be surprised if you wind up with a novel.

Robin Hemley's short stories have won various awards, including two Push-carts, STORY magazine's Humor Award, The Nelson Algren Award from *The Chicago Tribune*, The George Garrett Award from *Willow Springs*, and The Hugh J. Luke Award from *Prairie Schooner*. His stories have been antholo-gized on National Public Radio's "Selected Shorts," and "The Sound of Writing" elsewhere. His story collections include *All You Can Eat* and *The Big Ear*, and he has published a novel, *The Last Studebaker*. His memoir, *Nola: A Memoir of Faith, Art, and Madness*, was published by Graywolf in September 1998, and he is currently working on a book of nonfiction for Farrar, Straus and Giroux. He is Associate Professor of Creative Writing at Western Washington University.

III
Point of View

Casting Shadows, Hearing Voices: The Basics of Point of View

VALERIE MINER

P oint of view is one of the most basic elements in the craft of fiction. Through this medium, storytellers see (hear, feel, smell, taste) from particular consciousnesses and metabolisms as well as from specific spatial and temporal perspectives. Since most contemporary fiction involves a "growth of perception" (among characters and readers), the selection of viewpoint is crucial. Who is telling what story? *Who* is integral to *what* because the narrator shapes content.

Many emerging writers ignore this element of craft, perhaps because point of view seems automatic. While it's true that one may have a natural affinity for first person or third person, experienced writers rehearse fiction with a variety of instruments. A single piece of music may be played by a violin, flute, piano, and oboe. In each case, the tune is the "same" but the music is "different" because of the chosen instrument. Likewise in fiction, while basic details of plot may be similar whether told from the first person or the third person, the *story* varies greatly depending on the narrator. Or narrators. With chamber performance or larger orchestration, music is different yet again as instruments are combined. So, too, in fiction, harmonious or dissonant narration can add dimension. Playing with the narrator's perspective acquaints writers with the range of their voices. Even authors who loyally stick to one point of view for their whole careers can learn something about the strengths and limitations of their preferred medium by occasionally fiddling with who is telling the story.

FIRST PERSON

First person usually employs the "I" voice and sometimes the "we" voice. A first-person narrator can give the impression that a story is "more real." This point of view implies intimacy and makes a dramatic story even more immediate. A first-person protagonist narrator often heightens readers' sympathy with certain characters because the story-telling appears more personal.

On the other hand, first person may reveal a solipsism in writers who only want to tell their "own" life stories. Or a voyeurism in readers seeking vicarious experience of other people's joy, loss, sexual ecstasy, ambition, and violence. Perhaps some satisfactions provided by the "truer" voice of the "I" narrator comes from the simple human impulse for gossip.

Skillful use of first person avoids an impression of self-centeredness. As Jack Hodgins says in his wise book *A Passion for Narrative*, "the most successful first person narrators talk less about themselves than about others. We learn about them indirectly." Grace Paley models this lesson in *Later the Same Day*, in which her character Faith discloses volumes about herself in a description of her grown sons.

> The boys were in different boroughs trying to find the right tune
> for their lives. They had been men to a couple of women and
> therefore only came to supper now and then. They were worried
> for my solitariness and suggested different ways I could wear
> my hair.

Authors less experienced than Paley can confuse first-person fiction with memoir. The current American fashion in autobiographical fiction and criticism is complicated enough to be the subject of an entire essay, but here I will raise only a few caveats. *Some* autobiographical fiction is no more than score settling or retrospective psychoanalysis. Not evils in themselves, but projects distant from the imaginative artistic search that attends to the instinctive unconscious. When we insist our "real life" stories into fictional frames, we often fail to distinguish between the "I" author and the "I" narrator. How can we *know* what we know if we only reassemble from lived and remembered experience? How can we transcend the moment if we don't imagine? Ironically, I find that the strongest fiction is autobiographical not in the form of "memory recorded" but in the form of premonition— when what we write predicts what will happen to us, when life follows art. While memory is at best a reconstruction, imagination sometimes bears the grace of prophecy.

One learns so much about the story, the character, and the writerly self by examining habitual use of point of view. For years, I tried to avoid the first person. Gradually I noticed that I had more empathy for my "he" and "she" characters than for my "I" characters, a problem directly linked, I believe, to a serious penchant for self-criticism and apology. Mea Culpa is my Latin name. Only when I concentrated on and practiced that crucial distinction between authorial identity and narrative persona was I able to do a book in the first person.

Recently I rewrote the final drafts of my seventh novel, *Range of Light*, in the first person after writing several drafts in the third person. First person allowed me greater access to the internal lives of the main characters, Adele and Kath, and also a more direct channel for expressing their feelings toward one another. To underline the subjective unreliability of this first-person narration, I often related the same incident twice, through the separate "I" voices of Adele and Kath. One challenge of this mode is that the language of the *narrated action* and *description* as well as the language in the dialogue must be character identified. For instance, Kath and Adele are walking in the same mountains at the same time of day and yet, in their internal monologues, the setting is portrayed differently by each of them, through the lenses of their idiosyncratic consciousnesses and through the distinct registers of their individual voices. My insight into each protagonist was deepened by listening so directly to Kath and Adele that now I don't know how I could have considered using the third person.

SECOND PERSON

Second person affords a different kind of intimacy, whether we imagine "you" as the listener, as the narrator's alter ego, as a particular third party or as an anonymous character tracing his or her way through the story. The "you" can be singular or plural: "you" as in "you, Robert Burns," or "you" as in "you, the Scottish people."

Perhaps the most familiar literary use of second person is in romantic poetry, when a loved one is addressed directly. ("How do I love thee, let me count the ways. . . .") The poetic tradition of the *apostrophe*—speech in which the absent (person, people, abstract thing) is being addressed—can convey intimacy not only with lovers but with friends, family members, objects or ideas. *Apostrophe* comes from the Greek, "a turning away." Here's an example from "A Deep-Sworn Vow" by W.B. Yeats.

> *Others because you did not keep*
> *That deep-sworn vow have been friends of mine;*
> *Yet always when I look death in the face,*
> *When I clamber to the heights of sleep,*
> *Or when I grow excited with wine,*
> *Suddenly I meet your face.*

Tone varies according to the nature of the relationship between the narrator and the person being addressed. Two very different forms of patrial address are found in Dylan Thomas and Sylvia Plath. In "Do Not Go Gentle Into That Good Night," we hear Thomas' exhortation.

> *And you, my father, there on the sad height,*
> *Curse, bless me now with your fierce tears, I pray*
> *Do not go gentle into that good night*
> *Rage, rage against the dying of the light.*

In "Daddy," Plath makes a declaration.

> *Daddy, I have to kill you.*
> *You died before I had time—*
> *Marble-heavy, a bag full of God,*
> *Ghastly statue with one gray toe*
> *Big as a Frisco seal. . . .*

Second person is also recognizable in common aphorisms, "You don't know what you have until you lose it." Yet Western fiction exhibits a fascinating resistance to this figure of speech. Writing second-person fiction is as much a taboo as dismantling the theatre's fourth wall (the imaginary wall between actors and audience). While the person "I" is comfortable to many authors, second person seems intrusive, almost as if the writer were asking, "To be or not to be, that is *your* question." Ultimately, of course, in our efforts to provoke readers, we're always trying to incite self-questioning.

Engaging the audience immediately through the second person has various advantages. To admit readers this directly into the story can be both demystifying and empowering. It is demystifying in the sense of inviting audiences into the rarefied chambers of the text itself, and empowering in allowing the writer to ask questions of and make demands of those readers. Storytellers using second person put the audience more on the spot, in much the same way as the dramatist Bertolt Brecht did with his "in your face" and "agitprop" tactics that challenged the artificial catharsis of traditional theatre.

One of my writing projects is a cross-genre book about my Edinburgh family in which I use second person to address my grandfather. Since Daniel Campbell died forty-two years before I was born and left no records, I am addressing a fictional character. Yet, I also feel that by speaking to him directly, first with anger at the way he treated his wife and children, then with increasing compassion for his own difficult life, I am coming to know the actual man, and so is my audience.

Second person can be written as scolding, informing, inquiring, arguing, reassuring. The effects range from immediacy to irreverence, congratulations, and distance. My favorite second-person fiction is Randall Kenan's story "This Far," in which Booker T. Washington's career is exposed to him as a series of failures, strokes of luck, successes, and compromises. "This Far" opens as the fifty-nine-year-old Washington is visiting two college friends and reflecting on their early days together.

> So ignorant and pitiful you were then, the shame of it still lingers like the smell of shit on the fingers, just like the hunger which still gnaws beneath your wool suit, tailor-made for you in London, beneath the solid-gold watch and chain that dangles from your vest pouch, a gift from E. Julia Emery, one of your many wealthy white patrons—but it gnaws and bites and growls just the same. You cannot rid yourself of it, can you?

Here Kenan achieves a kind of intimacy (between narrator and protagonist, between reader and protagonist) unavailable in most traditional third-person historical fiction. Washington's wardrobe is more vivid because the narrator addresses the wearer himself. Likewise, the feeling of shame is made palpable as the owner of that shame is confronted directly. Some readers will relate more closely to Washington and to the narrator as the word "you" conflates the character who is being addressed with the reader who is also being addressed.

Two frequently cited models of second-person fiction are Lorrie

Moore's *Self-Help* and Jay McInerney's *Bright Lights, Big City*. An excellent example of using second person to introduce characters to their own stories is the short-short "Girl" by Jamaica Kincaid, in which a daughter comes to terms with her complicated mother by "recalling" mama's alarmed instructions about womanhood. Another short-short story, "Bread" by Margaret Atwood, confronts the reader with questions of survival and responsibility.

> Should you share the bread or give the whole piece to your sister? Should you eat the piece of bread yourself? After all, you have a better chance of living, you're stronger. How long does it take to decide?

THIRD PERSON

The two most common forms of contemporary fiction are third-person limited and third-person omniscient. Normally, third person is singular. But the omniscient version can switch back and forth between observations about "he" or "she" and then refer to "they" when observing families or societies.

In a third-person limited narrative, the story is told from the point of view of a participant in the action, although that character is not directly speaking. This approach is more intimate than third-person omniscient because the point-of-view character must be present for any action or dialogue and all feelings are filtered through that individual's consciousness. For instance, if you're writing third-person limited from Michael's point of view, this doesn't work: "When Michael was out of the room, Andrea walked over and whispered a secret to Mary."

Third-person limited does allow more latitude than first person for physical and emotional description. "When Michael returned, he smiled ruefully at Andrea and ran a pink comb through his purple hair." In the first person, Michael would seem self-conscious describing his smile as rueful and explaining that his hair is purple. Gish Jen makes fine use of third-person limited in her novel *Mona in the Promised Land*. Here the very American Mona reflects on the infuriating cautiousness of her immigrant Chinese parents.

> Make sure, more sure—the endless refrain of her parents' lives. Sometimes Mona wants to say to them, "You know, the Chinese Revolution was a long time ago; you can get over it. . . ."

Third limited can be used in multiple voices as I do in *All Good Women*, a novel about four friends set during World War II. Once each protagonist's voice is distinguished, occasionally all of them speak in the same chapter. By having multiple points of view, I retain the option to describe action when one of them is absent. I can directly describe Wanda's experience at the internment camp and Ann's work in London with refugee children and Moira's and Teddy's lives back on the San Francisco home front. I don't have to keep them all in the same room. Or the same country.

THE COMPLEXITY OF OMNISCIENCE

What is the distinction between shifting third-person limited and third omniscient? With the limited point of view, *less* (knowledge on the part of a fallible narrator) can lead to *more* (reader empathy with the struggling point-of-view character). If the narrative voice in *All Good Women* were omniscient, I could describe a scene in which none of the protagonists was located. I could relate histories and futures unknown to them. The omniscient speaker often knows more (about tomorrow, for instance, or about the motives of minor characters) than can be expressed in the third-person limited point of view. The omniscient voice can distance readers from the protagonist and may even establish a sense that the narrator and the reader are in league together—beyond the ken of the main character. The omniscient point of view was often used in the Victorian novels of Charles Dickens, George Eliot and Anthony Trollope. Many twentieth-century readers mistrust such authority and prefer a non-omniscient voice (which reveals private confusion and other vulnerabilities) to a god voice (which knows more than characters or readers). It is much harder to convey a "growth of perception" through an omniscient narrator whose knowledge is unassailable and eternal.

But novelist Dorothy Bryant doesn't think these complications should stop us, and she says so in *Writing a Novel*.

> We seem, most of us twentieth-century writers, to have lost
> scope, to have lost the ability to move about as freely as Tolstoy
> did, or Thackeray or Hardy or Austen. Critics write all kinds
> of philosophical explanations for this loss: the powerlessness,
> impotence, alienation of modern man reflected in the interior,

limited point of view, etc. Maybe. But I think we lost range through lack of use. We traded omniscience for other effects. The only way to get it back is by trying again, probably in a different form.

A recent, successful omniscient novel is Brian Moore's *The Magician's Wife*, about French colonialism in North Africa in the 1800s. At first, readers view a scene observed by Emmeline and Lambert, which could indicate a third limited point of view. Then, as the horsemen move out of the characters' view, it is clear that the narrative voice is omniscient.

> At eight o'clock the following morning Emmeline and Lambert saw, circling below in the courtyard, four horsemen: Deniau, Hersant, and two young lieutenants of a Zouave regiment. Two additional horses were held by grooms, waiting their arrival. Once mounted, their procession trotted out into the streets of Milianah. There, ten Arab riders, wearing red burnouses and armed with rifles, moved in an escort. When they reached the gates of the town, a further twenty armed Arabs dressed in red burnouses joined the cortege. Two hundred yards farther on, a third escort surrounded them, and as they reached the open plain, yet another twenty riders joined them. . . .

Perhaps one reason the omniscient works so well here is that Moore is writing from the hindsight of a century. Present-day readers expect to be more knowledgeable about the shifts of history than characters living through that history. Thus, the "authority" of the omniscient narrator is a consequence of temporal reference point and not of supernatural power.

SHIFTING, MULTIPLE-PERSON POINTS OF VIEW

Yet another option is the shifting multiple-person viewpoint, as used in Rosellen Brown's intriguing novel *Before and After*, about a family in which the seventeen-year-old son is a fugitive suspected of murder. Brown writes about the Reisers' ordeal in the first-person voice of father Ben, the third-person limited voice of mother Carolyn, and the first-person and third-person limited voices of their daughter, Judith. Missing is the point of view of Jacob, the absent young murder suspect. Jacob's silence and the shifting voices of his family heighten the haunting suspense.

When done well, the multiple-person, multiple-point-of-view narration can reach beyond catharsis to illustrate the multiplicity of truth. Such complex narrative strategy requires a lot of the reader, much in the way multimedia art stimulates audience members to use various physical senses and understandings of temporality. At any one point in this kind of narration, the reader doesn't know whether to turn his head or look up or duck or close his eyes. In contrast, by the final draft, the *writer* must always have her eye on the speaker.

Poet Diane Glancy has divined the ideal narrative form for *Pushing the Bear*, a novel about the Trail of Tears. At first, the short, dissonant segments of testimony from a vast number of Cherokee forced to march from North Carolina to Oklahoma seem jarring, confusing. Readers hear, but have trouble listening to, concentrating on, so many urgent, competing, contradictory voices. How can we follow? Whom do we follow? Where are we going? Glancy compels her audience to experience the very questions native people asked of themselves and each other throughout the death-and-disease-ridden trek. *Pushing the Bear* disrupts conventional story expectations by juxtaposing the words of main characters with voices from completely new players who may appear only once or twice. Glancy's fragmented story line keeps readers in the painful present of the Cherokee ordeal.

PERSONA

Person is born of persona. Successful fiction requires the writer's understanding about the standpoint, character, and tone of the narrative persona (the speaker, the actual teller of the story). *Persona* derives from the Latin word for the mask worn by classical actors. The carrying or wearing of a mask was the ancient equivalent of using makeup and costumes in contemporary drama to enhance the identity and/or credibility of characters. In fiction and poetry, "persona" is the personality assumed by the narrator.

Strategizing point of view entails not only choosing among first-, second-, third- and multiple-person voices but also understanding the character and purpose of the narrative persona. Is the narrator the main character or a more peripheral observer of/participant in the action? From what point in time and space is the narrator recounting the story? Is she in the next room or in another country?

Our narrators can be dull, incendiary, coy, anxious. Persona comes across in the language of description and action as well as in dialogue, in the idiosyncratic uses of vocabulary, grammar, and figurative language. Narrative idiom can reveal not only nationality, region, race, education, class, age, but also many subtleties within those identifications. Is our narrator verbose? Apologetic? Hesitant? Bold? Rash? Measured? Does he stutter, emphasize certain words or syllables, drone on and on? A narrator's distance can imply detachment, cautiousness, or forgetfulness. The persona's confiding tone can make readers either sympathetic or suspicious.

Even the third-person omniscient requires the creation of a narrative persona. It may have been simpler in a more homogeneous literary scene like nineteenth-century Britain to assume one's readers subscribed to the same worldview, to write from an omniscience rooted, for instance, in a Christian moral framework, an increasingly industrial economy, and an imperialistic sense of entitlement. But the Empire is fading, and more human beings are reading. This diverse, modern audience understands that there are distinct brands of omniscience. Is our narrator Yahweh? Krishna? Venus? Buddha? Jesus? Higher Power? Zeus? Einstein? What one knows has a lot to do with *how* one knows, with the values through which one filters attitudes about forgiveness, justice, generosity, contradiction, tolerance, humor. The choice of an omniscient narrator in a psychologically sophisticated, culturally complex world requires disclosure.

"Who's calling, please?" It's a natural everyday question. Likewise, readers are curious about both the who and why of the narrators they encounter. Narrative motive is key to audience sympathy and attitude. Today's audiences want to know (or be able to discern) at some point if we are being told this story to win an argument, to enlighten us spiritually, to persuade us philosophically. Every narrator has blind spots and gifts of insight. The central question is not, Is this point of view reliable or unreliable? but rather, How unreliable is the narrator, and in what interesting ways?

As with most elements of craft, point of view has no rules, just intriguing and sometimes perplexing possibilities. We can temporarily borrow a map from a fellow writer, but the real adventure of point of view doesn't begin until we strike out on our own and trek cross-country, discovering new territory, listening for elusive voices, and observing the angles of those shadows.

EXERCISES

1. Rewrite a story you have written in the first person by using the first-person voice of a different character. What impact does this shift have on plot? Tone? Theme? What do you learn about the story by doing this?

2. Borrow a classic scene from literature—Lear's disowning of Cordelia, Achilles' mourning for Patroclus, the banishment of Adam and Eve from the Garden of Eden—and write both a first-person account of this moment and an omniscient account of the moment. What freedoms, insights, and restrictions did each point of view carry?

3. Try writing a shifting, multiple-person, multiple-point-of-view story about a familiar experience: family at Thanksgiving dinner, shoppers in a department store on Christmas Eve, people working out in the weight room of the local Y, fans enduring or enjoying a baseball game. Aim for cohesion in the midst of this "confusion." What holds a story like this together?

Valerie Miner is the author of nine books, including *Trespassing and Other Stories, Movement,* and the novels *Range of Light, Winter's Edge,* and *A Walking Fire.* Her work has appeared in *Ploughshares, Prairie Schooner, The Gettysburg Review, Village Voice, T.L.S., The Nation,* and many other journals. Currently Professor of English at the University of Minnesota, she also travels widely giving readings and lectures.

A Container of Multitudes, or When "I" Isn't "Me": The Art of First Person

ALYCE MILLER

L et's face it, first person seduces. It may start with little more than a whisper in the ear: "Pssst. Come closer, I'm within you." Familiar, it mimics the insistent voice of the self-dramatized, the cathartic un-staged soliloquy of private diaries and journals, unintended for public consumption. But if we follow it into fiction, it becomes the voice of someone less familiar, even unknown, appearing with intimate urgency. "Quick," it says, "I must tell you my story. Get me down on the page before I get away." And it is all you can do to get to your pen and tablet in time.

No wonder "I" is often preferred by beginning fiction writers. It offers itself so willingly. We are accustomed to dramatizing ourselves in speech and writing as "I." What could be simpler than merely tran-scribing the voice as it speaks?

"I" WEARS THE MASK

As Eve Sedgwick points out, we are many people, and not always who we think we are. As writers, we take on roles, not unlike actors and actresses, who work to "become" the characters they portray. In other words, they inhabit personae, often very different from themselves. *Persona*, as mentioned in the previous essay, is the Latin word for mask. The mask of the self. The mask we take on when we say we are ourselves or when we become other people. In actuality, first person is a narrative choice that allows us to inhabit, or be inhabited by, at close range, a vast array of characters, in a perfect blend of subject and object.

Consider the mask worn by Daniel Defoe when he gives voice, to Moll Flanders. Consider that David Copperfield is *not* Charles Dickens, but an assumed identity.

Inhabiting "I" involves hearing the poetry of that particular voice, and, much like dramatic monologue, it generally occurs around a dramatic incident. It involves what Charles Johnson calls "ego-less listening." The "I" of fiction is transformed out of self through imagination. The fictionalized "I" is always an enactment.

"I" AS PERSONA

Writers have traditionally adopted personae that are very different from themselves, crossing gender, class, sexual, racial, cultural, and social lines as required. While writers of first person often speak of the importance of having empathy or understanding for every character, likable or trustworthy, or not, they also must reach beyond their own immediate experience and language to discover who the character is. Writing first person is not merely an exercise in lining up all the facts. It is an act of discovery, a yielding, a listening.

Personae are as varied as the color spectrum. "I" might be the voice that engages companionably, begs to be trusted: "Call me Ishmael." Or the self-pitying voice in its bid for sympathy: "This is the saddest story I have ever heard. . . ." It is the wistful retrospective narrator reflecting on the past: "One day, I was already old, in the entrance of a public place a man came up to me." It is the voice of memoir that pledges truth: "I know that in writing the following pages I am divulging the great secret of my life. . . ." It is the connection to others: "After long and fruitless waiting I have determined to write to you myself. . . ." It is the amoral perpetuating its own twisted logic: "That's my last Duchess painted on the wall. . . ." It is the innocent child's voice matter-of-factly recording without interpreting: "We didn't always live on Mango Street."

POINT OF VIEW MATTERS

Point of view may be the single most important choice a writer makes. Who tells the story, and from what perspective? Point of view offers the controlling framework that shapes any fiction and determines its dimensions. It also establishes the tone and mood of the piece, the information known and revealed, as well as the idiom in which it's given, and the ordering and sequence of events. What is important to one teller may not be of interest to another. The main consideration in choosing any point of view is evaluating what will be gained and what will be lost with any teller.

First person often seems the most natural of all the points of view. It can feel less mediated than the more "literary" voice of third, which implies the presence of an "author." However, it's important to clarify that all "I" narratives *are* mediated, that lack of mediation is an illusion. Since through our daily conversations we are accustomed to narrating our own lives through "I," we may be deceived into thinking first person is easiest to write. But first person comes with enormous challenges as well as limits.

All events and observations must be consistent with what the first person character sees, knows, and believes to be true about the world. In other words, everything is filtered through the consciousness of the narrating "I." There is little or no room for slippage in perspective the way point of view can be shifted around a little more in third. Still, this often tighter focus, which limits what can be told, can be exploited in interesting ways through implied irony, discrepancy, and contradiction. For example, let's say the first-person narrator reports something as true, but another character or a fact comes along to contradict, interesting tension arises, as well as doubt on the part of the reader who must now read more critically as the piece progresses.

Tonally, first person has endless possibilities, depending on the character in whose consciousness the story is lodged. And there are interesting ways to offset the first-person focus, through dialogue with other characters, other characters' observations, or straight reporting. All of these can give readers a control point from which to make evaluations.

TO TRUST OR NOT TO TRUST "I"

The reliability of any narrator is always at stake but becomes far more critical with first person. By reliability, we refer to how much the narrator can be trusted. This often is determined by the reader's own worldview and how closely the narrator's vision compares. We tend to question the judgment of a narrator whose take on the world is very different from ours.

The first-person narrator is automatically recognized as not as "objective" as a third-person voice, since often the first-person narrator has a vested interest in how the reader interprets the events. You as the writer will have a fairly strong sense of how closely this narrator's perceptions will line up with reader interpretations of the information as presented. A deliberate discrepancy between what the first-person narrator imagines to be true and the reader's under-standing or perspective can provide interesting distance and even enhance the conflict. Distance between reader and narrator can de-velop in a number of forms: morals, values, worldview, experience, and general outlook.

For example, I often use Eudora Welty's well-known story "Why I Live at the P.O." in my classes to illustrate unreliability. The story plays with the instability first person allows against the elusive notion of "truth." Tonally, the first-person narrator, Sister, immediately draws us in to a personal and highly opinionated dialogue. In the style of a dramatic monologue, Sister is eager to convince us that her family members have mistreated her, and to demonstrate that she has be-haved impeccably in spite of it all.

The question of course is not only how much distance exists be-tween the "I" of the fiction and the experience, but the "I" of the fiction and the reader.

Vladimir Nabokov opens *Lolita* by dropping the reader into the middle of a private, impassioned reverie, evoking the "I" through a litany of possessive pronouns: "Lolita, light of my life, fire of my loins. My sin, my soul." We have no idea who's speaking and why until a few paragraphs later wherein Humbert decides to locate himself: "I was born in 1910, in Paris." The character of Humbert could not have been written successfully in the third person. The author would have gotten in the way, and Nabokov was smart enough to know that. We need the "I" of Humbert's mask, we need his own language, voice, and words, his own self-parody and self-criticism, unfiltered through a narrating voice. The unmediated Humbert is far more powerful. Not unlike Humbert, whenever we use "I," in daily speech or in writing, we are inventing ourselves anew in a form of impersonation.

"I" AS ACTOR OR OBSERVER

Two terms are frequently used to discuss first-person stances: *central* and *peripheral*. Humbert Humbert is a good example of a central first-person narrator, one whose active consciousness is at the core of the material and whose narrating voice is indispensable from the events. It is, as we say in creative writing workshops, "his story" and his perspec-tive. A peripheral "I" is the character as observer, who may be part of the events but does not influence them and does not become their focus. A peripheral first-person narrative suggests that the focus lies elsewhere than on the observing "I" of the story. It often is characterized by a detachment, the voice of the spectator, and may in actuality carry a certain moral weight or judgment.

The peripheral narrator Nick in F. Scott Fitzgerald's *The Great Gatsby* fits the role of observer/commentator. Somewhere in between central and peripheral is the narrator of James Baldwin's "Sonny's Blues," who claims the story is about his brother, Sonny, though it is about himself in relation to Sonny, too. In fact, the change that takes place in the story (the final epiphany) occurs for the narrator, not Sonny.

Peripheral first offers the opportunity to back away from the real, unspoken "I" of the narrative and approach it at a slant. Sonny would have had no reason to narrate his own story, because he is not the one seeking understanding. Likewise, while Gatsby is the real protagonist, his mysterious past and invented present could not have accumulated with the kind of tension they do if he were the speaking "I." Too much mystery would have been explained away. Gatsby observed is far more intriguing than Gatsby as speaking agent.

On the flip side, an observed Humbert would not have worked for obvious reasons. Part of the pleasure of reading *Lolita* is uncovering the gaps in Humbert's logic and perceptions. The novel is, among many things, a cat-and-mouse game with the reader. The central "I," often a mechanism to engage the reader closely with a character who shares common ground, dislodges and jolts in *Lolita* as we are ping-ponged between hilarity and revulsion. Simultaneously amused by Humbert's critique of American consumer culture and revolted by the skewed logic of his obsession with nymphets (though the two things are cleverly related), the reader is thrown into moral ambivalence. Captivated by his intellect, wit, and charm, we are participants in an immoral discourse that openly revels in violating all dominant norms. We find ourselves complicit just for reading the book and being engaged by Humbert, making it uncomfortably impossible for us to judge Humbert without judging ourselves.

FOCUS OF PERCEPTION

Any discussion of point of view must raise the issue of not just who speaks but who actually sees and what it is they perceive. Narrative depends structurally on who knows what and when. Any discrepancy (either through a character's ignorance or another character's deliberate withholding of information) is the stuff of dramatic tension: misunderstanding, contradiction, speculation, and sheer invention. First person provides an interesting challenge to the writer to further that tension between speech and perception. Often it is the reader, in first-person narratives, who is given the role of perceiving what the speaker cannot.

Focus of perception is a handy term I've swiped from Gerard Genette and other narrative theorists to open up to my students the concept that point of view is far more complicated than merely identifying first, second, or third person. Knowledge, when and where and how, is key to fiction and is intricately tied to tension and conflict. It is from this tension of who knows what and speaks what they know that plot develops, not the other way around.

VARIOUS SHADES OF FIRST PERSON

Ever heard of writing a first-person narrative without mentioning "I" at all? To achieve a very claustrophobic effect, Alain Robbe–Grillet chose an obsessive narrator for his novella *Jealousy*. The narrator never refers to himself as "I," but it is clearly he who speaks and who observes the mundane details of what he (falsely?) assumes to be evidence of his wife's infidelity. In the terrific novel *Housekeeping* by Marilynne Robinson, Ruthie, the "I" narrator, escapes the presumed limits imposed by "I" and moves frequently into a kind of omniscience through speculation and dream. This fluid and flexible use of first person allows the narrative to access other kinds of truths not based in fact. It acknowledges that all stories are invented. And that is one of the single most distinguishing advantages of fiction over nonfiction—it offers alternative truths.

Toni Morrison in *Jazz* makes use of an omniscient "I," normally an oxymoron in point of view. Her narrator—ostensibly an "I" who is never named, but who is truly, in a trick of homonyms, an "eye," like a camera—expresses a point of view that seems to belong not simply to one consciousness or one experience. The "I" of the city is located in a voice that collaborates with the characters and even the reader to make sense of the events.

THE FAMILY OF FIRST PERSON

First person can often feel like a close relative of third-person limited, which undoubtedly shares certain characteristics. In third-person limited, as with first person, the narrative is confined to the perceptions and understandings of one main character. Unlike first person, however, limited third does give a little more breathing room, because the language belongs more obviously to the narrating voice, and a separate intelligence which is separate from the character. There is some room for subtle editorialization and authorial comment. In first, there is the illusion that the language belongs to the speaker, and it is the writer's task to not only develop but remain consistent to the idiolect of that narrator.

The reason I suspect many contemporary writers like "I" is that not only does it allow us to experience a character from the inside out, it automatically raises the question of reliability. In our age reliability is always a critical issue in any narrative, political, ideological, fictional, or otherwise. Contemporary readers, no longer satisfied with being preached to or openly manipulated by an "author" in the intrusive way our nineteenth-century counterparts were, may actually trust the "I" more because it is easily recognized as "unstable."

This is part of the draw of "I." The "I" voice to a beginning writer can feel less formal, less intimidating. It opens a door and summons you to follow. "I" offers the illusion of writer alone with the telling. It mimics the wonderful secrecy of the writer alone with "self," in all its multiplicity, whatever form that may take. Simply put, the most interesting and successful "I" is "other" discovered as "self." And for a while, as writers occupying "I," we act as both ourselves and not ourselves, as both subject and object, inhabiting our other selves a little more fully.

EXERCISES

1. Getting "I" out of your system: Write several pages in first person from "your own" perspective, giving your personal view of a very emotional, real-life event. Now try writing about the same event from the point of view of an invented, but detached, outsider "I" who observes peripherally with a kind of detachment, and therefore brings objectivity to the situation. Give yourself a couple of pages to build momentum. Consider what happens in terms of tone, language, and presentation. Now rewrite the same situation one more time choosing for peripheral first person an "I" speaker also involved in the event (with something at stake) but whose perspective and investment would be different from or even opposite of yours. Notice what happens to language, perspective, representation of experience, and so on, as the

"I" position shifts. Is there irony present more obviously in one than another? What about tension? Was one easier to write than another? Which one is more interesting and why? What challenges did each "I" bring? What advantages?

2. Write a "true" statement about yourself involving an action. (Example: "I traveled to Egypt last year with my aunt Cynthia.") Follow that opening line with a couple of pages of developing details. Pause and consider the language and tone. How close is the "I" in that piece to the "I" you use when speaking casually to acquaintances in real life about yourself? Now write a false statement, involving an action, about yourself. (Example: "I have never left the county I live in.") Allow the "I" to develop from that opening sentence. Since it is not a true premise, you will find yourself beginning to inhabit an "I" that is not just like yourself. Make the most of these possibilities and see where they lead.

3. Imagine someone who is your complete opposite in some specific way. For example, if you are a very tidy person, take on the "I" voice of someone who is, among other things, a slob. But remember, no character is merely a sum of attributes, so you will want to avoid simply creating a portrait of a slob. Now choose an action (driving a car to see a friend, preparing a meal, getting ready for work), and inhabit that "opposite I" up close without criticism or judgment for several paragraphs or pages. Make the character likable and interesting. Don't announce he or she is a slob, but allow that detail to become part of and inform a larger situation. This is harder than you may think.

Note: Try any of the above exercises in a third-person version as well, and see what happens rhetorically. As with any exercises, try all of these more than once, and then take time to reflect on what you have observed about point of view in the process of writing.

Alyce Miller's collection, *The Nature of Longing*, won the Flannery O'Connor Award. Her novel, *Stopping for Green Lights*, was published by Doubleday. Her short fiction, essays, and poetry have appeared in numerous magazines. Her work has also won the Kenyon Review Award for Literary Excellence in Fiction and the Lawrence Award. She teaches in the MFA program in writing at Indiana University in Bloomington, Indiana.

And Eyes to See:
The Art of Third Person

LYNNA WILLIAMS

W e've all had it: the small flash that signals the beginning of
fiction. It's a snatch of dialogue overheard in a Chinese restaurant: "I'm not kidding; ten years we've been married, and he thinks
intimacy is eating dim sum." It's the sour cherry taste of the last red
lollipop left in the bowl at Halloween, a newspaper photo of a six-
year-old girl alone on a seesaw, a shoplifter calmly stuffing a grapefruit
into his book bag at Kroger. It's an old memory, a just-seen image,
an idea that pops into our heads with no known provenance. But
something about it makes us say, "That's a story," and in that wonderful moment of declaration—of *naming* as a story what is still only a
moment, a circumstance, a single image—we're opening ourselves to
the rest of the process, to *making* a story, whole and complete. But
how do we get from story "trigger" to story draft, from impulse to
understanding, from beginning to end?

A major part of the answer is deciding on the work's point of view,
which is nothing less than the choice of perspective (or perspectives)
from which the reader will see the action unfold. But as important as
the choice of point of view ultimately will be to how the story is read,
it is key, too, to how the writer begins to locate the story that exists for
him or her within the first glimmerings of an idea. Once a point-of-
view decision is made, the writer creating the story can begin to find
his or her own way *into* the developing narrative; point-of-view choice
influences virtually every other decision to be made in constructing a
story, but its first importance may be how it draws us, as writers, deeper
and deeper into the material, making us see the possibilities.

Consider the snippet of dialogue quoted above, in which a wife
jokes about her husband's idea of intimacy. Make the story first

115

person, and the construction of the wife's voice almost certainly will assume center stage. The exploratory question, Who *is* this woman? becomes bound up in how she speaks. The writer's first understanding of the character and situation comes through the act of giving her speech.

> Robert and I are taking a year-long Intimacy in Marriage seminar at the little shingled box of a YMCA out on Mansfield Highway. The first time we drove into the parking lot, all I could think about was that it looked like a place parole violators would be comfortable going for a swim.

Make the point of view second person, and establishing the tone of the piece becomes key. Stories in the second-person point of view typically take full advantage of a kind of observational commentary, as well as wry humor. So getting into a second-person "mind-set" in the first stages of story development requires coming up with an entry point into the material: some way to make the most of the possibilities for observation. In our Chinese food/intimacy example, we could decide to begin by asking the question, *Where* is this woman? The answer, Manny's Egg Roll Palace inside the Great Mall of China, suggests a number of observations that might be made by the "you" of the story; exploring those possibilities can contribute to our understanding not just of the character and the situation but to *her* (and thus our) understanding of the truth about her marriage.

> At Manny's Egg Roll Palace, you watch as Robert makes googly eyes at the little Chinese girl toting a tray of fortune cookies around the dining room. When you can't stand to watch anymore, you switch to wondering where Manny, the emperor of egg rolls, was introduced to red Naugahyde. You haven't noticed before, but every surface in the restaurant—chairs, tables, even one wall—is covered with it. You are not proud of this, but suddenly you wish the little girl was covered in it, too; your husband, Nature Boy, might think twice about coveting a child upholstered in a synthetic material.

But what if we begin our exploration of the woman at Manny's from a third-person point of view? What happens then? First things first: The woman sitting at a corner table picking apart a vegetarian egg roll becomes a "she." And knowing that, if we're aware of the possibilities of this point of view, we can immediately enter the lunchtime scene with *her* perspective, one that prompts us to ask not just, Who *is* this woman? but, What does she *see*? And with that second question, we've entered the real territory of third person in contemporary fiction, in which sight is one of the primary means of developing the consciousness of the character and thus, ultimately, of developing the story.

THIRD-PERSON UNIFIED

Third person is an enormously flexible point of view, so we have a number of choices available to us in deciding how the point of view in our fledgling story will work. (Valerie Miner's essay discusses the third-person omniscient point of view.) For now, let's explore a point of view sometimes called third-person unified, because that term suggests the "single vision" that distinguishes this kind of third person. Simply put, in third-person unified, the point-of-view character is the consciousness of the story: We have access to that character's eyes, and mind, and only hers. The narrowing of vision brings us closer to the character in this type of third person than in any other. Unlike third-person limited, which will be discussed later, third-person unified does not take advantage of the possibilities of objective narration. In this point of view, everything, even the "telling" that goes on in exposition, is filtered through the point-of-view character's consciousness.

So back to the Chinese restaurant. In beginning to think about what our character and story might be in this instance, when we position ourselves *with* the "she," seeing what she sees, every detail we invent can add to our knowledge of the character and point us toward the real story. Suppose as she (let's call her Ellen) and her best friend sit down to lunch, Ellen takes in the faux-leather menus, which are the size and thickness of a Dr. Suess storybook, and the teenage boys waiting tables, and the little Chinese girl racing from table to table with a plate of fortune cookies. In our imagining of her, the woman who sees these details will be different from one who would notice where the fire exits are, that the cloth napkins smell like nail polish remover, that the health certificate framed on the wall has a plastic rose hiding the inspection score. And as the details accumulate—as *her* vision takes hold in *our* imagination—what she sees suggests paths for the story to take: For example, notice that the details she notices first all have to do with children. This pattern suggests a number of avenues to explore: What's behind the jokes about her husband's definition of intimacy? Are they childless? Possibly considering adoption? Is she afraid her husband thinks everything in life is too easy? If he thinks intimacy is eating dinner together, what does she think his notions of parenting will be? When she tries to picture him with a child, what memories come to her? The Chinese meal they ate on their honeymoon? What happens when the little girl with the fortune cookies stops at her table?

The questions above, suggested by what our point-of-view character sees, also suggest lines of inquiry, ways in which the "thread" of the story can be unraveled. Answering that first question may require coming up with answers to all the others, which may be what's needed to establish what the story is really about. Some of the other questions above speak to a need for information about the couple's life together in the "now" of the story. Another suggests the possibility of a flashback. And dealing with the final question posed above, a "What happens when?" question, moves us naturally into the writing of a scene in which we'll see the point-of-view character talk to the little girl. That dialogue exchange, even at a very early stage in the story's development, can go a long way toward helping to establish what's important here, what most needs to be explored further. If we write that scene, we'll almost certainly hear not only Ellen speak but other characters as well: the girl with the fortune cookies, perhaps one of the waiters, or the girl's father as he comes out from the kitchen to check on her, or our point-of-view character's best friend at the table. But as the characters talk, we'll keep the angle of vision firmly rooted in our point-of-view character's perspective, making any understanding she gains from the encounter our own. With the little girl standing at the table, what does our point-of-view character notice about her? What connections does Ellen make between what she sees and her own experience of children? With what she knows of her husband's experience? If the girl's father comes out of the kitchen, what does our point-of-view character look for in him? Is she any closer after that scene to understanding the nature of intimacy between parents and children, husbands and wives?

From a bit of overheard dialogue, we've begun to fashion a character both from what she sees and what she makes of it. What's required of the writer now is the closest kind of attention, as we continue to *work* the character's point of view—using her different levels of vision—to get at the truth of this character, this story. As fiction writers, what's asked of us may itself be a new kind of seeing, as we try to represent truthfully the set of eyes we've created and positioned within our developing story idea.

Robert Browning, in his poem "Fra Lippo Lippi," has the Renaissance painter remark on how often we come to love something we've seen a hundred times only when we see it painted on a canvas. Something of the same sort of transformation can take place when we create a character's third-person unified point of view. This is the moment in story development when we should find ourselves slowing down, weighing the value of everything seen, trying to assess what it means, what use can be made of it.

In that process, we may find ourselves in closer and closer communion with the point-of-view character. Browning's "Fra Lippo Lippi" again: "Art was given for that; / God uses us to help each other so, / Lending our minds out." If we keep at it, those lines can describe what happens in our understanding of the "she" in the Chinese restaurant: For the length of our story, her mind is lent to us for the purposes of art.

In this kind of union, we can achieve such closeness that, even though the story is cast in third person, we arrive at something very like the voices that distinguish first person. In this example, our point-of-view character is watching one of the teenage waiters deliver a platter of dim sum two tables over.

> The boy put the platter down with a slight flourish, and one of the dim sum—a fat one—slid off onto the table. It lay, beached, between the salt and pepper shakers, and in the orangey fluorescent light, she imagined she saw tiny fins, fish whiskers, gills opening and closing. Ellen felt her hand rising to her mouth and, quick, conjured up a cheeseburger. It was no good, though: the cheese melted over her fingers, and then she was staring at Cheese Pond. Cheese Pond, where fish lived in families. She hated fish; she hated food that looked like fish; she hated anything small, anything defenseless, anything that couldn't make its own way in the world.

In reading those lines, we can see how the merger of language and vision supports a sense of both her character and her situation. The point-of-view character is the only consciousness present in that paragraph, and in the story. She's our ticket: Her movement through the story is our own. Developing her point of view—honoring, and exploring, its possibilities—is a major step in moving the story forward.

Third-person unified is a standard in contemporary short fiction; it's less common in novels, where a greater range of perspectives may be necessary for us to get at the real story. J.M. Coetzee's *The Master of Petersburg* casts no less a personage than Fyodor Dostoevsky as the point-of-view character. The story has Dostoevsky grappling not only with the death of his stepson but with the sometimes warring obligations of art and life. At one point, Dostoevsky asks, "What am I to do?" and then, "If I were only in touch with my heart, might it be given me to know?" That second question is well worth remembering when working with the third-person unified point of view. It demands that we do the work necessary to be in touch with our characters' hearts; in building that closeness, the heart of the story can reveal itself to us.

THIRD-PERSON LIMITED

But what if, in developing Ellen's story, the close-in quality of third-person unified begins to seem a little too close? What if, in working with the material, we begin to feel we need some breathing room, some moments when we're not anchored in the point-of-view character's consciousness? If that's the case, the answer may be a shift to a third-person limited point of view. It may seem very similar to the point of view discussed above, since Ellen will continue to be our angle of vision on events, and we'll still have access to her thoughts. But in this use of third person, we'll also be able to take advantage of objective narration; that is, neutral exposition that is not tied to the character's consciousness.

> Manny's was inside the Great Mall of China, which was just an open-air food court surrounded on three sides by a video store, a discount shoe warehouse, and two martial arts establishments. In past lives, Manny's had been a spareribs place, and a pizza place, and once, years before, an all-night wedding chapel. But now it was an egg roll palace, and two giant egg rolls, with stick legs and tap shoes, danced a welcome on the plateglass window out in front.

It's not hard to to see how, in third-person unified, Ellen's perception of the dancing egg rolls in tap shoes could be used to further develop the character. In third-person limited, Manny's location and history can be presented in a "neutral" gear, free of any characterization by Ellen. Physical descriptions, background, summary, anything we need to know but don't need cast in the point-of-view character's perception, can be given to us through this kind of objective exposition.

One way of determining whether this type of third person is suitable for a developing story is to consider whether only providing a unified point of view has resulted in a kind of fictional claustrophobia. The addition of objective narration can sometimes act in the same way as throwing open a window does on a stifling hot day; it gives us some breathing room that may not be available if everything is funneled through one character.

Point-of-view decisions, like other decisions in fiction, are often a question of balance. Ask yourself what the potential benefits of a particular point of view are, and then what the costs might be. When using third-person limited, it may be the case that the addition of objective narration provided a much needed counterweight to the point of view character's perspective. Or it may be that sticking to one point of view, even in the use of exposition, establishes a more powerful connection to the character—and thus is worth a little claustrophobia. But to make those kinds of costs versus benefits decisions for one story, as opposed to another (and for second person versus first, or between the kinds of third person), requires a thorough understanding of the ways in which different points of view operate.

SHIFTING POINT OF VIEW

So far our focus has been developing that initial bit of overheard dialogue from the point of view of one character. With short stories, the wisdom traditionally had been that one point of view is sufficient, that to employ multiple points of view almost guarantees a short-changing of *all* the points of view. But what if we find that one perspective simply isn't enough? Making that determination involves thinking through the obligations of point of view in fiction: Can we see the action unfold satisfactorily from one perspective? If not, then what other perspective is necessary? For example, we may, in working with

Ellen's point of view, begin to suspect that the perspective of the little girl's father is somehow important to the story. Perhaps when he comes out from the kitchen to check on his daughter, Ellen begins to romanticize him as the perfect father, seeing in the small actions of his hands, working to straighten the little girl's collar and smooth her hair, a blend of love and duty she fears won't ever be present in her own husband. The story could work the possibilities inherent in this situation solely from Ellen's point of view. The decision to shift point of view to the father would require us to believe that *his perspective*—not just his character, but his eyes—offers something the story must have. We can hear his voice in dialogue, without switching to his point of view. But to actually see what he sees requires a shift in point of view.

If we can get the complete story from Ellen's point of view, then the answer is simple: Don't give us any other point of view. The decision to shift point of view must be based on the conviction that we cannot see the story unfold properly from a single perspective. We know that Ellen wants children. What does this father of this little girl see when he looks at his daughter, and again when he takes in Ellen at her table staring at the child? What's his point of view, as opposed to Ellen's, and how can they combine to make one story?

> When Lee didn't come back to the kitchen for more fortune cookies, he pulled off his apron and went into the dining room after her. He didn't see her at first, and he made a fist with his left hand, to balance the sudden tightness in his chest. She was never where she was supposed to be, but he looked again, and there she was, spinning through the center of the dining room with the red lacquer tray above her head. The customers in her path ducked to avoid the cellophane-wrapped fortune cookies, flying at them from the tray. It was like this all the time now; it was as if she had shaken off gravity with her baby teeth. He stooped to retrieve a fortune cookie and, slowly, in his own time, moved toward his daughter.

The story has a new dimension now; not only can the father's point of view be explored, but the tension between his and Ellen's different points of view can be exploited for dramatic effect. I should say that it seems unlikely that this story, as talked about here, actually would require more than one point of view. The decision to use multiple points of view should be based on the conviction that only by providing more than one perspective on the action can we actually get at truth of the story.

Ernest Hemingway confronted the question, How many perspectives does this story require? in the short story "The Short Happy Life of Francis Macomber" and came up with four perspectives, plus "descriptive" narration. One of those points of view belongs to the lion that Francis Macomber runs away from in terror. It's no small undertaking to provide access to a lion's perspective, but it's necessary to the story.

Still, stories needing point-of-view shifts are rarer than those that do not. Again, it's a question of benefits versus costs. In novels, when there's a landscape of some length to be filled in, the benefits are usually clear. The "bigger" the story, the more natural it may seem to bring a variety of perspectives to bear on it. We may end up with multiple "takes" on one event, or introduce different narrators while moving the story forward. Even though it's much more common to employ point-of-view shifts in novels, the risks, in one sense, are much the same as they are in short fiction: If too many points of view are offered, we may be undercutting, and underdeveloping, the one or two points of view that are most necessary to tell of the story. In both genres (but especially in short fiction), if we switch point of view too often, and for reasons that aren't compelling, we may sever the readers' connection to the characters and, eventually, the story.

Overall, it's important to be prepared to shift point of view when it's called for; a rigid adherence to the "old" rules about only employing single points of view in short fiction, for example, may shortchange a particular story. But, and this may be the case more often, it's good to be a little wary of an initial enthusiasm for shifting point of view. Sometimes it may seem easier to switch than to fight; that is, to stand our ground and work through the process of fully understanding one character's heart and mind—one character's story.

Whether we're committed to developing one point of view in third person or more than one, though, using sight as a way into both character and story can open a new world of possibilities. In biblical language, the "light of the body is the eye," and, as we develop our story, a character's vision, literally and figuratively, can light our way.

EXERCISES

1. Think of a story you tell often: the time your sister climbed onto the roof in her sleep, say, or the day you chased a robed monk down Michigan Avenue to return an umbrella. Now make yourself the point-of-view character in that story, but in a third-person unified point of view. In writing the story, concentrate on re-creating what you saw in as complete detail as possible. Use other senses as well: hearing, taste, touch, smell. Don't rush this; take your time, and focus on providing as much concrete, physical detail as possible. Don't worry for now if everything you're seeing belongs in the scene.

2. Write a dialogue exchange between two characters, grounded in the third-person point of view of one of those characters. This is an exercise in providing a context for dialogue; set the physical and emotional scene for us from the character's point of view as the conversation takes place.

3. Write a passage in which the third-person unified point of view is so close to the character that it reads like first person. Render both the point-of-view character's thoughts and the exposition in his or her language. Try to get so close to the character that tag lines like "he thought" seem unnecessary.

Lynna Williams' short fiction has been published in *The Atlantic Monthly*, *Lear's*, and a number of literary magazines; five of her stories have made the annual 100 Best Stories list in *The Best American Short Stories*. Her first collection, *Things Not Seen and Other Stories*, was named a *New York Times* Notable Book of the Year. She is at work on a novel, *The Faith of Gazelles*. A former reporter and political speechwriter in Texas and Minnesota, she is now an associate professor of English/Creative Writing at Emory University.

IV
Plot, Structure, and Narrative

Incremental Perturbation: How to Know Whether You've Got a Plot or Not

JOHN BARTH

Storytellers, it goes without saying, tell stories. Fiction writers write them, playwrights and screenwriters script them, opera singers sing them, ballet companies dance them, mimes mime them. But what's a story?

Damned if I know, for sure. "A whole action," says Aristotle in effect in his *Poetics*, "of a certain magnitude." "A meaningful series of events in a time sequence," say Cleanth Brooks and Robert Penn Warren. "That which is extracted from a novel to make a movie," says William H. Gass.

Yes, well. But . . .

Most working writers of fiction—myself included when the muse and I are at it—operate less by articulated narrative theory than by the hunch and feel of experience: our experience of successfully (sometimes unsuccessfully) composing, revising, and editing our stories and, prerequisite to that, our experience of the tens of thousands of stories that all of us audit, read, spectate, and more or less assimilate in the course of our lives. In his 1984 Hopwood Lecture at the University of Michigan, Norman Mailer confessed his tendency "to mumble about technical matters like an old mechanic." "Let's put the thingamajig before the whoosits here," said Mailer, "is how I usually state the deepest literary problems to myself." Me too.

But it's another matter when, as teachers of novice fiction writers and coaches of more advanced apprentices in the art, we find ourselves in the position of trying to explain to them and to ourselves why the manuscript before us, whatever its other merits, lacks something that we've come to associate with stories, and is in our judgment the less satisfying for that lack. "Gets off on the wrong foot," somebody in the room may opine. "Something askew in the middle there." "The ending bothers me."

Okay: But exactly what about the beginning, the middle, the ending fails to satisfy? What keeps the thing from achieving proper story-hood? Sigmund Freud remarks that he didn't start out with such peculiar notions as the Oedipus complex; he was driven to their articulation by what he was hearing from the psychoanalytical couch. That's how I feel with respect to dramaturgical theory.

WHAT'S DRAMATURGY?

In my shop, *dramaturgy* means the management of plot and action; the architecture of story, as distinct from such other fictive goodies as language, character, and theme. Be it understood at the outset that mere architectural completeness, mere storyhood, doth not an excellent fiction make. Every competent hack hacks out complete stories; structural sufficiency is hackhood's first requirement. On the other hand, about a third of Franz Kafka's splendid fictions, for example, and a somewhat smaller fraction of Donald Barthelme's, happen to be "mere" extended metaphors rather than stories—metaphors elaborated to a certain point and then, like lyric poems, closed—and they are no less artistically admirable for that. More typically, however, the productions of these two writers, unconventional as may be their material and manner, are rigorously conventional in their dramaturgy. Kafka's "Memoir's of the Kalda Railroad" and Barthelme's "Bone Bubbles" are examples of nondramatic extended metaphors; "A Hunger Artist," "A Country Doctor," by Kafka and "The Indian Uprising," "Me and Miss Mandible," by Barthelme (and most of the rest) are classically constructed stories.

The fact is that most of the fiction we admire is admirable dramaturgically as well as in its other aspects. If we admire a piece of prose fiction despite its nonstoryhood, we are, precisely, admiring it despite its nonstoryhood. Even the late John Gardner—by all accounts a splendid writing teacher despite his cranky notions of "moral fiction"—used to advise, "When in doubt, go for dramaturgy." Amen to that.

Back to Aristotle: The distinction between plot and action can be useful to what we might call clinical dramaturgical analysis, since a story's problems may lie in the one but not the other. As a classroom exercise, one can summarize the story of Sophocles' Oedipus the King, for example, entirely in terms of its plot with little or no reference to its action: "A happily married and much-respected head of state comes to learn that his eminent position is owing to his having unwittingly broken two major-league taboos, and in a day his fortunes are reversed." Clearly, any number of imaginable sequences of action might body forth that summarized plot. One then proceeds to examine for efficiency and effect the particular sequence chosen by Sophocles to do the job. Indeed, one may summarize the drama contrariwise, entirely in terms of its action with little or no reference to its plot: "A delegation of Theban elders complains to King Oedipus that a plague has fallen upon the place. The King sends his brother-in-law to the Delphic oracle to find out what's going on. That emissary returns with news of the gods' displeasure. The chorus of elders sings and dances apprehensively," et cetera.

Aristotle's stipulations that the action be (1) "whole" and (2) "of a certain magnitude" can be at least marginally useful, too: A "whole" action includes everything necessary to constitute a meaningful story and excludes anything irrelevant thereto. Got that? "Of a certain magnitude" means that the action of fiction ought not to be inconsequential, however much it might appear to the characters to be so. But if we ask, What's the meaning of meaningful? or, What do you mean by consequential? it turns out that meaningful means "dramaturgically meaningful" and consequential means "dramaturgically consequential," and around we go (likewise with Brooks and Warren's "meaningful series of events," even without their redundant "in a time sequence"). One is tempted to go back to Mailer's "whoosits" and "thingamajig"—but these preliminary distinctions and definitions are worth bearing in mind as we try to spiral out of their circularity, mindful that what we're interested in here is not "mere" theory but practical dramaturgy: applied Aristotle.

THE CURVE OF DRAMATIC ACTION

Not all fictive action is dramatic, either in the colloquial sense of "exciting" or in the practical sense of advancing the story's plot. And drama, to be sure, involves character and theme and language as well as action, although it's worth remembering that the Greek word *drama* literally means "deed," an action performed by a character, and that Aristotle declares in effect that it's easier to imagine a drama without characters than one without action, the without-which-nothing of story. Dramatic action is conventionally described as rising to some sort of climactic peak or turning point and then falling to some sort of resolution, or denouement. In short, as a sort of triangle—not really of the isosceles variety sometimes called "Freytag's triangle" after the late-nineteenth-century German literary critic $\wedge$; but more like a stylized profile of Gibraltar viewed (in left-to-right cultures, anyhow) from the west $\diagup\!\!\diagdown$; a ramp, let's say, which the story's rising action rather gradually ascends to a peak and then precipitately descends (punch lines are normally shorter than their jokes). Add to this ramp a bit of an approach and a bit of an exit $\frown\!\!\diagdown\!\!\lfloor$ and you've graphed the ingredients of story as conventionally formulated: exposition (the information requisite to understanding the action, or, as I prefer to put it, the "ground situation": a dramatically voltaged state of affairs preexisting the story's present time); conflict (or, in my shop, the introduction of the "dramatic vehicle": a present-time turn of events that precipitates a story out of the ground situation); complication (of which more presently); climax; denouement; and wrap-up (the little coda, closing fillip, or dolly-back shot often appended to the denouement like a jazz drummer's "roll-off" at the end of a number, and usually suggestive of what the story's completed action portends for the principal characters).

Seems arbitrary, doesn't it, this curveless classic curve: an uncomfy-looking bed of Procrustes upon which the action of fiction must be stretched or chopped to fit, or else. Or else what? Why not a story whose action graphs like this $\searrow\!\!\!\diagup\!\!\!\sim$ or this $\diagdown\!\!\!\diagup$ or that tracks more or less like Laurence Sterne's diagrammed flourishes of Uncle Toby's walking stick in *Tristram Shandy* $\mathcal{W}\!\!\mathcal{W}\!\!\sim$ or that simply flat-lines start to finish _____? In fact, that question touches a genuine mystery, in my opinion—and, of course, one can readily point to stories like the aforementioned *Tristram Shandy* that appear to proceed aimlessly, randomly, anyhow un-Aristotelianly; that digress repeatedly while in fact never losing sight of where they're going: up the old ramp to their climax and denouement. For practical purposes, however, the matter's no more mysterious than why one doesn't normally begin a joke with its punch line, a concert program or fireworks display with its pièce de rèsistance, a meal with its chef d'oeuvre, a session of lovemaking with its orgasm: Experience teaches that they simply aren't as effective that way, and "the rules of art," as David Hume remarked, are grounded "not in reason, but in experience." Edward Albee has declared his preference for stories that have a beginning, a middle, and an end, "preferably in that order." Quite so—once one allows for another classical tradition, this one best articulated not by Aristotle but by Horace in his *Ars Poetica*: the tradition of beginning in medias res, in the middle of things rather than at their chronological square one. To tell the story of the fall of Troy, says Horace, we need not begin ab ovo ("from the egg" laid by Leda after her intercourse with Zeus-in-the-form-of-a-swan, and from which hatched, among others, fair Helen, whose face launched a thousand ships); we might begin not even with the opening hostilities of the Trojan War itself, but rather—like Homer—in the ninth year of that disastrous ten-year enterprise, and then interstitch our exposition retrospectively as we proceed.

In other words, the dramaturgical beginning need not be, and in fact seldom is the chronological beginning, and a story's order of narration (or a play's order of dramatization) need not be the strict chronological order of the events narrated. Dramatic effect, not linear chronology, is the regnant principle in the selection and arrangement of a story's action.

ISOMORPHS

Apprentice story makers may need reminding, however, that the world contains many things whose structure or progress resembles ("is isomorphic to" has a nice pedagogical ring) that of traditional dramaturgy. I have mentioned jokes, concert programs, pyrotechnical displays, multicourse meals, and lovemaking when things go well; one could add coffee brewing (an old percolator of mine used to begin my every workday with a rising action that built to a virtual percolatory orgasm and then subsided to a quiet afterglow), waves breaking on a beach—you name it, but don't confuse those same-shapes with stories. In truth, such isomorphism can be seductive. Many an apprentice piece hopefully substitutes the sonority of closure, for example, for real denouement; the thing sounds finished, but something tells us—a kind of critical bookkeeping developed maybe no more than half-consciously from our lifetime experience of stories—that its dramaturgical bills haven't been paid. Similarly, mere busyness in a story's middle does not necessarily advance the plot; an analogy may be drawn here to the distinction in classical physics between effort and work. Dramatic action, as afore-established, need not be "dramatic," although a little excitement never hurt a story; it does need to turn the screws on the ground situation, complicate the conflict, move us up the ramp. Otherwise, it's effort, not work; isomorphic to storyhood, perhaps, but not the real thing.

SO HOW DO WE TELL?

By never again reading your own stories or anybody else's—or watching any stage or screen or television play—innocently, but always with a third eye monitoring how the author does it: what dramaturgical cards are being played and subsequently picked up (or forgotten); what way points (and how many, and in what sequence) the author has chosen to the dramaturgical destination, and why; what pistols, to use Anton Chekhov's famous example, are being hung on the wall in act one in order to be fired in act three. By learning to appreciate the often masterful dramaturgic efficiency of an otherwise merely amusing TV sitcom, for example, while on the other hand appreciating the extravagance-almost-for-its-own-sake of François Rabelais' *Gargantua and Pantagruel*. Maybe even by reciting like a mantra the definition of *plot* that I once upon a time concocted out of the jargon of systems analysis: the incremental perturbation of an unstable homeostatic system and its catastrophic restoration to a complexified equilibrium.

COME AGAIN?

With pleasure. The "unstable homeostatic system" is that aforementioned ground situation: an overtly or latently voltaged state of affairs preexisting the story's present time; one that tends to regulate itself toward equilibrium but is essentially less than stable (otherwise there could be no story). The Montagues and the Capulets have been hassling each other in Verona for a long time: a taunt here, a street scuffle there, but nothing the two families can't absorb; the city of Thebes appears to be doing quite satisfactorily under its new king, who fortuitously routed the Sphinx and married the widowed queen (somewhat his elder) after the old king was mysteriously slain at a place where three roads meet; et cetera: no ground situation, no story, however arresting the action to come, for it is its effect upon the ground situation that gives the story's action meaning. On the other hand, if the system merely continues on its unstable homeostatic way, there'll be no story either. One more dustup between Mercutio and Tybalt? Another child born to Oedipus and Jocasta? What else is new?

"And then one day," as the narrative formula puts it, the dramatic vehicle rolls into town: Young Romeo Montague falls for young Juliet Capulet, and vice versa; a murrain descends upon Thebes and environs and is determined to be owing to the gods' displeasure at the unsolved murder of old King Laius. Because most stories originate in some arresting experience or event—wait'll you hear what happened to me last night!—it's a common failing of apprentice fiction to be more interesting in its action and characters than in its theme and its ultimate sense, to launch an arresting or at least entertaining (potential) dramatic vehicle—a UFO lands on Fred and Mildred's patio one Sunday morning—without a clearly established and thought-through ground situation, as ripe as Shakespeare's Verona and Sophocles' Thebes for . . .

INCREMENTAL PERTURBATION . . .

Which is to say, for the successive complications of the conflict. The star-crossed lovers declare their love, but . . . That crazy old prophet Tiresias reluctantly claims that Oedipus himself was old King Laius' murderer. The conflict complications comprising a story's middle may in some cases be more serial than incremental: One can imagine rearranging the order of certain of Don Quixote's sorties against reality or of Huck and Jim's raft stops down Old Man River without spoiling the effect. Even in those cases, however, the overall series is cumulative, the net effect incremental; the unstable homeostatic system is quantitatively perturbed and reperturbed, until . . . In the most efficiently plotted stories, these perturbations follow not only upon one another but from one another, each paving the way for the next. In what we might call a camel's-back story, on the other hand, the complicative straws are simply added, one by one, as the story's middle performs its double and contradictory functions of simultaneously fetching us to the climax and strategically delaying our approach thereto. In both cases, however—as Karl Marx says of history and as one observes everywhere in nature—enough quantitative change can effect a comparatively swift qualitative change: The last straw breaks the camel's back; one degree colder and the water freezes; at some trifling new provocation, the colonies rebel. Here's how we'll arrange your tryst, guys: Juliet'll take this little potion, see, and then . . . You say the ditched baby had a swollen foot, like, uh, mine? And that the uppity old dude I wasted back at that place where three roads meet was actually . . . ?

So how many perturbatory increments does a story need? Just enough: Too few leads to unconvincing climax, faked orgasm; too many is beating a dead horse, or broken camel. And how many are just enough? Just enough—although one notes in passing the popularity of threes, fives, and sevens in myths and folk stories.

The climax or turn, when it comes, happens relatively quickly: It's catastrophic in the mathematicians' "catastrophe theory" sense—a comparatively sudden and consequential effect triggered by comparatively small incrementations, like an avalanche, or the click of the thermostat—whether or not (as Aristotle prescribes) it involves the fall of the mighty from the height of fortune to the depths of misery. Even in the most delicate of epiphanic stories, the little insight vouchsafed to the protagonist (or perhaps only to the reader), the little epiphany that epiphs, does so in a comparative flash—and, for all its apparent slightness, is of magnitudinous consequence.

Which consequence we measure by the net difference it effects in the ground situation. Like some pregnancy tests, the measurement is only one-way valid: If nothing of consequence about the ground situation has been altered, no story has been told; the action has been all effort and no work. If the ground situation has unquestionably been changed (all the once-living characters are now dead, let's say), then a story may have been told. The follow-up test is whether that change—be it "dramatic," even melodramatic, or so almost imperceptible that the principals themselves don't yet realize its gravity—is dramaturgically/thematically meaningful, in terms of what has been established to be at stake. The "equilibrium" of a story's denouement is not that of its opening: The surviving Capulets and Montagues are sadder but perhaps at least temporarily wiser in the "glooming peace this morning with it brings"; the lovers, however, are dead. Order may reign again in Thebes, for a while anyhow, under Kreon's administration; but Jocasta has hanged herself, and Oedipus has stabbed out his eyes and left town. It is an equilibrium complexified, qualitatively changed even where things may appear to all hands (except the reader/spectator) to be back to normal.

Otherwise, what we have attended may have its incidental merits, but, for better or worse (usually worse), it's not a story.

EXERCISES

1. Write a scene that begins its action with its characters in a literal geographical valley and arrives at its climax when its characters have arrived at a literal geographical peak. Write a scene in which the opposite occurs. Develop this scene into a full-length story.

2. Plot a scene in which there are three distinct "incremental perturbations." Develop the scene into a full-length story.

3. Borrow the plot of a famous work of classic(al) literature or myth, and plan a contemporary story that follows along the same dramaturgical lines. Develop the plot outline into a fully fleshed-out story.

Novelist **John Barth**, whose fiction includes *The Floating Opera*, *The Sot-Weed Factor*, *Lost in the Funhouse*, and *On With the Story*, is Professor *Emeritus* at the Johns Hopkins Writing Seminars.

Time and Order:
The Art of Sequencing

LAN SAMANTHA CHANG

As a child, I was a thirsty reader of fairy tales and legends. One of the stories I loved best was the Grimm brothers' "Little Snow-White," which begins like this.

> Once upon a time in the middle of winter, when the flakes of snow were falling like feathers from the sky, a Queen sat at a window sewing, and the frame of the window was made of black ebony. And whilst she was sewing and looking out of the window at the snow, she pricked her finger with the needle, and three drops of blood fell upon the snow. And the red looked pretty upon the white snow, and she thought to herself: "Would that I had a child as white as snow, as red as blood, and as black as the wood of the window-frame."

Almost every child knows this story, and knows what happens next. The queen does bear a daughter who is as white as snow, as red as blood, and as black as ebony, but the queen dies in childbirth, and the king remarries. His new wife is beautiful, but vain, and therein little Snow-White's real problems begin. What I did not notice about this story as a child, and what now fascinates me as a writer and a reader, lies in its sequencing: The fairy tale does not backtrack. Never once in "Little Snow-White" does its ancient narrator recount any portion of the story that took place before its opening. There are no backward jumps, or flashbacks; there are not even any prolonged descriptions of the characters' memories. This story unfolds forward in time, as simple and magical as my childhood enjoyment of it.

Little did I know, as a six-year-old, what would happen when I grew up and tried to become a writer. Little did I realize that the stories I would want to tell would move forward in time but also backward: to a country that my parents had left before I was born, to a cast of characters that I had never met, to a long ago when their most powerful and evocative stories lay. I did not know what havoc my desire to explore the past would wreak upon the narrative shape of a simple unfolding.

The story I wished to tell would have begun something like this.

> Once, in a small Midwestern American town, there lived a family that seemed very much like any other, except that the parents had come to the U.S. from a country on the other side of the world. And to the children of that family it seemed that their mother and father lived in a persistent dream. Although they went to work and picked the children up after school like the other parents, they were not quite living in the present. When the mother was practicing the piano or preparing vegetables, here is what she was remembering. . . .

Where to go next? The story wants to move backward in time. At some point, it must move back to the parents' lives in another place for the reader to understand and feel the conflict; it must move backward for the reader to continue discovering the heart of the story. Like the hearts of the mother and father, part of this story lies in the mystery of the past.

SHAPING A PATTERN IN TIME

So perhaps it is my material that sparked my interest in sequencing. By sequencing, I mean the order in which the writer puts the story's episodes and scenes. Every story shapes a pattern in time, and its writer must find that shape.

A writer who studies sequencing is concerned with some of the most basic and essential elements of storytelling: selection, order, the passage of time, and the creation of narrative. Anyone who has told a joke will understand the importance of getting the facts in the right order. Manipulating sequence can greatly increase a writer's range, her flexibility and her authority. A leap backward can dazzle the reader and develop his understanding of the characters. A complex story may move back and forth in time, creating a spellbinding pattern. A subtle, chronological telling can draw the reader smoothly into the author's world, holding him rapt with an awareness of its possibilities.

When a writer sets a moment, when she writes in a certain tense, and when she strings two scenes together by using narrative, she draws upon her power, as a storyteller, to manipulate time. For example, two scenes, separated by brief transition, a description, or a summary, hang together because the writer has decided that they should, because she is making a choice. The writer has brought the reader to a place where the laws of time have disappeared and have been replaced by story time, with its own laws, where a moment can take pages to explain, but where a year, or ten, might pass in the flicker of a white space. Italo Calvino, in his essay "On Quickness," writes, "Sicilian storytellers use the formula '*lu cuntu nun metti tempu*' (time takes no time in a story) when they want to leave out links or indicate gaps of months or even years."

A writer announces this jump to story time with the first sentence of her work: "They were new patients to me, all I had was the name, Olson. Please come down as soon as possible, my daughter is very sick" (William Carlos Williams, "The Use of Force"). "Last night I dreamed I went to Manderley again" (Daphne du Maurier, *Rebecca*). "Many years later, as he faced the firing squad, Colonel Aureliano Buendía was to remember that distant afternoon when his father took him to discover ice" (Gabriel García Márquez, *One Hundred Years of Solitude*). Once the story time has been established, it is the writer's choice to linger, recall, or move forward. At this point, she begins to consider an inspiring, and even bewildering, range of options. What must she tell the reader about this character—his actions in the past, his behavior in the future—in order to move the story forward? She might decide to make a small leap to the next scene: "An hour had passed before he remembered to turn on the oven. . . ." She might jump ahead by years.

FLASHBACKS

She might, as I mentioned earlier, move backward. In the previous essay, John Barth notes Horace's exhortation to begin in the middle—in medias res. But after you have crafted your first scene, or even your first sentence, you must begin to consider ways to show the more important events that have taken place *before* the story opens. A flashback can give the reader a clear picture of these events by dramatizing a conversation or a crucial memory. It can jump to an incident of

137

years before and linger there for a paragraph or several pages before bringing the writer back to the present.

A flashback might immediately follow an opening sequence, as it does in Alice Munro's "Friend of My Youth." In this complexly told story, the adult narrator seeks to understand her relationship with her mother, who died after a long illness. The story opens with a description of the narrator's recurring dream about her mother, hinting at some of the conflicts that still exist even though the mother is dead. After the description of the dream, the story resumes with a recounting of events that took place before the narrator was born.

> When my mother was a young woman with a soft, mischievous face and shiny, opaque silk stockings on her plump legs (I have seen a photograph of her, with her pupils), she went to teach at a one-room school, called Grieves School, in the Ottawa Valley.

Much of "Friend of My Youth" takes place in the past. We are told the story of two sisters with whom the mother boarded while she was teaching at the Grieves School, and we learn how the story of these sisters affects the way the narrator remembers her mother. A glimpse into the past can be a powerful tool. A flashback can shed light on the way we see the present; it can also give later scenes dramatic power. Perhaps it is for this reason that flashbacks are often a seductive option for the new writer. Many beginning writers tend to overuse flashbacks, because they want to convey important information concerning the past lives of their characters, and they do not yet know how to show this information in the present time.

In a well-told story, a great deal of information can be relayed in the present. For example, a story about a man suffering in the wake of a difficult separation does not have to include a flashback of the troubled marriage. Consider the opening of Raymond Carver's short story "Why Don't You Dance?" which is told entirely in the present. Note the efficient way that Carver manages to inform us of the demise of the relationship and to move the present story forward at the same time.

> In the kitchen he poured another drink and looked at the bedroom suite in his front yard. The mattress was stripped and the candy-striped sheets lay beside two pillows on the chiffonier. Except for that, things looked much the way they had in the

bedroom—nightstand and reading lamp on his side of the bed, nightstand and reading lamp on her side.

His side, her side.

He considered this as he sipped the whiskey.

Think hard before you decide to use a flashback. Consider what kind of story you would like to tell. If you are writing a very taut, action-oriented piece, then a flashback may interrupt the action. Like any interruption from the present story, a flashback can distract the reader; it can sometimes cause the reader to lose interest in, or even forget about, the present narrative.

If you use a flashback, you must also signal your move in time so the reader won't be confused by the sudden change, or even miss it. Also, consider its placement in the story. A well-placed flashback is "launched" from the present time by a significant and related event (in "Friend of My Youth," it is the narrator's dream about her mother and the hint of her troubled relationship). Ideally, the image or episode in the flashback will then launch itself back into the present story, adding drama and weight to the narrative. In other words, the story and the back story should speak to each other, answering each other's narrative questions and posing new ones.

FLASH-FORWARDS

Most stories advance forward steadily, in scene after scene, or in a gradually summarized narrative passage of time. But occasionally you may want to give the reader a sudden, clear-eyed glimpse into the future by using a flash-forward, or prolepsis.

An example of a flash-forward occurs in Harriet Doerr's novel *Stones for Ibarra*. The novel begins as Richard and Sara Everton, a San Francisco couple, travel to Mexico to reopen an abandoned copper mine in the village of Ibarra. Then the reader receives a glimpse into the future.

"It's on the outside edge of nowhere," said the friends. "You can't mean to spend the rest of your lives down there."

But it is indeed the Evertons' intention to spend the rest of their lives down here. They will not know until July that in Richard's case this will amount to six years.

"Count on at least six active years," they will be told by the doctor, who diagnoses an irregularity, or, put more clearly, a malignancy, in Richard's blood the summer after their arrival in Ibarra.

But by then they are already white washing the old house and pumping water from the third level of the Malguena mine. . . .

One of the most well-known stories that employs flash-forwards is William Faulkner's "Barn Burning," which contains this powerful passage where the narrator suddenly zooms into the future.

> That night they camped, in a grove of oaks and beeches where a spring ran. The nights were still cool and they had a fire against it, of a rail lifted from a nearby fence and cut into lengths—a small fire, neat, niggard almost, a shrewd fire; such fires were his father's habit and custom always, even in freezing weather. Older, the boy might have remarked this and wondered why not a big one; why should not a man who had not only seen the waste and extravagance of war, but who had in his blood an inherent voracious prodigality with material not his own, have burned everything in sight? Then he might have gone a step farther and thought that that was the reason: that niggard blaze was the living fruit of nights passed during those four years in the woods hiding from all men, blue or gray, with his strings of horses (captured horses, he called them). And older still, he might have divined the true reason: that the element of fire spoke to some deep mainspring of his father's being, as the element of steel or powder spoke to other men, as the one weapon for the preservation of integrity, else breath were not worth the breathing, and hence to be regarded with respect and used with discretion.
>
> But he did not think this now and he had seen those same niggard blazes all his life.

What can be gained using a flash-forward? It can provide us with a startling and revealing vision of the characters' futures as their present conflicts unfold, helping us understand the present story in a larger context. It can invest the narrative with a weighty sense of significance and destiny, as in *Stones for Ibarra* and "Barn Burning." Or, in a first-person reminiscent story, such as Tobias Wolff's "Smorgasbord," it can call attention to the narrator's maturation; it can emphasize what he has learned in the interval between the events of the story and the telling of it.

I had trouble getting to sleep. The food I had eaten sat like a stone in me, and I was miserable about the things I had said. I understood that I had been a liar and a fool. I kept shifting under the covers, then I sat up and turned on my reading lamp. I picked up the new picture my girlfriend had sent me, and closed my eyes, and when I had some peace of mind I renewed my promises to her.

We broke up a month after I got home. Her parents were away one night, and we seized the opportunity to make love in their canopied bed. This was the fifth time that we had made love. She got up immediately afterward and started putting her clothes on. . . . Sometime later I heard a soft knock on my door. I was still wide awake.

You should consider using a flash-forward only when a glimpse of the future will add to the tension and enrich the present story. In most cases, a flash-forward can detract from the narrative tension, answering so many of the reader's questions that the narrative suspense will trickle away. Perhaps this is why flash-forwards are sparingly used in today's short fiction.

FRAME STORIES

Once you have made your first, rusty moves into the story's future and past, like a tentative skater learning to go forward and backward on the ice, you may find yourself in the territory of memories, images, dreams, and visions. You may develop a fuller and more complete idea of what your story is about and discover that the material lends itself to a certain narrative shape; you may gain confidence and want to try more complicated moves.

A frame story employs a prolonged flashback that becomes the center of the narrative. It typically opens by immersing the reader in a present-time dramatic scene before jumping into the flashback. "Friend of My Youth" is a frame story—that is, it returns to the present after a series of prolonged flashbacks. The flashbacks are crucial—they reveal the power of a particular time in the past and why it is still affecting the narrator in the present.

Another example of a frame story is Stuart Dybek's "Paper Lantern," which opens with a description of a meal eaten by three scientists at a Chinese restaurant (the scientists are working on, appropriately, a time machine). The researchers return to the laboratory and discover it in flames; they left their Bunsen burner on.

All along empty, echoing streets, sirens are screaming like victims.

Already a crowd has gathered.

"Look at that seedy old mother go up," a white kid in dreadlocks says to his girlfriend, who looks like a runaway waif. She answers, "Cool!"

And I remember how, in what now seems another life, I watched fires as a kid—sometimes fires that a gang of us, calling ourselves the Matchheads, had set.

I remember how, later, in another time, if not another life, I once snapped a photograph of a woman I was with as she watched a fire blaze out of control along a river in Chicago. . . .

"Paper Lantern" goes on to describe the narrator and his lover as they watch the flames, and what happens after. This long flashback, which makes up the body of the story, explores the relationship before it moves back into the present, where the laboratory is still burning. Let us examine the way that Dybek creates the return from the past to the present.

I'd kept [the photos] all these years, along with a few letters—part of a bundle of personal papers in a manila envelope that I moved with me from place to place. I had them hidden away in the back of a file cabinet in the laboratory, although certainly they had no business being there. Now what I'd told her was true: they were fueling the flames. Outlined in firelight, the kid in dreadlocks kisses the waif. His hand glides over the back of her fringed jacket of dirty white buckskin and settles on the torn seat of her faded jeans. . . .

At this point the reader realizes how the story and the back story join together: The photographs of the woman with whom the narrator watched the fire are burning along with the laboratory. This transition illustrates one of the most important aspects of a frame story: It shows how the past and the present are linked.

FIGURE EIGHT

Perhaps you discover that you are working on material that keeps returning to the same image or central event. You might choose a sequencing strategy of looping time around this central moment, shaping the story into a "figure eight," the way James Baldwin does in "Sonny's Blues," or Stephanie Vaughn in "Able, Baker, Charlie, Dog." Both stories begin at one point in time, then leap backward, returning gradually, in scenes, to the time of the story's opening, then continuing forward to show more scenes that follow the events of the opening and have been irrevocably affected by it.

"Able, Baker, Charlie, Dog" opens as the narrator, a child of twelve, watches her father, in his army officer's uniform, walking toward the house, returning home from a day at work. This scene is followed by a long jump backward as the narrator describes briefly the beginning of her parents' marriage and then depicts her relationship with her father when she was four years old, then six years old. We come closer to the year of the opening scene, which takes place in Fort Niagara, when the narrator's father learns that he has been passed over for a promotion. Shortly afterward, the narrator watches him walking again, carefully picking his way across the ice floes near Niagara Falls. She describes his leaving the army that year, then jumps ahead in two more scenes that show his aging and death. At the end of the story, thinking about her father's life, she remembers again the way he looked as he walked across the ice.

REVERSE ORDER

You may decide to move the entire story in reverse order, marching the characters into the past, as Lorrie Moore does in "How to Talk to Your Mother (Notes)," which traces the relationship between mother and daughter, beginning years after her death and ending with an early childhood memory. This technique depends on the power of the stories behind a story and is sometimes used in novels, such as Charles Baxter's *First Light*. Once again, the backward shape works best when it works with the writer's subject matter. Martin Amis said that he wrote his novel *Time's Arrow* in backward chronological order because looking backward "was the only way to understand the Holocaust."

OUT OF SEQUENCE

Occasionally, a story works best when the information is scrambled, or given out of sequence. William Faulkner's well-known "A Rose for Emily" illustrates some of the ways that telling a story out of sequence can increase its power. "A Rose for Emily" relies in part upon the suspense created as information is slowly given to the reader. The story offers certain facts about the life of a Southern woman, Miss Emily Grierson, ostensibly narrated by the people of a small southern town where she lived. Faulkner is able to create a meandering narrative by using his narrator, the townspeople, with their bits of incomplete information, their tendency toward rumor and anecdote.

Early in "A Rose for Emily," we learn of Emily's ability to "vanquish" the town elders when they are reluctant to discuss with her a bad smell that comes from her house. There follows a series of the townspeople's impressions of Emily, related anecdotally. At one point, she buys rat poison. Only later does it become completely clear that the rat poison was used to murder a man and that his body was the cause of the smell. If the townspeople's observations (the death of Miss Emily's father, Miss Emily's inability and refusal to pay taxes, Miss Emily's northern beau, the purchase of rat poison, the bad smell) had been related in chronological order, the fact of the murder would have been all too clear. A more straightforward telling would have eliminated the suspense.

Another example of a story told out of sequence is Alice Munro's "The Progress of Love," which begins, again, with the death of the narrator's mother and loops through the future and different versions of the past, revisiting two family myths and examining the way that members of the same family can see its history differently. The story jumps more than a dozen times, creating a rich and complex pattern that can be confusing to the reader on his first encounter with it. But a careful study reveals its many layers of meaning, fully developed.

Given the number of jumps in "The Progress of Love," it's difficult to understand how the author has managed to achieve a coherent narrative, let alone such a powerful piece of work. How does she do it? For one thing, the flash-forwards and flashbacks all circle the events that took place in one significant summer, when the narrator was twelve. "The Progress of Love" also works because each jump brings the story to a moment in time that gives the reader a piece of information crucial to the narrator's present telling and comprehending of her family's story. In other words, the chunks of the past and future that are spliced throughout the story are never irrelevent; they never swerve from the narrator's overall purpose.

FINDING THE SHAPE OF YOUR STORY

Occasionally, the shape of a story may come naturally to you. You may instinctively sense that it can be told in a simple, linear fashion.

Or you may sense that it reaches back and forth, or moves in circles around an important event, and decide early to abandon a linear approach.

But more often, you won't be able to see a structure even after you finish a draft. You will finish writing with the vague sense that its shape is not quite right, that you have completed not a story but a vague, amorphous blob. This is a natural and often typical part of the writing process. A writer often does not find order in her work until well into the revision.

The most important and crucial way to find your story's pattern in time is to become familiar with the material, to learn how it is trying to tell itself. You must learn what your story is *about*. For example, if you find your drafts returning to the idea of family myth and family memory, you may find yourself, like Munro in "The Progress of Love," making many jumps in time. If your story unfolds primarily through action, you may consider the advantages of writing without flashbacks, keeping the narrative line taut and suspenseful.

Almost always, a story's pattern in time is determined by its subject. For example, Faulkner was able to tell "A Rose for Emily" out of sequence because he was writing about the way that a group of people—in his case, the people of a Southern town—tend toward rumor and gossip, piecing together the lives of their neighbors. This is developed through his use of the first-person plural ("we") narrator.

Toni Morrison's *Beloved* is another example of the way that the subject can affect sequencing. In this novel, Sethe and Paul D, former slaves, rediscover each other years after they have been freed. They attempt to create a new life. But they cannot forget the torments they have experienced as slaves. Then Beloved appears, a mysterious young woman who brings back their troubles and rips their lives apart. Who is she? Is she a ghost? Only when Sethe and Paul D have worked through their painful histories can they move forward.

In structuring this novel, Morrison used two main story lines, a past and a present narrative, jumping back and forth between them. In the present story, Sethe and Paul D meet and try to live their lives. But the narrative continually flashes to the other story line, which describes the years when they were slaves. The many flashbacks refuse to let the reader forget what the characters can scarcely bear to remember. Well into the novel, a character reminiscent of the back story appears in the present story and Sethe and Paul D's lives fall apart, reflecting the novel's underlying statement that if you don't deal with your past, it will come and get you.

CHRONOLOGICAL ORDER

Last but not least, a writer should never forget the power of chronological order. This narrative device, which has been the engine behind our oldest stories, is as important and magical as ever. As long as we live forward in time, we live in thrall to the power of time as it unfolds around us. In his essay "The Magic Show," Tim O'Brien writes, "By its very nature the future compels and intrigues us—it holds promise, it holds terror—and plot relies for its power on the essential cloudiness of things to come. We don't know. We want to know." The innovative writer Gilbert Sorrentino favors chronological order whenever possible, "because then the reader doesn't know what is going to happen next."

The beauty of forward movement in time can be seen in James Joyce's "The Dead," in which he describes a Christmas party in Ireland in naturalistic detail, with the characters, conversations, and even the meals faithfully rendered as the evening unfolds. The tale from the woman Gretta's past, revealed at the story's climax, is given entirely in a conversation taking place in the present. Only because we have been seduced by the evening's gradual unfolding, watching its characters, young and old, are we able to understand the signficance of the history that unfolds in Gretta's story as she tells it. Little by little, through the most subtle details, lines of dialogue, and small conflicts, the narrative has built up its authority and moves toward its beautiful, transformative ending.

At the heart of sequencing lies what is one of the writer's most important tasks: to show the passing of time and its effects on the lives of humans, on society, and the world. The storywriter shows us our lives, the way that time marks and changes us, bearing witness to our different stages. Time is a fiction writer's medium, and she must learn to move her story through time in a way that will illuminate characters, the passing of entire lives as well as moments of stillness.

EXERCISES

1. Write a short story in which the action takes place in strict chronological order. The action of each scene should unfold moment by moment in the present, as if it is taking place before the reader's eyes. You are not allowed any flashbacks (backward movements in time). Or, if you would like to write a short-short, try to make all of the action take place in one scene, without significant gaps in time or changes in setting.

2. Choose a draft of a short story that you would like to revise. Find a pair of scissors and cut the draft into its major scenes and narrative sections. Now practice reordering the scenes and sections to make some of the narrative shapes mentioned. Where would be an effective point for a flashback? Would it be possible to shape the pieces of this story into a "figure eight," and would that be the most powerful way to tell the story? Why or why not? How would the story change if the scenes were given in strict chronological order? The purpose of this exercise is for you to gain a clear idea of each piece of your story and to develop flexibility in your understanding of sequencing.

3. Write a short story in which the scenes and episodes take place in backward order.

Lan Samantha Chang is the author of *Hunger: A Novella and Stories*. She has received a James Michener-Copernicus Fellowship, a Wallace Stegner Fellowship, and a literature grant from the National Endowment for the Arts. She has taught fiction writing at Stanford University and The University of Iowa Writers' Workshop.

An Architecture of Light: Structuring the Novel and Story Collection

PHILIP GERARD

It astonishes me that intelligent people who would not hold a wedding, plant a garden, or even slap together a utility shed without exhaustive planning nonetheless regard the novel as a spontaneous literary event that just *happens* onto the page—a suspenseful, thrilling, long story arising full blown and unraveling flawlessly in chronological sequence without any planning whatsoever. All the writer needs is inspiration.

I choose these examples advisedly: wedding, garden, shed.

A novel, like a wedding, *is* an event—a celebration even. A book is just a wad of wood pulp until a pair of intelligent eyes scans its lines, and then it begins *happening* in a cognitively literal way inside a stranger's imagination. It's a marriage, if you will, between writer and reader—both are on for the long haul. But it's a marriage nobody is sure will succeed, either as a memorable event or a long-term partnership of mutual trust and passion.

You cannot just announce a wedding and wait to see who, if anyone, shows up. The author approaches the event with some definite hopes about how things will turn out, what shape the event will take, what promises will be made to which sort of suitor. There are no guarantees, but there is a meaningful shape to the ritual—and the anticipation of a seduction to follow.

To plant a garden is an exercise in preparation—choosing good ground and then preparing it. Just so, the novelist must search out an area fertile enough to promise a story of a certain scale and then must prepare it to yield something grown from a seed, something that wasn't there before on the bare ground—a long fiction. It will grow under the husbandry of the author—good old-fashioned word, *husbandry*, whose linguistic roots include both *freedom* and *bondage*. That's the central tension of writing the long form: creating boundaries within which you can invent freely.

This is useful to remember: If the thing is organic, it will grow beyond your designs for it. But you must have designs for it, or it won't grow at all.

And the utility shed metaphor comes from Henry David Thoreau, who reminds us that writing, after teaching, is the humblest of professions:

> The youth gets together his materials to build a bridge to the moon, or perchance a palace or temple on the earth, and at length the middle-aged man concludes to build a wood-shed with them.

The novel, like the shed, is functional. However fine the art of it, whatever lovely ideas, characters, and lyrics inhabit it, the novel must *work*. It is, in a dignified sense, utilitarian. We'll talk later about the special work it does.

So the novel is an organic event that requires prepared ground to do its work.

BEING AN EXTRAORDINARY STORYTELLER

Another way of saying it: I believe the novelist must have a pretty definite idea of what the novel is to be about, what shape it will take, where his interest lies, even where it is liable to wind up. As novelist John Irving reminds us in "Getting Started":

> If you don't know the story before you begin the story, what kind of storyteller are you? Just an ordinary kind, just a medio-cre kind—making it up as you go along, no better than a com-mon liar.

This is an old-fashioned notion but one we tend to forget in an era when many novels are really more like novellas—single-character stories of barely one hundred pages, limited in time and scope and concern, each following a single thread to its end without *War and Peace*-style complications—and so perhaps can be approached like the short story, which reveals itself to the writer as it unfolds. In the short story, as Edith Wharton puts it, there's almost no delay between the flash and the bang—like a painting, it can be apprehended nearly all at once (more on this later).

But in a novel, there are likely to be many flashes and bangs, lots of noisy characters scurrying about, clamoring for attention, making a mess of things, long waits between the author's promise and the reader's reward. So you must orchestrate that distance, make the best use of that delay, keep the characters and events sorted out, keep the reader reading ("the persuasion of continuity," critic Northrop Frye calls it), save the biggest bangs for last, and make the reader feel, after much time and labor, that she has apprehended all of it and the experience has been worth it.

You can't just wing it: A good part of writing the novel is done before you start writing.

THE PROBLEM OF THE CATHEDRAL

Whenever I teach Forms of Narrative Prose to my graduate students, I begin the first session with a riddle: If the cathedral is a solution, what was the problem it was meant to solve?

"To give glory to God," my students say, wondering if they have blundered into the wrong seminar, or, "to create a majestic object of beauty." They're caught in our narrow Romantic aesthetic, so reflexively they are not even aware of it: Beguiled by the stunning inspirational effect of the finished cathedral *on them personally*, they fail to imagine themselves in the place of the artisan contemplating how to build the damned thing.

That is, they are reacting like readers, carried away by the majesty of the finished artifact—rather than like writers, charged with creating that effect.

From the architect's point of view, the prosaic problem solved by the cathedral is most significantly not a problem of faith, ego, legacy, or beauty—there is nothing either personal or sublime about it. It is a problem of *architecture*—of *structure*, not *beauty*; of *craft* not *art*. But if it is solved with sound engineering, art and beauty are made possible.

For thousands of years, builders were obsessed with the problem of creating a large interior space. This sounds simple, but think about it again, and you'll understand the challenge of the novel.

It was easy enough to construct a gigantic roofless space—like the Roman Colosseum. But how do you hold up the roof on the cathedrals of Chartres and Notre Dame? How do you hold up the middle?

A corollary problem that distinguishes the cathedral from, say, a warehouse: That space must be *lighted*—something important, some *sacred communication*, must occur inside it. In an age before electric or even gas lamps, this was no small challenge. And if you are depending on load-bearing walls for support—walls that must be very thick if you're building a tower to heaven—you have to figure ways to cut large, high windows without making the whole shell so structurally weak it topples from the sheer weight of itself.

In my seminar, usually by a series of my primitive blackboard drawings and some lively discussions, we rediscover that a whole series of innovations, from the Roman arch to the flying buttress and including the cruciform shape of the cathedral itself, are all engineering inventions to help hold up the roof—the middle.

So let us refine the problem solved by the cathedral: How do you build a large indoor lighted space?

Answer. You create an architecture of light. Which is exactly what the novelist must do.

ONE-LINE NOVEL

In other words, you've got to create a large, durable, multifaceted story structure that will illuminate what's inside—the characters whose actions and interior lives tangle and disengage, sprawling across continents and years.

You've got to stop being a romantic and think hard about *structure*. Just piling on more of everything—building thicker and thicker walls—won't do. You've go to do some careful calculations to arrive at a blueprint that makes possible mystery and beauty.

One useful place to begin is to encapsulate the thrust of your novel into a signature—as in music: defining the key, the pace, the range of tonal possibilities. Think of *Moby Dick*: Madman goes hunting for a white whale. *Anna Karenina*: Beautiful woman marries the wrong man. *Huckleberry Finn*: Two guys float down a river on a raft, trying to escape to freedom. The signature, expressed as one simple defining sentence, may sound trivial, but it can focus your effect.

It doesn't slight the larger, complex concerns of the novel, the twists and nuances of character and action. It does not *summarize* the novel—it will take your whole novel, every chapter, scene, and word, to tell your large story. But it does define the structural arc of the story, the blueprint for holding up the long middle. Such a signature declares, as Captain Ahab might, "The path to my fixed purpose is laid on iron rails, on which my soul is grooved to run."

It's your purpose, the driving line of the novel. Every other creative decision you make derives from that purpose. It's not for a second what we're interested in on a deeper level, but it will drive the surface tension, which will pull along all the other tensions: Jim and Huck's raft is a vehicle for moving Mark Twain's story down the river. It carries the characters places where interesting things happen, and it causes an alliance that matures into friendship, complicated by the social fact that Jim is black and Huck is white, that their world is full of pretenders and hypocrites, and so on.

Sometimes, in the course of the novel, Huck and Jim stray too far from the river. But whenever the story digresses too far and the reader's interest begins to flag, you can practically hear Twain's panicked voice shouting, "Back to the raft!" and the characters scramble aboard to resume their journey—and their story.

Think of the signature as the cable that hauls the roller-coaster cars up the long, slow hill of suspense, around the hairpin turn of reversal, down the stomach-clenching fall. We don't care about that cable—we probably don't even realize it's there. But it makes the ride work. Without it, none of the thrills would be possible.

OUTLINING

One way to write a novel is to outline it first. A lot of writers don't, but I maintain that once you have conceived a structural template, you have much more freedom within that to relax and allow the story to surprise you—since you're not struggling so hard to make sure it has dramatic coherence. In your outline, you have already established an overall coherence. The arc of the story hangs together. You've framed your cathedral.

The kind of outline I mean is basic, spare, and consists of six parts:
1. working title (you can change this later: *The Great Gatsby* started out as *The High-Bouncing Lover*)
2. signature (your roller-coaster cable: poor boy, Gatsby, tries to win heart of rich girl, Daisy)
3. list of major characters (who: in *Gatsby*, there are only three who matter to the story, four more who matter to the plot, and a handful of bit players)

4. list of major locales (where: in *Gatsby*, five locales serve all the action)

5. numbered chapters, each containing a one-sentence description of the central event (chapter one: Nick meets Daisy, Jordan Baker, and Tom)

6. your concept of the ending—not in exact terms, but a recognition of what the ending must address (does the poor boy win the rich girl?)

As you write, and as your understanding of your own story develops, almost everything will change. Locally—within chapters and scenes, moment by moment—you will be surprised and inspired, events will take remarkable, unexpected turns, new characters will arrive out of nowhere. That's as it should be. You should be writing for the same reason your reader is reading: to find out what happens next.

THE ARCHITECTURE OF CHAPTERS

This takes two forms: the arrangement of chapters within the larger framework of the novel, and the progress of scenes within each chapter.

Dramatically, the "rule" of chapters is the rule of scenes in any fiction: Each one should have a clear reason for inclusion. It should not just provide more information, a more thorough résumé of character, or lush descriptions of place. It may do all those things, but first it must have an indispensable role in moving the story along.

In chapter one of *The Great Gatsby*, we meet the narrator, Nick Carraway, and get a mixed message about how much to trust him. We are quickly spirited away to Daisy Buchanan's mansion, where, in a setting that seethes with restlessness, trouble waiting to happen, we meet Daisy and her cohort Jordan Baker, about whom (Nick teases us) he once heard a "critical, unpleasant story," and Daisy's husband, Tom, a rude, bigoted man who receives a mysterious and upsetting telephone call.

Chapter two lets us in on the secret of the call—it was Tom's mistress, Myrtle, and now we're riding the train with Tom, Myrtle, and Nick through the Valley of Ashes, under the watchful billboard eyes of Dr. T.J. Eckleburg, toward New York and a very bad party.

It's not till chapter three—almost fifty pages in—that we actually

153

meet Gatsby, though everybody we've met has remarked on him, adding gloss to his legend. By now, we have all the players on stage, all the significant relationships laid out—including the adulterous affair that will lead to tragedy; we've even been over the literal road where the tragedy will happen. When the tragedy unfolds in fast, confused flashes, we won't have to stop and take in mere description or become oriented to a new locale. Every scene has had its own minor tension—Daisy and Tom spatting, Jordan throwing a tantrum, Tom driving too fast—and we can already see the dramatic convergence of the parts in the mystery of Gatsby's identity.

Storytelling is the art of unfolding knowledge in a way that makes each piece contribute to a larger truth.

Unlike a short story, a novel chapter must be both complete and unfinished—that is, it must seem to be one discrete thing, a self-contained dramatic whole, or there'd be no reason to separate it as a distinct chapter, and yet it must create enough new anticipation to make the reader carry her interest over to the start of the next chapter.

Each chapter seems to accomplish its "business" and then asks a question, raises an issue, piques a curiosity, that introduces other "new" business and teases the reader to turn the page rather than stop: Tom and Daisy are having a rocky marriage—we know that for sure now—but who was that on the phone?

Suspense

Remember: Suspense is made up of curiosity and delay. There's a question we really want to know the answer to, and the writer doesn't allow the answer to emerge until the interest has been heightened, the reader knows enough to appreciate the significance of the answer and to fret over it and can't bear to wait any longer.

Here is how suspense works in a novel: Your wife says, "I've bought you something, but you can't open it until Christmas." Anticipation.

She lets you ponder that for a whole week and then says, "You know, the thing I bought? We really can't afford it. But what the hell." Mild anxiety.

Another week goes by. She says, "You know that present I told you about? Well I hope you like it, because I can't take it back." Greater anxiety—and curiosity. More is at stake.

A week later, she says, "I'm wondering if I ever should have bought you that present." A touch of panic? What does she mean? You lie awake counting off the possibilities, worrying each one through. In the context of marriage, they matter. What's she trying to tell you?

A week before Christmas, she places your present, wrapped in beautiful paper and ribbons, under the tree. You pick it up and shake it, curious. She says, "Oh, no! I hope you haven't broken it!" So you place it gently back under the tree—guilty, resentful, feeling a little foolish.

Suspense is what's going through your mind, every minute from the moment you learn of the present until the moment you open it, and every teasing worry brought on by the new information. Every emotion—frustration, gratitude, anger, anxiety, love, doubt, impatience—is part of your experience with suspense.

Christmas Day arrives. She makes you wait till after breakfast, till after you've opened all the other presents, till after she's opened hers from you (will it measure up?). You take a deep breath and pull at the ribbons, tear the paper. Inside is—paper! And something else—a plane ticket. For Paris, France! You're baffled—you don't even speak French and have never expressed a desire to go to Paris. As you're about to say thanks anyway, she looks at you and smiles slyly. "No, no," she says, "that's not your present! Your present is *in* Paris!"

Are you *not* going to get on that plane?

And when you do, are you *not* going to say to yourself, "Wait a minute—how could I have broken it by shaking the package?" and start worrying all over again?

THE TWO MOST DAUNTING CHALLENGES: FINISHING AND FINISHING

While you're working on the novel day after day, month and year after month and year, it seems more real than the world beyond the page. Scenes and characters take on a vividness that is almost painful, often exciting, and quite beguiling.

When it is working.

When your novel is not working, it just lies there in pieces on the page, leaking vital fluids all over your desk.

In either case, your course is clear: If it's working, just let it keep working. Keep accumulating the pages. If it is not working, you'd better pause and remember what you were trying to do in the first place (your signature) and then do some hard diagnostic work to find where it has gone wrong. If you set out to send two guys down the river on a raft and they've wound up in a salon in Copenhagen discussing Kierkegaard for no particular reason, then perhaps you took a wrong turn somewhere. Trace the line of the story back to the wrong turn, and take a different turn.

The most common reason, I think, why writers get stuck in first drafts is that the line of the novel just peters out. It wasn't a large enough scenario. It didn't contain a big enough possible world. The characters weren't interesting enough to sustain deep reflection on their interior lives. There just wasn't enough *there* there.

A false start. Better to find out after fifty pages than five hundred.

So the first big challenge—and don't underestimate it—is simply sustaining a long, interesting story from start to finish. Not just linking a bunch of scenes or anecdotes or ruminations or slice-of-life moments, but building a big story that is all one thing, that finishes what it starts, that arcs convincingly from clear beginning to recognizable end—a big luminous creation in which you've managed to hold up the roof so the people inside can conduct their sacred communication with the reader. If you've done that—even if the novel is dreadful, predictable, hackneyed, overwritten, and full of missed chances and ragged threads of unsolved story—you have written a novel. You've done something most people can't do. Will never do. Wish they could do and had done. Would trade their drawers full of great beginnings for.

Next, write a *good* novel.

So the novel that is working and the one that is an utter dead fish present clear paths of action. The tough one is the draft that *sort of* works but also has dead spots, riveting scenes and flat scenes, a plot that seems plausible one day and ridiculous the next, characters you love and then grow tired of and then love again, until tomorrow when they seem utterly uninteresting.

I don't know what to do about such a first draft, except to finish it and find out where it ends up and then try to reenvision the thing. Some writers will tell you to not write another word until you've figured out the design flaw—but that may stop you for good. Sometimes you just have to struggle through to the other side, building whatever makeshift bridges you can out of soft scenes and tired sentences until you can replace them with sounder stuff.

Probably this is an indication that there is something basic wrong with the conception of it, but exactly *what* is wrong may be impossible to recognize until you've arrived at either a right or wrong ending and can read the novel whole. If you're lucky, the flaw will stand out in sharp relief. If you're luckier, it will be fixable.

If the novel is based on autobiographical experience, the flaw is probably in staying too close to what happened, instead of what, in the most interesting of all possible worlds, *might have* happened.

Almost as big a trap is trying too hard to force your novel to a preconceived ending. That's the central paradox of writing the novel— you have to know where it's going, but when it speaks to you, shows you a better direction, you have to be ready to abandon your plan and listen to the story. It's enough to drive you crazy.

The other obstacle to finishing is again a prosaic one—*continuity*.

This affects the writer in two ways. First, it's extremely easy to lose track of complex turns of plot, the life histories of characters, the dramatic logic of the story. The famous example of this occurred in Raymond Chandler's *The Big Sleep*, in which the murder of a chauffeur springs all the other links in the chain of plot. When filmmakers were adapting it for the screen, they came across a curious fact: On close reading, it's never clear in the novel *who* killed the chauffeur or why. Yet the entire plot of the book depends on it. So they called Chandler and asked him, and he obligingly looked at his novel again. Beats me, he said.

William Faulkner hung a map of Yoknapatawpha County over his writing desk, to keep his fictional geography clear. He even changed the population count from time to time, to keep up with the migrations, births, deaths, and lynchings in his novels.

Most of us have faulty memories, and simply keeping track, in a precise way, of the intricacies of what has happened so far—especially as the book grows into the hundreds of pages and several layers of drafts—is difficult. Again, it's not a matter of art but of the working craft. Like an outline, it's scaffolding you dismantle after you've built your cathedral.

For the big stuff to work credibly, you've got to get the little stuff absolutely right.

The second way in which continuity challenges the novelist is through real-life time: A novel will typically take years to complete, and the writer will change. At some point, a major change may mark a before-and-after transition in the writer's life—the death of a loved one, a gain or loss of faith, marriage or the breakup of a marriage. The writer of chapter seventeen may not be the same writer who wrote chapter one—the writer may need to scrap the old work and work from a new vision entirely.

Whenever I begin a novel, I always feel a clock being started—the catch is that I have no clue how long the clock will run till the alarm bell goes off, but there is a certain urgency *that must be ignored*, since the only way to write a novel well is to proceed as if you had all the time in the world.

Likewise, mundane interruptions to the daily habit of writing the novel can pose serious threats to finishing: a job, family obligations, illness, jury duty. Anything that keeps you away from the pages for more than a day or two can impair your ability to keep track of the thing, let alone to do something wonderful and artful with it. One solution is to "visit" your novel in progress even on those days when you are prevented from working on it—remind yourself of the last few pages you wrote, or of a scene that's been nagging you. You're just touching it to make sure it's still there, poking your head inside that little universe to remind yourself how the air tastes and of the quality of the light.

WAR AND PEACE: EFFECTS OF SCALE

In *The Fiction Dictionary*, Laurie Henry writes, "Because of its greater length, a novel will have more characters, take place over a longer period of time, and involve more movement among settings than a novella or short story." This expression of the causal relationship between the novel's *length* and its other characteristics has always struck me as backward—based on a fundamental misconception about how the novel operates.

The novel does not have more characters and scenes *because* it is bigger—as if the novel were just a bigger bin in which to throw more stuff. Just the other way around: The novel's length is an artifact of the different way scenes, characters, and events are used.

For instance, *War and Peace* is commonly regarded as a big, sprawling novel; in most editions, it runs to seven hundred pages or so. Yet scene by scene, the novel is not crammed full of detail and chatter. To the contrary, the party scenes that open the novel are almost minimalist in style. We get a brushstroke for each character, not full descriptions and résumés. Likewise, in the battlefield scenes, we don't get complicated military detail—we get Prince Andrei glimpsing a single cannon here, a commotion over there. We know one thing only about the Russian foot soldier: He is barefoot. And all the scenes take place in a very few locales, to which the action returns again and again: the drawing room, the country estate, the barracks, the battlefield.

Yet consider the progress of the first three big scenes in the novel:

1. Anna Pavlovna's society party, at which the main business is the women's relentless politicking for appointments in the army for sons, brothers, and cousins, where we meet Pierre, huge and out of place, the illegitimate son of the famous Count Bezúkhov;

2. the Horse-Guard barracks, where Pierre visits his dissolute friend Kuragin, in the midst of a debauch: An officer named Dolokhof wagers he will guzzle an entire bottle of rum while balanced on a windowsill high above the stone courtyard and not holding on, while his drunken companions tease a chained bear;

3. old Count Bezúkhov's deathbed chamber, where the underhanded fight for his inheritance is won accidentally by his bastard son, Pierre—the same Pierre we have seen in high society and a drunken debauch—who is then certified by the Tsar as the new lawful Count Bezúkhov.

A character's fortune has changed completely before our eyes without even being the main business of the book so far—though it does reflect that business: the reckless Russian nobility preparing for a fall. Shortly thereafter, we go off to war, and the drawing room characters are now in the army, making a mess of the campaign, as we suspected they would, careening merrily toward the debacle at Austerlitz. The novel oscillates (surprise) between scenes of war and scenes of peace, and the implicit, tragic joke is that the pampered nobility can hardly tell the difference—until it's too late and their own estates are burning.

The line of development is unmistakable and large in scope: from career politics, to debauchery, to the illegitimate legitimized, to disastrous war. It is this line of development that requires a large canvas— you just can't fit Austerlitz into a short story without overwhelming the form. The scenes are used in succession to create this line of development, which requires many scenes, and thus many pages, to play out.

The effect is of accumulation—not of sheer detail, but of detail meaningfully augmented by repetition, which deepens our understanding of the events. As in a symphony, motifs reemerge in minor keys and in variations, creating a sense of movement and return. No wonder Maxwell Perkins, the famous editor, once wrote to author James Jones of the remarkable structural virtues of *War and Peace*: "I think it would be much better to read that book over and over, to the neglect of books on the art of fiction."

The material itself makes it large, not just long, and in turn produces effects of scale.

THE WORK OF THE NOVEL

So what is it that a novel does, exactly? Milan Kundera (author of *The Unbearable Lightness of Being*), in *The Art of the Novel*, defines it as "the great prose form in which an author thoroughly explores, by means of experimental selves (characters) some great themes of existence."

Great—you don't hear that word much anymore. But the novel is *great*—in the sense of being larger than other things of the same kind, namely novellas and short stories. Not just longer—*larger*. Because the reader lives with it for an extended period, the novel comes to take on an accrued reality, like a snowfall. The fully realized world of the novel is a big undeniable fact operating in the reader's mind. It deeply engages the reader on every level—intellectual, emotional, artistic, and spiritual. It leaves a broad, deep footprint on the reader's imagination.

In other words, the novel is the only fictional form that takes advantage of a particular and powerful aspect of narrative time—the real time out of the reader's life devoted to its reading—time during the reading of the long story in which the reader's mind is already processing that story, coming out of it and going back into it repeatedly, feeding real life back into the experience of reading and also feeding back in the experience of reading the earlier chapters.

An effect of *scale* is operating—one of many such effects in the novel. A cathedral, complete in every detail but only as large as a country chapel, might evoke admiration, but it could not evoke grandeur, the breathtaking realization of interior space created on a larger-than-life scale. Indeed, the effect would likely be the opposite: the somewhat ironic appreciation of the miniature that makes models so appealing for their fine fragility—or for their implicit joke about scale, as in the case of the ship in the bottle.

The novel doesn't deliver the hit-and-run satisfaction of the short-short, or even the brilliant flash of insight or grace that a short story offers. The form presents a prosaic challenge in literary engineering. Executed well, it makes us gape, openmouthed, awed and captivated. It does not astonish so much as it overwhelms us. It makes us raise our eyes, because the ceiling vaults so high, almost out of sight, suspended by an ingenious, invisible structure, and there under the vault live its most memorable secrets.

THE SHORT STORY COLLECTION

The short story collection, like the novel, works by a kind of accumulation of effect. Most writers don't start out consciously creating a series of interlinked stories as a book. Rather, they write a story, then another one, then several more, then one day begin to recognize that their stories have something essential in common, and they begin to think about creating a book of stories.

Often the process begins when an interested editor or agent asks to see a sheaf of stories with an eye toward making them into a book. The agent or editor almost instinctively groups certain stories and throws out others. These stories are "all of a piece," the editor says vaguely. The next steps will be three.

1. revising the stories selected for inclusion
2. writing some new stories specifically designed to fill out the collection—which requires understanding why the stories are "all of a piece"
3. finding the best order in which to place the stories

Of the three, the last seems to me least important, though many writers and their editors would disagree vigorously. My reasoning is that, except for story cycles that actually function somewhat novelistically—we'll get to them—story collections aren't necessarily read from start to finish. Enough readers read at random within the collection that worrying too much about the order of stories may distract the writer and editor from more important considerations.

Nonetheless, since the stories have to appear in *some* order, it's worth reflecting on what ideal effect you're after. That is, if your ideal reader were to read your collection carefully from start to finish, in what order do you want the individual effects to add up? This presumes, of course, that you can identify a single overall effect for each story. A typical pattern is to begin a collection with the most provocative story—not the best, since you'll want to save that for last—but the one that will capture the reader's attention. It's not the place for a story that is slow getting started or frustratingly obscure. You want to establish common ground with the reader and the exciting promise that there is a wonderful experience to follow.

The first point—revision of individual stories—is addressed in Jane Smiley's essay. The hard, key question is number two: What do these stories have in common?

The answer may be easy to recognize because of a superficial similarity of themes, subjects, even characters. So in each story of Wendy Brenner's delightfully wry collection *Large Animals in Everyday Life*, which won the Flannery O'Connor Prize in 1995, we encounter animals—dogs, cats, even a woman in a bear costume. Hence the title. But of course it's not the appearance of animals per se that defines the collection, but the zoo of quirky human characters.

A book of stories is the crystallization of a vision, a complete thought realized through a series of facets. Each story is a facet, another window into the thought—which though complete (there's nothing more the author can add, not at the moment) will remain unfinished, tantalizing, provocative. That's the nature of stories, and of story collections. The reader has to fill in the spaces between stories.

Another way of thinking about a collection is to recognize which story is the *tonic*, literally the *keynote*, as in a musical chord. Which story gives the pure clear note that determines the interest of the collection? Frequently (but not always), that story becomes the title story, the organizing principle, the touchstone that determines whether other stories are included. And just as in music, the tonic story may occur anywhere within the chord, depending on how you "voice" the chord.

Just as scenes within a story tend to cluster around a single defining moment without, necessarily, a "line" of plot, so collections tend to form around a keynote story that defines the concerns of the whole collection—for example, Raymond Carver's wonderful collection defined by the title story, "What We Talk About When We Talk About Love." Every story resonates with that central theme, with characters talking about everything except love.

WRITING A BOOK

It's axiomatic but worth remembering: Nobody writes a book. What you write every day is a piece of a book, a fragment, a scene. But it's just as useful to configure your ambition, early in the process, to encompass the long form, be it a novella, a novel, or a story collection. When you sit at your writing desk every day, you are two writers— one who is working closely on the piece at hand, completely immersed in the moment of the scene; the other who is holding in the back of his mind a large vision of connectedness, of the piece contributing to the effect of the whole.

But you can't apprehend a book all at once, either reading it or writing it, and so of course the writer, like the reader, simply concentrates on what is at hand, lives in it utterly, spellbound to find out what happens next.

EXERCISES

1. Pick a reasonably short novel with which you are familiar. Forgetting for the moment about content and style, outline the *structure* in as bare-bones a way as possible. For each chapter, identify the salient event that defines it and drives the story by unfolding new knowledge in a dramatic way. Trace the locales, and note which ones are used over and over again. Identify the climactic chapter.

2. Read three novels considered successful by reason of either popular success or critical acclaim. Boil each one down to the single sentence that defines its structural signature: "Man goes on a journey" or "Stranger comes to town."

3. Pick a novel you have never read. Read only the first and final chapters. Without reading what lies between, identify what the novel is about—the big issue that will be reflected in its signature. Now read the novel start to finish, making notes on every device that helps "hold up the middle."

Philip Gerard is the author of five books, including *Desert Kill: A Novel*, *Cape Fear Rising*, *Hatteras Light* and *Creative Nonfiction*, as well as numerous short stories and essays. He teaches in the MFA in Creative Writing program at the University of North Carolina at Wilmington and for two years served as President of the Board of Directors of the Associated Writing Programs.

The Lingerie Theory
of Literature:
Describing and Withholding,
Beginning and Ending

JULIE CHECKOWAY

There are many excellent ways to learn about narration—reading John Gardner's *The Art of Fiction* and Gerard Genette's *Narrative Discourse*, for example—but perhaps the most accessible lessons about writerly matters such as description, overwriting, and the opening and closing of stories are to be found, you may be surprised to learn, by reading (well, *reading* is probably imprecise) the Victoria's Secret catalogue, that ubiquitous, ninety-page(!), glossy circular that most women (and some men) find in their mailboxes about once a week.

Over the years, I've tried not to pay too much attention to those catalogues. Mostly, I've just pulled them out of my mailbox, eyes averted like a Puritan, and deposited them straight into the recycling bin. Just flipping through those pages can make the average gal crave Prozac—how those women manage to look that glamorous in just their underwear can be downright depressing. (For many men, I imagine, it's another matter, of course.) But not too long ago, when I began to understand how much writing fiction is an act of artful seduction, I began to look at the VSC with different eyes.

To backtrack, one of the most pressing problems I've found in my students' writing has to do with how much information to share in the process of narration, in other words, how to balance the desire to tease with the need to reveal. How much material, ask my students— undergrads and grads alike—do I need to tell the reader to reel him in? How much material should I withhold? And why?

These questions have inevitably to do with the issue of seduction. Aside from their characters, stories have two principal personae—the storyteller and the story hearer—who are engaged in a complicated and very personal relationship. In his book *Story and Situation: Narrative*

Seduction and the Power of Literature, the literary critic Ross Chambers reminds us that the storyteller's primary job in narration is to "exercise power" over the story hearer, to make him want to listen, and all one has to do is to remember the tale of Sheherezade to know that Chambers is right. In Sheherezade's case, you may remember, the act of storytelling lays bare the relationship between storyteller and story hearer, and makes it self-evident that the act of storytelling is, as Chambers argues, "not self-directed but other-directed." To succeed at controlling the "other," Chambers says, a storyteller speaker must both "achieve authority" and "produce involvement." In the telling of the tales of *A Thousand and One Nights*, for example, achieving authority and producing involvement are matters of the utmost urgency: One small move of narrative inefficiency, and Sheherezade will certainly lose her life.

Not all narrative situations are as dire as Sheherezade's, but many beginning writers forget that the storytelling requires a combination of the kind of urgency *and* craft that Sheherezade demonstrates. The challenge is, how do you "achieve authority" (let the story hearer know that you know what you're saying) and at the same time "produce involvement" (not give so much information that the story hearer becomes alienated or overwhelmed)?

All writers struggle at some point with the problem of balance between authority and involvement, seduction and revelation. Specifically, beginning writers wonder how much description to employ, and more advanced writers ask how much plot is too much or too little. And there is no better place to find answers than in the Victoria's Secret catalogue—or in any ad for lingerie—where the arts of seduction and revelation are so successfully practiced. After all, the secret of the effective lingerie ad is the secret of effective storytelling—to provide, moment by moment, the *illusion* of imminent exposé, to give the viewer (read: reader) the uncanny sense that something fundamentally compelling is always *just about to be* revealed. Lingerie ads and storytelling balance the veiled and the unveiled, the seen and the unseen, the shown and the about-to-be-shown. In short, it is the art of the tease, the craft of selective "coverage," that, not just in lingerie but in storytelling, works to enthrall.

A BASIC GUIDELINE: HOW MUCH IS TOO MUCH

Fiction writing may seem like a solitary activity, but it involves an intimate relationship between the writer and the reader. To succeed in the act of narrative seduction, to tell stories well, the writer must first realize that she, like Sheherezade, is never alone. The reader is always a writer's companion and partner.

It can be easy to lull yourself into thinking this isn't true. I've taught writing for over fifteen years, and I've yet to have a beginning fiction class in which at least two or three new students don't declare at one point or another, "But I don't care if the audience understands this piece. I'm writing for myself anyway." Certainly, self-satisfaction in one's work is an important part of writing, but I try to remind my students that the best and most worthwhile writing is a fundamentally desperate act of communication, a reaching out, an attempt at engagement, persuasion, entertainment, or enlightenment, and that thinking about it that way will probably serve them better in the long run.

But as desperate as this act of reaching out is in its impulses, to be effective it has also to be controlled. If you look at lingerie ads, for example, they aren't just full of wild abandon. Instead, they're really characterized by a crafty restraint. Unlike pornography, which reveals everything, the lingerie ad *suggests* revelation rather than performs it. Any good lingerie salesman would tell you that overexposure wouldn't work to sell his product. "Taking it all off," performing the striptease to its logical conclusion, would only draw the viewer's attention away from the primary narrative—the lingerie itself.

The same is true in storytelling. A writer has to be extraordinarily careful to keep the reader's attention on matters at hand, to reveal only what is necessary, to avoid overexposure, dramatic cliché, and narrative hyperbole, or nakedness, but to keep the storytelling as urgent and as tantalizing as possible from beginning to middle to end.

THE PROBLEM OF OVEREXPOSURE IN WRITING DESCRIPTION

One of the first things I do in any beginning fiction writing class is to put a complicated geometric drawing on the board (I just make one up) and ask my students to describe it so precisely that anyone reading what they've written could, theoretically, reproduce my (bad) artwork. It's an exercise someone once passed on to me from her years in girls' summer camp, an exercise meant to teach cooperation and communication between prepubescent campers, but it also teaches apprentice writers about the importance of precise description if they want something beautiful or unusual in their heads—a landscape, a scene, a character's internal thinking—to be understood by a reader.

Clear description is fundamental to good fiction writing, and becoming as concrete as possible in description should be an apprentice writer's first goal. The writer Natalie Goldberg does a very good job in her books *Writing Down the Bones* and *Wild Mind* at getting new writers down to brass tacks. Some of her freewriting exercises ask students to write precisely and concretely about places they haven't been in years—houses, summer camps—and about people long lost to them—kindergarten teachers, former best friends. Goldberg encourages writers to do what Rainer Maria Rilke wisely suggests in his *Letters to a Young Poet*—"to raise the submerged sensations of your ample past"—in an effort to become practiced at getting the details right. Relatedly, Goldberg asks writers to "drop to a deeper level" in their description. "Not just *car* but *Cadillac*, not just *bird* but *wren*," she says, encouraging students to go through their own first drafts and become fundamentally more specific about what they have seen in their mind's eye.

I use Goldberg's exercises and prescriptions about description as a way of getting students unblocked and fluid (Goldberg encourages students not to censor themselves, not to edit themselves too soon, to feel free to "write the worst junk in America"), but I soon run into a problem that I wish she had addressed. Writing description makes students nervous; it raises to the surface two of the most fundamental anxieties of all writers: *How much is too much?* and *How much is too little?* ("In my description of this house, should I mention that the paint is flaking and that the tree outside is dying? Should I say that the tree is an elm and that it is dying of Dutch elm disease?" "In my description of this character, should I tell his entire life history, including the fact that by the age of ten he still didn't have any adult teeth?")

It's important, I think, to respond to such anxieties carefully and not with the standard, "Oh, you'll just *know* how much to tell," or that smoke screen about that nebulous le mot juste (the correct word) as if one could pull such things mysteriously out of the insubstantial air. True, some writers know intuitively how much description is enough and how much is too much, but for others, it's an acquired skill, and there are several useful strategies to remember in order to master it.

The first is the old saw that fiction is, at its heart, economical (stories more than novels, of course), and that one must choose material for the fiction with a conservative, even sometimes miserly, touch. Description should therefore not be wasteful or redundant (unless you're trying to make some thematic point by doing so). One needs only to describe a house once, for example, as long as nothing has changed the second time we visit it in the fiction. One needs to say only once that the paint is flaking and that the tree is dying (unless you're aiming for a stylistic lyricism through the repetition of words or phrases). And, as my former teacher John Barth—himself a maximalist—used to say, description needs to be "illustrative" rather than "exhaustive," meaning that you need to give the reader information that is useful and thematically important (meaning description that contributes to the piece's mood and is related in some way to its content) rather than information that is merely compulsively comprehensive or too intently microscopic.

Ernest Hemingway is, of course, famous for his restraint in description. Here is a passage from *The Sun Also Rises*.

> We crossed the bridge and walked up the Rue du Cardinal Lemoine. It was steep walking, and we went all the way up to the Place Contrescarpe. The arc-light shone through the leaves of the trees in the square, and underneath the trees was an S bus ready to start. Music came out of the door of the Negre Joyeux. Through the window of the Cafe Aux Amateurs I saw the long zinc bar. Outside on the terrace working people were drinking. In the open kitchen of the Amateurs a girl was cooking potato chips in oil. There was an iron pot of stew. The girl ladled some onto a plate for an old man who stood holding a bottle of red wine in one hand.

Here, because Hemingway's novel takes place in the aftermath of World War I, in a reduced and pared-down Paris, the description of the Place Contrescarpe is sparse but still complete enough to paint a vivid portrait. To give the reader a sense of the atmosphere, Hemingway attends to the tactile ("It was steep walking"), the visual ("The arc-light shone"), the auditory ("Music came out of the door"), and he peoples the scene with extras (or supernumeraries, as W.D. Wetherell calls them in his essay in this book), each of them engaged in a concrete activity—drinking, cooking, ladling, or holding. In each of his short, declarative sentences, Hemingway is nonetheless concrete and specific in ways of which Goldberg and Rilke would most likely approve.

Thomas Hardy, a far more baroque writer than Hemingway, is nonetheless still economical in his descriptions, although he is more self-consciously poetic, certainly, and has a tendency to focus more minutely on moments and dissect them for the reader. Here, for example, is a description of the winds on the heath in his novel *The Return of the Native*.

> Throughout the blowing of these plaintive November winds that note bore a great resemblance to the ruins of human song which remain to the throat of fourscore and ten. It was a worn whisper, dry and papery, and it brushed so distinctly across the ear that, by the accustomed, the material minutiae in which it originated could be realized as by touch. It was the united products of infinitesimal vegetable causes, and these were neither stems, leaves, fruit, blades, prickles, lichen, nor moss.

Because place is so central to *The Return of the Native* (the novel's characters struggle valiantly to stay within it or escape from it), description and understanding of weather is of the utmost importance in Hardy's novel, and warrants more time than it would in Hemingway's, more unpacking. Here, the wind is described in metaphorical terms, as a whisper. Here, the wind is also a mystery, originating somewhere on the heath but *not* in the most familiar objects—stems, leaves, blades, and so on. This passage from Hardy is an intense moment of focus on a single object (the wind) but not just for the sake of focusing on it, and not overdone. Rather, the passage illustrates economically the uncanny qualities of the wind, the way that, to the characters, it is both a source of mystery and a kind of bane.

One way to decide if a particular passage of description is necessary or not is to think of the story or novel as an arrow pointing toward what Edgar Allan Poe called "the unified effect," meaning that moment when all a story's elements come together. Does the particular passage of description point *toward* the unified effect or away from it? If, for example, Hemingway were to have gone into greater detail about how steep the walk to the café was, would a lengthy description reveal thematically something about a long or laborious metaphorical "climb" that the characters were taking in the novel or would the description have been a red herring, a momentarily interesting distraction? What would have happened, for example, if Hardy had excluded from *The Return of the Native* his passage on the wind? What effect would have been lost and could not have been replaced in any other way?

OVERCOMING OVERWRITING

Sometimes writers get so excited about specificity and description that they begin to confuse them with mere wordiness. This is called over-writing and is a common early malady in apprentice writers. Some apprentice writers, usually those who love language, come down with a raging fever of overwriting, and it takes some months—sometimes years—for them to recover. Though I talk with them about the impor-tance of moderation in descriptive writing, the need to choose illustra-tive rather than exhaustive detail, inevitably they do not or simply cannot heed my warning. From minimalists with writer's block, most transform into maximalists, composing actual sentences like, "The moisture on my forehead drizzled down my tremulous face." And, "He glared with his forehead wrinkled and teeth clenched like a primi-tive beast trying to bite through its prey's hide."

Overwriting is a form of excessive love, but it is to be expected from time to time. It is important and even necessary for writers to fall in love with the craft of writing, with the sound of language, with the fact of their own finesse and let themselves go every once in a while. I myself was so in love with metaphors and similes and sounds when I started out, that, for a couple of years, I simply couldn't help myself and didn't care if anyone understood what I was saying. Here's one of my own early sentences: "Looter wears blue because it is the color of hacking coughs and the color of vertical, wet betrayal." Writ-ers far more famous than I have done it. Here's one of Eudora Welty's early first sentences: "Monsieur Boule inserted a delicate dagger in Mademoiselle's left side and departed with a poised immediacy."

The solution to overcoming overwriting, if you are ever diagnosed with it yourself or if you recognize it in others, is simply to exercise restraint and to remember the notion of economy. Welty's sentence, short of its too-fancy verbs and its excess of adjectives, might simply have read, "Monsieur Boule stabbed Mademoiselle with a dagger and left the room in a hurry." "The moisture on my forehead drizzled down my tremulous face," might easily have read, "I began to sweat and shake." My own awfully overwritten sentence might have more easily read, "Looter wears blue because the conductors in the train station do." I have no idea what I ever meant by saying that blue was "the color of hacking coughs . . . ," so I won't even touch that.

In an effort to conquer her overwriting, an acquaintance of mine used to cut her dearest overwritten sentences (the ones that Annie

Dillard says in *The Writing Life* come with "price tags" attached) out of her manuscript with scissors and deposit them in a manila folder she called her Goddess File. Any time she was blue and just wanted to see what a brilliant writer she was, all she had to do was open up the Goddess File and admire snippets of her handiwork. If cutting back on adverbs and fancy, unnecessary verbs or keeping a Goddess (or God) file doesn't work for you, you might just have to camp out and wait the overwriting out. In time, it will pass. But bring supplies along. Bring canned goods and a pup tent. Gather firewood. Sometimes it takes a while.

Overwriting continues to occur when a writer continues to be interested in seducing only himself, when he has become drunk on his own language, inebriated by his own ideas. In the end, overwriting is a date with only yourself, the ultimate lonely hearts endeavor. It's a lingerie ad posed so elaborately and with such confusing signals and focuses that no viewer will ever be able to, or will want to, fully take it in.

THE DANGER OF TAKING IT ALL OFF— A FORM OF OVERWRITING

Overwriting can occur at the level of the sentence but it can also occur in a story as a whole. To whit: I once had a student named Bill, a freshman who had an extraordinarily vivid imagination. Bill wrote mostly fantasy, a very complicated genre in which to work. More than anything, he was an inventor. He invented fascinating worlds in which characters had Roman or Greek names and wore togas and sandals but dashed around in spaceships between gleaming cities built in the clouds. The work had potential but, in reading it, I was always reminded by what Flannery O'Connor wrote in her brilliant collection of essays, *Mystery and Manners*. She said that the writer of surrealism has *more* of an obligation than the writer of realism to be absolutely, perfectly clear about what is unclear.

Bill's stories weren't clear at all. Quite the opposite. In the space of one paragraph he'd introduce about fourteen major characters and thirty different settings, all of them possibly compelling and interesting but none of them dealt with yet as if they were. Bill's stories were so highly detailed—we learned everything about his fantasy world, including what kinds of ammunition they shot out of their guns, what snacks his characters ate at midnight, what kind of material their togas were made of— that the sheer rush of information made the reader dizzy. Once, thinking that Bill was merely constrained by the form of the short story, I suggested that he consider writing a novel, but when he attempted to do so, the result was the same: In every paragraph he bombarded the reader with so much unrelated and unthematic information that none of it, in the end, made any sense. In fact, in one workshop, a classmate threw her hands in the air and, in the sort of display of aggravation I never welcome in my class, said, "Enough already. That's enough. You're killing me with info!" Secretly, I felt exactly the same way. When I read Bill's work, I felt suffocated, talked *at*, not written *to*. I felt ignored, in fact. It was as if Bill didn't really care if I were there or not.

Bill was at that stage of writing that Frank Conroy has called "self-absorption"—when the beginning writer (and sometimes the more advanced writer) doesn't give an owl's hoot if anyone understands him but merely performs brilliant but inaccessible arabesques for only his own delight. In fact, chronic overwriting usually afflicts the smartest and best-read of fiction writers; it's a phenomenon, in part, of having too much knowledge.

Bill's main problem was impulse control. Like a flasher, he wasn't able to restrain himself from revealing to everyone at any time everything he felt he had to show. He wasn't ready to *select* what information he *should* share, the way Hemingway said that writing a story is like making an iceberg—building the structure beneath and making sure that only a certain, deadly portion shows above the surface of the water, suggesting the foundation below. (For more on the iceberg theory, see the essay by Kim Edwards.)

And as far as Bill's flashing went, I didn't ever get much out of it. I'd rather that Bill had practiced for his audience a more complicated and tantalizing dance of the veils.

OPENING AND CLOSING THE CURTAIN—BEGINNING AND ENDING STORIES

At the risk of continuing to be risqué, let me remind you that the lingerie ad, like the short story, is neither the beginning of a striptease nor its end but more like what occurs in the middle. The subject of the lingerie ad was once dressed and will, presumably, not be dressed at all very soon, but right now, in the picture in front of us, we see him or her in a frozen moment in time—in the act of disrobing.

Fiction is also a frozen moment in time. Fiction generally catches characters in the middle of their lives, at the point at which their habitual way of being in the world is about to give way. The playwright Edward Albee once said that the beginning of a piece of fiction is like the opening of a curtain on a scene that was already in progress before the curtain parted, and the closing of the curtain doesn't mean that the action of the story really ceases, merely that we are now limited from watching it any longer.

The challenge facing the story writer—and the model in the lingerie ad—is to imply a great deal about what happened before ("I was once dressed") through exposition or implication ("There are my trousers on the floor") and to imply, as well, what may happen once the curtain closes again ("I will soon be undressed. See how my bra strap is slipping off my shoulder?") but—and this is important—to remember to keep the reader's attention totally and completely focused on what is happening *right now* in the present action of the story or in the moment of the photograph ("Look at me. Look at me. Look at me now!").

Beginnings

So, to start, how *do* you decide where to open a the curtain on a story? How can you know where to begin?

The answer is largely dependent upon the story you wish to tell and on the unified effect you wish to reach by the story's end. Sometimes the beginning is the polar opposite of the ending, as in John Cheever's "The Enormous Radio," in which Cheever wishes to reveal that Jim and Irene Wescott are not all that they seem. The logical place for him to open is with the comprehensive description of how the husband and wife *appear* to others and to make clear by the last paragraph that they are, in fact, liars and cheaters far from the middle-class ideal of respectability.

> Jim and Irene Wescott were the kind of people who seem to strike that satisfactory average of income, endeavor, and respectability that is reached by statistical reports in college alumni bulletins.

Other beginnings are meant to serve as the planted seeds of a story's ending, the original kernel. Shirley Jackson's "The Lottery," for example, which ends with a human sacrifice, begins in this way.

173

> The morning of June 27th was clear and sunny, with the fresh warmth of a full-summer day; the flowers were blossoming profusely and the grass was richly green.

Jackson's ending may seem, like Cheever's, to be a reversal of the original picturesque view, but it is also true that the annual human sacrifice (like sacrifices of old) at the end also seems to insure or reinforce the fertility and physical beauty that is so carefully described at the beginning. So, in short, it's important to ask yourself what sort of relationship you'd like your opening and ending to have. Should the opening be a situation you wish to reverse by the end, or should it be a seed you plant that grows into profusion by the final paragraph?

A related question is where *in time* to begin. Should you begin far back in a character's past and move forward, or should you begin in the present and make use of flashbacks only where necessary? The answer is to be found back in our discussion of description and overwriting. *If* the material with which you want to open the story is from the character's deep past, then there *has* to be an important relationship between what has happened in the past and what is about to happen. In other words, is the material with which you open the story an arrow pointing toward the unified effect? Is it important, for example, to let the reader know—as the first piece of information in a story—that your character didn't utter a word until the age of four, that by the age of ten his permanent teeth had not yet come in? Is there some information or scene or moment or event from the character's past that is so consequential to the action of the story that its only logical place is at the very beginning?

An example of such a story is Frank Conroy's "Midair," in which a traumatic event in the main character's childhood must be told in its entirety and at the very start of chronological events, in order for the ending to work. (More on that later.) Another example is the nonfiction book *The Autobiography of Malcolm X*, in which the first chapter traces carefully and chronologically the birth of the civil rights leader and the various traumas not only of his own past but of his parents. This chronology sheds light on the reasons for Malcolm X's political and religious conversions later in life. So generally speaking—and there are certainly exceptions to this rule—a story should start in the distant past *only* when the narrative to follow is a kind of "long-range conversion" story, the story of a character's rather massive change.

Most stories open, though, not at the very beginning of events but in the middle of the action, in what is commonly known as *in medias res*. Stories start this way because that is where the energy is, that is where the *oomph* or the push is to get the story going, to get it in motion on the page. Some examples: "I know what is being said about me and you can take my side or theirs, that's your own business. It's my word against Eunice's and Olivia-Ann's, and it should be plain enough to anyone with two good eyes which one of us has their wits about them. I just want the citizens of the U.S.A. to know the facts, that's all" (Truman Capote, "My Side of the Matter"). "During the whole of a dull, dark, and soundless day in the autumn of the year, when the clouds hung oppressively low in the heavens, I had been passing alone, on horseback, through a singularly dreary tract of country. . . ." (Poe, "The Fall of the House of Usher"). "When Blake stepped out of the elevator, he saw her" (Cheever, "The Five-Forty-Eight"). "Powerhouse is playing!" (Welty, "Powerhouse").

A tip: Because you may be a writer who does character sketches or background first when you're writing a story or a novel, you may find your most powerful beginning not in the material you wrote first but in the material you wrote once you really found the story's voice. Character sketches or background material can be used as exposition later in a second draft rather than up front, where it can tend to look and feel heavy and not pull the reader immediately into a story. Look for places in your drafts—as above—where the voice is especially strong and seductive, where it seems to be speaking with urgency and energy to a listener. Where it has power. That, in many cases, will be the best place for you to begin.

Endings—The "Just Say No" Theory of Narrative

The problems of seduction and revelation arise again when a writer comes to composing the ending of his story. "Great is the art of the beginning," said Thomas Fuller, "but greater the art of the ending." Endings present a complex challenge. Should the ending be the absolute and final-word summation of all that has gone before, or should it be clever, coy, full of riddles and trickery? How much revelation is too much? How little is too little?

I have always had a bad habit of wanting the endings of my own stories to wrap up breathlessly all the loose ends, and over the years, I've discovered this is a terrible idea. Maybe the big-bang summation works in movies—the male and female lead embracing amongst the smoking rubble of their lives, the sun miraculously setting behind them, some gorgeous vista coming into view, big pan shot, then the credits—but fiction ain't a Hollywood movie. In fact, one of the wisest things I ever heard anyone say about plot came not from a fiction writer but from a poet, the Pulitzer prize winner Philip Levine, who said that it is in fact useless for writers to try to compete with Hollywood plotting, because Hollywood—with its pyrotechnics and special effects and beautiful people, its ultimate flashiness and its promise of eternal satisfaction—will always, always win out over literary fiction.

The trick, Levine said, was to remember that literary writing is fundamentally different from film, and though some of the more interesting innovations in point of view in twentieth-century fiction have borrowed from film, I can't agree with Levine more that Hollywoodizing your work (in terms of plot) is incredibly dangerous. That is not to say that some books of fiction don't make fine films or that a writer shouldn't sometimes keep an eye to the fact that a novel or story could be optioned for film, but to write *in competition with film* will lead to the sort of hyperbole in fiction that will ultimately fail to satisfy a reader.

Unfortunately or not, writers in the late twentieth century are deeply influenced by film and television, and inevitably, this can show up in our fiction in the ways that our endings are constructed. If we're not careful, we can fall into the trap of creating big bangs and huge arguments, and killing off our characters, not to mention manufacturing cheap-trick endings (more on that in a moment).

From a technical standpoint, apocalypses are very hard to write. They involve a lot of choreography and casting (blood, frogs, vermin, enormous wars, floods, fires, armies of horsemen) à la Cecil B. DeMille, but ultimately, I'd argue, they're not as humanly interesting as what happens before or after them. It's important to remember that some of the best stories ever written aren't about big bangs. The big bangs occur *prior* to the stories or in their *aftermath*. In other words, some of the best fiction out there (particulary short stories) is not apocalyptic but *pre*apocalyptic or *post*apocalyptic.

The problems with apocalyptic writing (the story in which the car actually crashes, the house burns to the ground before your eyes, the relationship completely falls apart) are (1) that it is filmic rather than literary and (2) that it moves away from the primary purpose of fiction:

to let us see into the hidden life of things. Inside character, inside the souls of folks, their secret lives. Filmic endings are generally simplistic and momentarily satisfying, like the completed striptease. Literary endings are often ambiguous; they let the story rest not in perfection but in the startling beauty of irresolution.

One story that avoids the apocalypse beautifully is Raymond Carver's very short short "Little Things," which he originally published under the title "Popular Mechanics." In that story, which is only a page or so long, a nameless couple fights over their baby. The couple is breaking up, and in the course of the story, each makes claim to the baby, and each begins to pull on the baby for dear life. Each grabs an arm. Carver's story is obviously a brilliant contemporary rewrite of the famous biblical King Solomon tale, but he is smart enough to end "Little Things" before the baby is actually hurt. The baby is slipping out of the mother's grasp. The father is also losing his grip. Surely the baby *is* about to fall and be injured, or perhaps even killed, but Carver doesn't show that. Instead, his last line is biblically resonant: "In this manner, the issue was decided." In his story, Carver keeps his eye on "little things" and not on the inevitable big bang. We know what's going to happen anyway. We can project forward. Carver restrains himself from taking us there. That's why that story works.

In my fiction-writing classes, I read all of "Little Things" aloud, except the last line, then have the students write an ending line of their own. I collect all the ending lines, slip in Carver's original, then read them all aloud. Then, as a class, we vote on which is the best ending. Inevitably, the line that wins is *not* the blood-and-guts line ("and then they swept up the baby's bloody body parts"), if not Carver's ending than an even better one, but always something subtle and resonant that makes the rest of the story quake when you think back on it.

But how to avoid falling into the trap of writing the big summation, of going too far with a story? First, remember that the big ending is a cliché. It's been done. And done and done. And that's why it, like all other clichés, occurs to many writers first. In my own experience, the best endings to my stories have come not from my first thoughts but my second, third, or fourth thoughts. That's why, for example, in the first weeks of my writing classes, I never allow my students to kill any of their characters on stage. It's too easy, I tell them, when you're not sure where to end a piece, to cause the undoing of your characters and let the death stand as closure. "No killing in the first half of the semester," I tell them. If they're really good, I promise them, they can kill a character or two later in the semester, but not until they've practiced some subtlety.

This is not to say, however, that I encourage writers to write anticlimactic stories. Rather, I'm arguing for a more complex climax—a climax that is emotionally significant as well as significant in action, a climax in which external action does not overshadow the fundamental human story but complements it.

TRICK ENDINGS

A related problem is the temptation to use trick endings. I may get in trouble for saying this, but I think that many of the most entertaining stories taught in high schools (I know—I taught high school for six years) do those students who become fiction writers a lot of damage. Two such stories are "An Occurrence at Owl Creek Bridge" by Ambrose Bierce and "The Necklace" by Guy de Maupassant. Both feature trick endings (in "Occurrence," we believe that Peyton Farquar has escaped from a hanging, but by the end, we learn that the elaborate escape sequence has been only a fantasy; and in "The Necklace," a woman works her entire life to pay for a borrowed diamond necklace she has lost, only to discover, too late, that the necklace, in fact, had been a fake). Trick endings may be startling and sometimes interesting wake-up calls for the reader, but, like apocalyptic endings, they ultimately draw the reader's attention only to the writer's ability to manipulate data.

Writer and editor Gordon Lish once said that the last line of a story should be like the little piece of string that one pulls when trying to build a ship in a bottle. You pull the little string and the whole structure, already fit snugly inside the vessel of the glass, goes up, masts and all, entirely constructed. *Voilà*! Lish's point is that the ending shows the thematic and structural connections between all that has come before.

In most good literary fiction, you're likely to find such last lines. In Conroy's story "Midair," mentioned previously, the main character, Sean, has been haunted and frightened his entire life by the memory of an occasion in his childhood when his father dangled him from the window of an apartment building. In the final scene, Sean is stuck in an elevator with a young man who is as frightened of heights as Sean himself was when he was a boy. But instead of panicking—as he has his whole life—Sean reassures the young man until the doors finally open. When the story ends, Sean emerges from the elevator, amazed at his own sudden calm: "Here in the darkness, he can see the cracks in the sidewalk from more than forty years ago. He feels no fear—only a sense of astonishment." Another example is the famous, restrained epiphany at the end of James Joyce's "Araby": "Gazing up into the darkness I saw myself as a creature driven and derided by vanity; and my eyes burned with anguish and anger." And the moment at the end of John Updike's "A & P": "His face was dark gray and his back stiff, as if he'd just had an injection of iron, and my stomach kind of fell as I felt how hard the world was going to be to me hereafter."

In these endings, the writers exercise a degree of healthy repression and restraint. No big car chases, no conflagrations, but, rather, a moment of highly charged and enigmatic linguistic beauty that suggests cataclysm rather than practices it. Usually this is a moment before change is about to occur, before resolution is about to be enacted. At the end of another brilliant Carver piece, for example, a story called "Fat," a waitress stuck in a miserable and unsatisfying relationship with a cook in a diner says, finally, "My life is going to change. I can feel it." By the end of the story, Carver has resisted the impulse to change the waitress' life. Instead, he suggests the pathos in her desire to change and in her inability to do so. He resists taking the story to its natural conclusion, to the jump off the cliff, and ends it instead with a breathtaking look out over the horizon and the suggestion of the possibility of things to come. "It isn't fair, it isn't right," cries the human sacrifice, Mrs. Hutchinson, in Shirley Jackson's "The Lottery." "And then they were upon her," reads the last line, although it artfully and intentionally avoids depicting the blood and gore of what is just about to occur.

One last piece of advice: Look for your ending a few paragraphs or pages above where you think it should end. Often, surprisingly enough, embedded somewhere in the body of the manuscript is the perfect and subtle ending for which you've been searching.

The fundamental secret, then, to the effective ending is to practice the restraint one sees in those Victoria's Secret lingerie ads—enough coyness to tantalize, enough enigma to tease, but never, ever, too much naked abandon. Resist, I say, at all costs, the impulse to perform a fictional striptease for the reader. Practice, instead, a kind of sexy modesty, which is, perhaps, in the end, the most seductive narrative style of all.

EXERCISES

1. Write a scene that takes place after a terrible fire or after a horrible car wreck. Use only limited flashbacks of the cataclysmic event, and focus on how the characters are living in the aftermath. Develop this into a story that similarly avoids an apocalypse.

2. Write a scene that avoids any apocalyptic event but still has plot and ends with the subtle line "And then she closed the window." See if you can then expand this into a full-length story.

3. Take a story you think you have finished and find an alternate ending that is perhaps more subtle and enigmatic. Look two or three paragraphs above your original ending.

Julie Checkoway is the author of *Little Sister: Searching for the Shadow World of Chinese Women*, the Director of the Creative Writing Program at the University of Georgia, and the President of the Board of Directors of the Associated Writing Programs. Her work has appeared in *The Iowa Review*, *The North American Review*, *Poets and Writers*, and other literary magazines. She has been listed in *The Best American Short Stories* anthologies and has written documentaries for television.

V
Style and Voice

You're Really Something: Inflection, Tone, and Pitch

CHARLES BAXTER

Before Spielberg, and before *Jurassic Park*, and before *The Lost World* was found and filmed and sold to millions, and before there was tie-in merchandising of *Jurassic Park* lunch boxes and T-shirts and video games, and before special effects and multimillion dollar box-office receipts, before all this, there was, and still is, along Highway 12 in southern Michigan close to the Ohio border, a humble tourist trap, Dinosaur World. Dinosaur World is a little roadside attraction in Michigan's so-called Irish Hills. It shares the neighborhood with a Mystery Spot, where the laws of gravity are violated and where, the billboards claim, scientists are baffled; a fireworks outlet called The Boom Box; the Dwight D. Eisenhower presidential railroad car set up next to a chocolate fudge stand; Chilly Willy's miniature golf course; and other odds and ends of local tourist interest, including a water slide and a go-cart track. Most of the businesses could use a few coats of paint. The place has seen better times. Like Norman Bates' motel, the area has suffered neglect ever since, to use the local phrase, "they moved the highway," meaning the freeway, which is now fifteen miles north.

When our son was seven years old, my wife and I decided to make a day of it and take him to Dinosaur World. We figured he was ready for the terrors of prehistoric killer raptors and reptiles. He thought so, too.

Outside Dinosaur World, a fountain of sorts spouts water tinted dark blue, thanks to heavy doses of dye. You pay the entry fee and are loaded onto a train of what seem to be about eight rusting golf carts, Cushman Cars, linked together. There are no rails. These carts are on kid-sized rubber wheels. While you wait for the guide, you watch the *Triceratops*, the one dinosaur available for free viewing. He is constructed out of chicken wire and some sort of painted plaster. His mouth opens and shuts every five seconds, like an elf in a department store Christmas window display, and the sound of reptilian indigestion emerges from a hidden loudspeaker in the bushes. At last our guide arrived. He was a high school kid. This was his summer job. It was August, and you could tell from the expression on his face that he had just about had it with Dinosaur World. He was exasperated and bored but was playing it cool. He looked at us, his customers and fellow adventurers, with ferociously undisguised teenage indifference.

"Welcome to Dinosaur World," he said in a flat monotone. "We are about to go into a land that existed before time began." He had said the line so often that it had turned, almost Germanically, into one word.

"Weareabouttogointoalandthatexistedbeforetimebegan." He plunked himself into the driver's seat of the head golf cart and began speaking into a microphone. "Fasten your seat belts," he said, unnecessarily. His voice came out in that distinctly distorted tin-foil PA system bus-tour manner. "Lemmeknowifthereareanyquestions."

The hapless train, moving backward in time in several respects, followed the asphalt road around the displays of chicken wire and painted plaster. The multinational technology of Disney World was far, far, *far* away. Every so often, the guide would stop to explain the prehistoric wonder before our eyes, reciting his memorized script with incremental boredom. At the climax of the tour, he said, mumbling into a microphone close by an eight-foot-high killer dinosaur, "This is the fearsome *Tyrannosaurus rex*." He yawned, and the three of us, my wife and son and I, burst out laughing. The guide looked slightly taken aback. "What'ssa matter?" he asked. "You're not scared?"

I can't remember what my wife and son did, but I shrugged. I had loved his use of the word "fearsome," however, and I resolved to use it someday in a story.

Feeling slightly defeated, we rode back to the gift shop, where Dinosaur World salt-and-pepper shakers and postcards were for sale. There we bailed out. I could imagine how the tour guide would sound when he was behind closed doors, talking to a fellow guide. "So they're, like, *sitting* there, and I'm like, doing the tour? and man, these assholes, begin to, y'know, *laugh*? and, jeez, it just totally fucking freaks me out. I tell you, man, Dinosaur World is *the* job from hell. You know what I'm saying? This place is the fucking armpit of the universe. Man, I cannot *wait* until football practice starts." All the inflection missing from his tour would have found its way into his inventory of complaints.

INFLECTION SIGNALS BELIEF

Samuel Taylor Coleridge's "willing suspension of disbelief" is a curious category. What makes it curious is not the "suspension" but the "willing." None of us at Dinosaur World expected to believe what we were seeing. We expected to be invited to a little party where the host acted as if *he* believed, or at least was interested in what he was seeing and was inviting us into that *as if*. The tour guide had an actor's job, and he had to perform a role and play a part. His job was to encourage us, to invite us, to will our suspension of disbelief. That was his task, his summer vocation. His role was to pretend, within limits, that he was inside a moment of time and that we could join him there. He was supposed to hypnotize us a little. This is the technical problem of narratives concerning fantasy materials. He was supposed to pretend to be interested, and he had to be the first person to believe. He had to perform his belief. All his information about dinosaurs was secondary. He didn't perform magic, and we didn't really expect him to. There was no true magic to be had, and we knew that. No: *He was supposed to act as if there were magic.* As Orson Welles once said, there are no magicians, there are only actors who are playing magicians. A great magician is a great actor. And great actors perform hypnosis on a small scale. They make us fall asleep into another world.

You get involved in a story when, among other reasons, you get attached to a set of narrated events, or when the tone of the narrative has so many signs of emphasis that it rouses itself to life and disbelief is suspended. The story starts to believe in itself. You also acquire the sensation that somebody has believed this story. That's called conviction, and it may be pleasant or unpleasant.

Inflection, the tone in which something is said, particularly when applied to extreme events or circumstances, can be so important to writers of fiction. It signals belief. It is not emotion recollected in tranquillity; it is emotion reenacted before your eyes. It is the story singing or groaning itself awake. And belief creates a feeling of being inside a moment and re-creating it. Writers of fiction not only stage events but often must suggest how those events and statements are to be inflected, that is, how they are to be acted, how they should be pitched, how they should be voiced.

My dictionary defines *inflection* as an alteration in tone or pitch of the voice. This might seem to be a small matter, but an alteration in tone or pitch can be the difference between being inside a moment and literally being out of it, or between fighting words and a statement of love, using the identical phrase, such as "You're really something." Say it one way, it's a caress. Say it another, and it's a slap. Say it flatly, and you're thrown out of the story.

Inflection, then, is two things: an indication of life-in-the-moment and an indication of how a phrase is to be understood. How a phrase is to be understood, or is understood, is often more important than what is literally said. It is the life of the story and its subtext. It is the difference between a tone of uninvolvement with one's own story and a sense that the story is alive, that it is going on *right now*, in front of us. A shift in tone constitutes a shift in meaning, from sincerity to irony, or exasperation to incredulity, and it is a shift that has the strange capacity to bring a scene to life, to suspend disbelief.

CONVEYING EMPHASIS

But here, as writers, we have a large-scale problem. The trouble is that every page is silent, unlike an actor speaking in the theater. Every writer, sooner or later, runs up against the silence of the page, where tone and pitch are only implied. Sooner or later, the reader's imagination must take over. Indications of inflection encourage the reader to become active.

In real life, you start to inflect statements when you don't quite believe that the words alone will carry the emotional meanings of what you need to convey. "So they're *sitting* there, and I'm like, doing *the tour?*" Inflection is often a substitute for eloquence—it can convey feeling despite a screen of poor or approximate word choices, because the words that it *does* employ are being subjected to so many tonal shadings. Multiple inflection typically gives the sense of the speaker's great involvement in what she is saying. It puts stress on the words, it weights them, it *enthusiastifies* them.

And it is particularly necessary to those who don't have access to official language and official eloquence—to teenagers, and the dispossessed, to minority groups, and those who are baffled and broken, the hopeless and downcast, the obsessed and the fantasists, outsiders of

185

every kind and stripe, and those who are feeling two contradictory emotions at the same time. Inflection is the home of fugitive feelings and of layered or compounded emotion. It is the eloquent music of colloquial language. It is the homing device of effective liars, magicians, outcasts, and hypnotists.

Is it possible that some fiction may be underacted? This is not a criticism we usually hear. After all, stories can be told without being brought entirely to life, and one of the signs of this semilifelessness, this zombie condition, this Dinosaur World narration, is that the whole story seems uninflected, as if the writer had not quite believed his own story, or was an agnostic about it, or didn't want to get involved in it, or was bored, or wanted to keep a safe distance from it or from the audience. Sometimes writers want to tell a story without being committed to it. How odd that is!

I am on an Amtrak train in Oregon. Right behind me there is a little girl commenting on the trip, town by town, mile by mile. When we cross a river and the bridge under the tracks is not visible underneath us, the girl says to her mother, "I'm frightened! We'll all fall into the river. We will be *destiny*." I immediately write down the sentence and am simultaneously plunged into despair about how to convey on a page the way the girl sang out the word "destiny."

THE ART OF ACTING APPLIED TO
THE ART OF WRITING

Inflection in fiction writing can probably be understood to include the writer's use of indicators about how a line of dialogue was spoken or emphasized or repeated or how it might be heard or misheard or misunderstood. Inflection can be built into the dialogue itself. After you've written the line, you sometimes have to decide how you want it to sound or to be acted. This is the art of acting as applied to the art of writing. Inflection provides a context for a line so that we know how the words "You're really something" are to be understood. When a statement is operatively vague, like "You're really something," inflection or its context fill in what the vagueness leaves out. Sometimes we know how to hear it by noticing how other characters react to it. And good acting often gives us an unexpected inflection, a reversal of what's expected, that makes a scene with dialogue come to life.

Often beginning writers are warned against telling the reader by means of adverbs how a person said something. When I was a kid, these writerly dialogue-adverb tags were called Tom Swifties, in honor of those Tom Swift young-adult books for boys. A Tom Swifty is an adverb tag that stupidly points up what is obviously there already. " 'I won't do it!' said Tom, stubbornly."

But most of the time, we are saying what we are saying in a manner that isn't obvious. And we are accompanying these statements with a large inventory of pauses, facial gestures, body movements that can intensify the apparent meaning of what we're saying. A conversation can go on entirely by means of body language, with no words at all. In dialogue, we emphasize some words over others and thereby give a special meaning to the sentence. In act two, scene two of *Macbeth*, for example, the woman who plays Lady Macbeth has to decide how to deliver the simple line "Give me the daggers" (she means the bloody knives that Macbeth has used to murder Duncan). If she says, "*Give* me the daggers," she's exasperated; if she says, "Give *me* the daggers," she's mocking Macbeth's weakness and emphasizing her own strength and ability to get the job done; if she says, "Give me the *daggers*," she's triumphant and bloodthirsty.

FLIPPING THE TONE

The plot of Francis Ford Coppola's remarkable movie *The Conversation* hinges entirely on how a single line of dialogue spoken by two young people is inflected, and how the movie's protagonist, Harry Caul, hears it or mishears it. The line is "He'd *kill* us if he had the chance." If the inflection, the emphasis, is on "kill," then the two people who are overheard in the conversation are frightened for their own safety ("He'd *kill* us if he had the chance"). If the emphasis is on "us," then they are plotting a murder themselves ("He'd kill *us*, if he had the chance"). In the second reading, by the way, it helps to have a pause, a comma, after "us." What happens, in that reading of the line, is that inflection flips the statement's apparent meaning.

Notice this flip in tone. Actors sometimes describe a "flip" as an unexpected reading of a line that wakes you up. The actor switches, or flips, the emotion so that the tone you had expected isn't there. Instead, the line is delivered, altered, with a tonal shading you hadn't expected but which was buried in the line nevertheless and makes the line more immediate. Christopher Walken has described seeing Laurence Olivier playing Dr. Astrov in Chekhov's *Uncle Vanya* and flipping the tone in Astrov's first long speech. In this speech, near the beginning of act one, Dr. Astrov comes on the stage and describes losing a patient, a railroad worker, who has died on the operating table under chloroform. Most actors playing this role deliver this speech using a commonsense tone of slightly depressive anxiety and unhappiness, reflecting Dr. Astrov's despair over his inability to do much good for anyone.

But that was *not* the inflection Olivier used, according to Walken. Olivier laughed during this speech, but it was not a laugh of relaxed good humor. Far from it. Olivier's laughter was exhausted and giddy, arising from the sort of spiritual fatigue that is so intense it has gone a little crazy, laughter that's close to hysteria. Walken says that watching Olivier laugh like that on stage was mesmerizing.

RENDERING SHIFTS OF TONE WITH PAUSES

Sometimes a slight shift in tone or pitch can be marked simply by a pause. Think for a moment of the last scene of Eugene O'Neill's *Long Day's Journey Into Night*. The aging Mary Tyrone comes on stage, completely stoned on morphine, and in her last speech, in front of her husband and two grown sons, drifting in a free-floating reverie, she remembers how, years ago, she met her husband. This last statement consists of four sentences.

> That was the winter of senior year. Then in the spring something happened to me. Yes, I remember. I fell in love with James Tyrone and was so happy for a time.

Now, on almost every occasion when I have seen this play, the actor playing Mary Tyrone is careful to insert a little pause between "happy" and "for." That little pause is an expressive air pocket of dead silence, during which reality, for that one microsecond, floods back into the mind of a woman lost in a fog of drugs and nostalgia.

> Yes, I remember. I fell in love with James Tyrone and was so happy [split-second pause] for a time.

She doesn't say that she was so happy, period. She turns it around at the last split-second. She was so happy *for a time*. Those three words signal the difference between the working methods of kitsch and a masterpiece.

COMBATING THE ZOMBIE EFFECT

Now let's look at the way inflection can be signaled in a work of literary fiction. In Katherine Anne Porter's "The Leaning Tower," set in Berlin in 1931, Charles, an American, has been staying at a hotel and then finds an apartment house where he would rather reside. His ability to speak German isn't good, so, like most foreigners, he has to study facial expressions and body language to make sure he has understood what he thinks he has heard.

In signing a lease for the apartment, Charles accidentally knocks over a little plaster Leaning Tower of Pisa in the landlady's parlor. The landlady tells him, "It cannot be replaced," and then the author adds that the line has been said with "severe, stricken dignity." Note the compounded emotion. This is a sign that Charles is paying attention to her intonation, but it is also a small indication of how she is reinforcing her distress, dramatizing it, theatricalizing it, with visual cues. We can see her physically stiffening. A few moments later, the landlady adds, "It is not your fault, but mine. I should not have left it here for—" She doesn't finish the sentence. The text tells us her next actions.

> She stopped short, and walked away carrying the paper in her two cupped hands. For barbarians, for outlandish crude persons who have no respect for precious things, her face and voice said all too clearly.

What Porter signals here is that conversations are *not* over when people stop speaking. Conversations continue for several moments in the silence that follows, often by means of facial expressions and body language. The largest, most emphatic point in the sentence may arrive not with the last word but with a refusal to say a word, allowing the silence to be suspended in the air. After all, which is worse or more effective in a quarrel? To say, "You're such a creep and a liar," or, "You're such a—"? You can argue with option A, but you can't argue with option B.

Anyway, in the following scene, Charles goes back to his Berlin hotel to move his belongings and to check out. Here he must deal with the "sallow wornout-looking hotel proprietress" and her "middle-aged, podgy partner." Charles had previously agreed to stay in the hotel for a month, but now, after eight days, he is leaving. What follows is a masterful scene of telegraphed malevolence and dramatized malice, indicated by both words and physical indicators.

" 'Our charges here are most reasonable,' the proprietess says, her dry mouth working over her long teeth." Why does Porter insert this detail of the mouth and the teeth? Partly, perhaps, to slow down the scene. To convey the woman's anxiety and suppressed rage. But also to put those "long teeth" into our mind's eye so that we don't take her as a purely comic figure.

"You will find you cannot change your mind for nothing," she continues, in what we are told is a "severe, lecturing tone." We would probably figure out this tone for ourselves, but the statement of it intensifies the feeling and adds a slight aura of danger, a sense of the woman's horror of flexibility and her pedantic vehemence. This sense is increased when the narrator illustrates the woman's facial change.

> She glanced up and over his shoulder, and Charles saw her face change again to a hard boldness, she raised her voice sharply and said with insolence, "You will pay your bill as I present it or I shall call the police."

Enter the proprietress' podgy partner, who, hands in pockets, smiles "with a peculiarly malignant smile on his wide lipless mouth." The author here is not only writing the words of the scene, she is directing them for us, showing us how they are to be played. Charles pays the proprietress all the money she has demanded, to the last pfennig, and then, the podgy man, whose "pale little eyes behind their puffy lids were piggy with malice," asks to see Charles' identification papers. I should stop here again and point out that now, in the late twentieth century, many writers are reluctant to characterize a character so judgmentally and so maliciously as Porter does the pudgy partner. Contemporary writers don't like to use phrases like "piggy with malice," maybe because we've grown sentimental about pigs and because judging characters that quickly is regarded as bad taste and mean-spirited. But it's an extreme situation, and it's important to note that the author's details are not purely malicious but are instead both malicious and dispassionately observed. This makes them a considerable pleasure to read.

Insisting on seeing the papers, the podgy man is then observed with a series of what we might now call close-up details. "He seemed struggling with some hidden excitement. His neck swelled and flushed, he closed his mouth until it was a mere slit across his face, and rocked slightly on his toes." After Charles has shown him the papers, the man says, " 'You may go now,' with the insulting condescension of a petty official dismissing a subordinate." In the next sentence, we learn that "they continued to look at him in a hateful silence, with their faces almost comically distorted in an effort to convey the full depths of their malice." Notice how, again, a silence is being drawn out, and how this silence is not peaceful, but hateful. It is a hateful silence. Notate your silences if you can. Fully expressive silences are by no means easy to create in fictional narrative. Finally, after Charles has left the hotel under their "fixed stare," he hears, "as the door closed behind him," the two of them laughing "together like a pair of hyenas, with deliberate loudness, to make certain he should hear them."

The cruelty here, and the malice, is very great indeed, and it's marked by all its small details of gesture, speech, and gratuitous meanness. But cruelty, as Henry James and Katherine Anne Porter knew, is increased and intensified by shades of detail. Cruelty often lives off small signs and hints, closed rather than open doors. Cruelty is not increased by brutality but is *diminished* by it. Cruelty and brutality are two different things. One is gestural and the other one isn't. Brutality makes everything easy—easy to respond to, easy to judge. Subtle cruelty, by contrast, as we all know, is a web meant to catch you in a couple of different directions and to keep you hanging as you are punished by small but incremental wounds. Brutality is rather common, and true cruelty is rather uncommon. You might say that Porter's scene demonstrates the effective malice of indirection, of cruelty slowly turning *into* brutality. She shows you, as clearly as she can, exactly how these people are signaling what they feel. The scene is intensely alive on all counts. Despite its great literary qualities, it feels immediate. No Dinosaur World zombie effect here.

COMPLEX INFLECTION

Let's move to another example, Eudora Welty's "A Visit of Charity." The ground situation is quite straightforward: Marian, a junior high Camp Fire girl, has been assigned to take a flower to a retirement home for old ladies and to sit there and chat for a while. This visit of charity is part of the procedure for Marian's earning of a merit badge. Simple enough.

I should stop here and say that this ground situation is not particularly promising, and in our own time, old ladies and old men have become objects of commonplace writerly pathos. There is no place like a retirement home or a hospital to turn up the needle on the pathos meter. Running into a scene in an old-folks' home is like meeting a bully at the end of an alley. It preprograms your responses. And I should know; I've used such places myself for those purposes. But it's hard to get real feelings, as opposed to preprogrammed ones, out of those settings now. If you locate a scene in a retirement home or a hospital without flipping it or defamiliarizing it in some way, every reader knows that her assignment is to feel sad and to weep dutifully. But when you know your assignment, you tend to resist it.

In this story Welty upsets the expected tone so that pathos is a minor element. Instead, there is a kind of dry wit at work, not pitiless but in the service of genuine but very dark compassion and understanding, and this dry comedy moves the proceedings in the direction of what I will call, for the sake of brevity, the abyss. Suddenly, the mystery of existence opens up in front of Marian and the reader. Welty does all this by carefully inflecting every moment of the scene. After a few pages, Marian's old ladies stop being pitiful creatures, old Southern ladies down on their luck, and seem more like Samuel Beckett's tramps, Vladimir and Estragon, in *Waiting for Godot*, struggling with time itself.

The reader is given, moment by moment, careful and close direction and detailing of the scene. Notice that this *is* a scene and is *not* summarized. Marian has walked into the room with her gift of the potted plant. There are two old ladies in the room, one lying down and one standing up. The one who is standing up has a "terrible square smile stamped on her bony face." Think of that: a *terrible* square smile. We're not told what makes it terrible. Nor are we told exactly how to visualize it. It seems contradictory. Her hand, "quick as a bird claw," grabs at Marian's cap. The room is dark and dank, and Marian starts to think of the old ladies as robbers and the room as the robbers' cave.

" 'Did you come to be our little girl for a while?' the first robber asked." The plant is snatched out of Marian's hand. " 'Flowers!' screamed the old woman. She stood holding the pot in an undecided way. 'Pretty flowers,' she added.

"Then the old woman in bed cleared her throat and spoke. 'They are not pretty,' she said, still without looking around, but very distinctly." After the first old woman repeats that the flowers are pretty, the old woman who is lying down says in return, batting the ball back, that the flowers are "stinkweed." So much for nice old ladies. Somewhat disarmingly, the old woman in bed is described as having a bunchy white forehead and red eyes like a sheep. When she asks Marian, "Who are you?" the line is interrupted by dashes to indicate slowness of speech, and the author tells us that the words rise like fog in her throat and that the words are "bleated." In the direction of a line of dialogue, you can't get more specific than this.

We learn that the woman in bed is named Addie. Addie and her unnamed old companion then commence to have an argument about a previous visitor and whether they had enjoyed that visit. Triangulated by the two ladies, Marian, the Camp Fire girl, begins, very mildly, to go off into the hallucinations of ordinary life created by the scene before her. At this point, Addie and the other old lady have a surrealistic discussion about who is sick and who is not and who did what as a child.

The standing woman speaks in an "intimate, menacing" voice, another unusual combination. This is interrupted by Addie's first long speech. It is directed, interestingly, toward both her roommate and, I think, obliquely to Marian. The author gets out of the way here and lets the speech speak for itself. In it, the sick woman berates the roommate, telling her she is nothing, that her life is empty, that she talks all the time.

At the end of this speech, the author notes that Addie turns her eyes toward Marian, eyes that have gone bright. "This old woman," the author notes, "was looking at her with despair and calculation in her face." We then get an image of her false teeth and tan gums. " 'Come here, I want to tell you something,' she whispered. 'Come here.' " Marian is frightened, we're told, and her heart nearly stops beating for a moment. Then Addie's companion says, " 'Now, now, Addie. That's not polite.' "

This scene, I would argue, is packed, completely layered, with seemingly contradictory emotions: Marian's fascination and terror, Addie's despair and calculation, her companion's fake sentimentality and cynicism—the scene is a mixture of despairing comedy, pathos, terror, and metaphysical giddiness. These elements are built into Addie's speech through the repetition of words like "empty," "talk," and "stranger," and the carefully deployed dashes and pauses. And they are then cemented by the brilliant inflection-tag following the speech, noting that Addie is now turning toward Marian with despair *and* calculation on her face. Please note this. Addie is not feeling one thing. She is feeling several emotions at once. One of them makes her pitiable; the other makes her dangerous. We then learn that today happens to be Addie's birthday.

As if this weren't enough, when Marian leaves, the nameless woman (the other half of this terrible octogenarian vaudeville team), who has been playing the straight woman to Addie's riffs of calculation and despair, goes into a riff of her own. We learn from the inflection ("in an affected high-pitched whine") that this woman may have fallen into a moment of senile dementia. Or, more likely, she may be playing a role for her own amusement to scare and disconcert Marian, maybe even to get some money out of her. You simply can't tell. And that's the way the author seems to want it—your uncertainty parallels the uncertainty that Marian must feel. You can see clearly and distinctly what you see, but *you simply can't be sure of what you're looking at.*

This transcendentally wonderful scene worries me. It worries me because I think it's true, moving, beautiful, and funny. And yet it worries me because I think that if it were brought into a writing workshop, someone or other might accuse it of being "unfair" to old women or "mean-spirited," or, even worse, "ageist." Why? Because it doesn't reinforce an orthodoxy: It doesn't reinforce what we are *supposed* to feel about the old, namely, that we are expected to pity them and to love or admire them more than we usually do. Nor does Welty's scene mock them, which would also be easy to swallow. In some sense, the scene has no *social* purpose at all. It has another purpose altogether in mind. It presents these women, as Beckett presents his tramps, with all the complexity of art, of realism flying off into the metaphysical and then flying back, flipping and inflecting the scene until it's so layered that you cannot describe the scene's feeling-tone in one word. You can't do that. It's impossible. What's going on with the two old ladies, triangulated by Marian, is too complicated for that.

WHEN UNINFLECTEDNESS WORKS
AND WHEN IT DOESN'T

There is much to be said for the uses to which the opposite—an uninflected voice—may be put. There may well be certain justifications for what might be called zombie voicings in literature, a deliberate tonal blank-out. Certainly it's notable in Kathryn Harrison's memoir, *The*

Kiss, and in virtually all the work of the novelists Craig Nova and Rudy Wurlitzer. And this tone of blank, uninflected death-in-life is put to interesting use in Tim O'Brien's novel *In the Lake of the Woods*, though just in the main body of that text, not in the footnotes. There is a certain Dinosaur World–narration effect all the way through O'Brien's novel, and I think, oddly enough, that it often works, given the subject of that book, which happens to be post-traumatic stress disorder. There is something about uninflectedness that suits trauma very well.

What can be bothersome about uninflectedness from the last two decades generally, however, is that it can seem like a decadent form of hipsterism, a retro form of cool, of being removed, which can harden into a posture. Against middle-class fake sincerity, fake patriotism, and fake fervor of every sort, uninflectedness and ironic withdrawal, at least since the Second World War, has been deployed massively and effectively in every form of postmodern art. It is, however, now completely mainstream.

The trouble with uninflectedness is that, because it is an attitude, it has a tendency to be inflexible. And this, it strikes me, is what has happened to some otherwise interesting contemporary writers who shall go nameless here, whose work sometimes seems to be trapped in the effort to turn attitude into subject matter (a fault, I might add, of a certain percentage of Ernest Hemingway's work).

CAUSING SLEEPLESS NIGHTS

The guide at Dinosaur World was at pains to demonstrate that he was above what he was saying, detached from it, *better* than it. And so he was. But as triumphs go, this is a very minor one, and in its way is as much a miscalculation as overacting would be.

In his recent memoir, *Crabcakes*, James Alan McPherson describes a moment during which he listens to two African-Americans flirting with each other. Then he remarks on what he heard.

> The kindly flirtation between the two of them reminds me of something familiar that I have almost forgotten. It seems to be something shadowy, about language being secondary to the way it is used. The forgotten thing is about the nuances of sounds that only employ words as ballast for the flight of

pitch and intonation. It is the pitch, and the intonation, that carries *meaning*. I had forgotten this.

Vladimir Nabokov once said that the price of being a writer was sleepless nights. But, Nabokov added slyly, if the writer doesn't have sleepless nights, how can he hope to cause sleepless nights in anyone else? If the writer doesn't indicate interest in the story through inflection, how can he expect the reader to be interested and willingly suspend disbelief? To close the book or finish the poem and to say, "You're really *some*thing"?

EXERCISES

1. Write two scenes in which the same sentence is inflected differently so that it has one meaning in the first scene and the opposite meaning in the second scene.

2. Write a scene with dialogue in which emphasis and repetition substitute for eloquence.

3. Write a scene in which crucial moments of dialogue are "flipped," that is, given an inflection that seems to go against the way they would customarily be said or spoken.

Charles Baxter is the author of six books of fiction, most recently *Believers*. He is also the author of a book of essays on fiction, *Burning Down the House*. He teaches at the University of Michigan and lives in Ann Arbor.

A Mystified Notion: Some Notes on Voice

SYLVIA WATANABE

The object of this chapter is to demystify the aspect of fiction we call voice. Here are some mystifications:

- that voice is something to be found
- that it is located somewhere off the page
- that some authors or stories have more of it
- that it can be borrowed and not returned
- that it never changes
- that it has to do with sincerity
- that it is about expression
- that the author can be found in it

As these imply, there is an inside and an outside to the notion: There is the voice of the individual piece of fiction, and there is what we call an author's voice. In practice, of course, things do not sort out this neatly, but much of the confusion about voice seems to involve the way we think of the author's relation to it. The rather old-fashioned notion of finding one's voice is really about "arriving" at an individual style, which is like putting the cart before the horse if you haven't written many stories.

THE AUTHOR'S VOICE

When I first began writing, I had a teacher, an admirer of D.H. Lawrence, who made a regular practice of instructing his students to go find their voices. When I asked, "What is voice? Where do I look for it?" he said, "Write real," then sent me off to read Lawrence.

For anyone, especially a beginning writer who is looking for a quick fix and who doesn't have the experience or patience to hone a style, this is the seeming contradiction: You can "write real," or you can borrow someone else's voice. You can express yourself, or you can find suitable objects of imitation. We'll return to the first of these approaches in a moment, but for now, let's look more closely at the second.

Imitation

In working with undergraduates, I rely on model texts to talk about the variety of contemporary fiction and to present different approaches to genre and form. After we've discussed a number of stories that deal with shifting voices and points of view, for example, I might ask my students to write a piece in which they come up with their own solutions to similar structural issues. I never assign the direct imitation of other writers' voices, which, in the long run, seems to lose more ground than it gains. As it is, students readily turn to this sort of imitation on their own, and any number of them show up at my workshops having recently participated in the Surrealist Automatic Writing Project and planning to continue more of the same, or trying to write everything in stream of consciousness, or having resolved to spend their entire writing lives sounding like Sylvia Plath or Jack Kerouac. Their imaginations have been closed to the larger possibilities of fiction, and sometimes it takes more than a workshop or two for them to open up again.

Occasionally a student like this isn't stuck on a single writer but moves from one to another, trying on voice after voice. My first term teaching, I worked on an independent project with a young man who showed up at my office every Friday with an incomplete draft in the manner of whatever author he happened to be reading that week in his Theory class, or in his Contemporary Fiction class, or in his Literature of the West class. Sometimes he came up with amalgams: Woody Allen Beckett. Lorrie Moore L'Amour.

One day he arrived with the beginning of a story about a nondescript character who didn't have a job, or a personality, or thoughts, who was always being mistaken for somebody else, and who bought all her clothes at secondhand stores. "I want her to be Everywoman," Lem said, "but I'm having trouble with the voice."

Where were we to begin?

Finally, I asked him how he imagined such a voice might possibly sound. We talked about particularity. I asked about metaphors: all those secondhand clothes. A light began to dawn. "That's what this is, isn't it?" he said, indicating his manuscript. Then he said he was going to do something he had never done before: He was going to write from concrete experience—about his boyhood in New York. A week later, he was back with a draft in the voice of J.D. Salinger Vonnegut.

I tell my students, if they must do it, imitation should exceed itself to be interesting. But when motivated merely by admiration, imitation stifles the kind of questioning by which we grow as writers, by which our craft proceeds. There is all the difference between the declarative, "I want to write like . . . ," and the question, "How did the author do this?" which leads to the next question, "How can I use it?" and the next. . . .

Expressive Writing

In contrast to the imitative approach, which attempts to reproduce the surface features of style, expressive writing focuses inward—on an author's deepest thoughts and emotions.

Here is some expressive writing:

> Spring is the season of birth and winter is the season of death. It was ironic that he decided to leave her in the spring. How long had it been? Months, years, weeks, minutes? She felt numb—everything around her felt surreal. Her life was filled with a vast emptiness. Just sitting and remembering the good times and the bad times, but mostly the good times, her eyes filled with tears. A single drop of moisture rolled down her cheek. The memories inside her shattering like shards of glass . . .

This is a collage of typical elements that appear in the drafts that cross my desk. Generalized, sincere emotion leaks out of every sentence, while concrete details about the characters' lives, relationships, and motivation are randomly given or altogether neglected. Being detached from the sense organs, this voice substitutes evaluative language for detail, and clichéd imagery for the evocation of feeling. This is a voice that everywhere expresses the intrusiveness of the author,

199

judging the characters and their situations, telling a reader how to think and feel.

One of the curious aspects of expressive prose, supposedly the most personal kind of writing, is its lack of personality. In its choice of subjects and use of language, it mechanically replicates—even down to specific images and turns of phrase—a recognizable genre with a recognizable voice. In doing this, the expressive approach appears to share more in common with imitation than would, at first, appear.

THE HABIT OF ART

There is, then, no shortcut to "finding" a voice; there is only the writing of fiction. A writer's style is a cumulative phenomenon that accrues over a body of work; it is the result of what Flannery O'Connor describes as "the habit of art." "Art is the habit of the artist," she says, "and habits have to be rooted deep in the whole personality. They have to be cultivated . . . over a long period of time. . . ." She is not only talking about a habit of work but the training of a sensibility—a writerly sensibility with writerly perceptions and a writerly feeling for language and form. It is this sensibility, and not, as the expressive approach mistakenly assumes, the author's "real" self, that is expressed through style. As a writer's sensibility changes over time, so, necessarily, does his or her voice.

But the story comes first.

THE STORY'S VOICE

Let's turn now to a specific instance, with an excerpt from "The River" by Flannery O'Connor. Pay particular attention to its *sound*. You might even try reading it aloud, and as you do, listen to the way the words and sounds go together. Note the predominance of one- and two-syllable words, the use of consonance and assonance, the rhythm of the sentences, the pauses created by the punctuation.

> The child stood glum and limp in the middle of the dark living room while his father pulled him into a plaid coat. His right arm was hung in the sleeve but the father buttoned the coat anyway and pushed him forward toward a pale spotted hand that stuck through the half-open door. "He ain't fixed right," a loud voice said from the hall. "Well then for Christ's sake fix him," the

father muttered. "It's six o'clock in the morning." He was in his bathrobe and barefooted. When he got the child to the door and tried to shut it, he found her looming in it, a speckled skeleton in a long pea-green coat and felt helmet.

This excerpt, which is in the realist mode and told from an omniscient point of view, consists of a dramatized scene in which we hear three distinct voices: that of the narrator, which begins and closes the excerpt, and those of the first and second speakers in the exchange of dialogue at midpoint. The register of the language shifts from somewhat informal, but clearly written sounding, usage in the exposition to usage that is more vernacular and spoken sounding in the dialogue. The two speakers are distinguished from one another by the marked regional and working-class idiom of the "loud voice" and the gendered, more genteel manner of the father. The register has been adjusted, or calibrated, so that the shift between exposition and dialogue is smoothly and believably accomplished. The immediacy of the dialogue emphasizes the ironic distance of the narrative point of view, while the narration, in turn, heightens the vividness of the dialogue. The interplay between the three voices works almost like the counterpoint in music, giving the excerpt a complex texture of sound.

What a difference it would have made if, say, O'Connor had attached the -ly suffix to "glum" and "limp": The child stood glumly and limply. The register would immediately move to a higher level of formality, with a corresponding change in the sonics, giving the opening an unpleasing, lisping effect. Or what if she had described the child as "morose" and "apathetic," or substituted "tessellated" for "plaid"? Again, we can see how these small shifts in diction would throw off the voice, requiring corresponding adjustments in syntax and, even, point of view.

The deceptive simplicity of the diction plays against the complexities of the underlying sentence structure. The first sentence begins in the active voice, with the child as the subject, but turns at the end, with the subordinate clause describing the father pulling the child into the coat. The next sentence perfectly accomplishes what writing teachers often tell students to avoid: It not only begins in a passive, it ends in one, too! The structure of the grammatical form here is an analogy for its meaning. The passive voice reflects the child's apathetic and disassociated state—his being reduced to an object, a mere body part, an arm hanging in a sleeve. A similar process is going on with the character who is identified in the dialogue simply as "a loud voice": We see nothing more of her at first than "a pale spotted hand that stuck through the half-open door."

Up to this point, everything has been narrated indirectly—through the shaping of the language and the careful construction and placement of the detail. With the exception of the two adjectives, "glum" and "limp," no emotion or judgment is expressed in the opening exposition; the cheerlessness and misery of the child's life are left for us to infer. But when we shift into dialogue, note how the texture of the voice immediately changes, becoming much more emphatic and direct: "He ain't fixed right." Here, the voice would have been affected very differently if the judgment had been written into the narration instead of given to a character.

ELEMENTS OF A STORY'S VOICE

From our discussion of O'Connor, we can begin to identify the specific aspects of a story's voice. These include choice of genre, articulation of point of view, treatment of exposition and dialogue, selection of detail, use of language (including diction, syntax, and the calibration of register), and the handling of sonics (the sound and rhythm of the prose). Voice, it would seem, abides everywhere in a story.

This large and abstract function is, in part, what makes voice more difficult to get a handle on than the seemingly concrete and isolable aspects of character, setting, and plot. However, as every writer knows, these neat divisions do not, in practice, work out so neatly; to take an obvious example, plot is often motivated by character, and character, in turn, revealed through plot. This interdependence is especially true of voice, which is present even in a story's silences. Not only is voice dependent on the other elements of a narrative, but all the aspects of voice are expressed through one another. Let's focus now on the relationship between voice and genre, point of view, and the use of detail.

Voice and Genre

Imagine, side by side, any Harlequin romance and any novel by Henry James. Or take another look at "Goldilocks" and "The Elf King" in a collection of fairy tales, then read the versions by Coover and Carter. The requirements of genre—whether we are writing within or against them—are, necessarily, an aspect of voice; different genres emphasize different aspects of voice. Conversely, a writer's choice regarding voice can completely transform a genre. The Coover and Carter are examples of this. You might also consider how the fragmentation of voice works in Coover's story "The Babysitter," which begins with a similar premise as "The River" but ends by destabilizing all the assumptions of the realist mode. To state the obvious: The telling of a story cannot be separated from the kind of story being told.

Voice and Point of View

Classical poetics distinguishes between three kinds of voices: the ego-poetic, the narrative, and the dramatic, each with a corresponding point of view and appropriate range of subjects. The first would be somewhat analogous to first-person or internal narration; the second, to omniscient or external narration; and the third, to limited omniscient or external narration with a limited filter—though none of these categories has an exact correspondence with any in our current lexicon of craft. The main point here, however, is that voice and point of view have been closely associated from very early on. In articulating point of view, voice contributes, as well, to the development of character. Perhaps the clearest way of talking about this relationship would be to look at a couple of examples. Here, then, are two different openings—the first to *Mrs. Bridge* by Evan Connell and the second to "Where Are You Going, Where Have You Been?" by Joyce Carol Oates.

> Her first name was India—she was never able to get used to it. It seemed to her that her parents must have been thinking of someone else when they named her. Or were they hoping for another sort of daughter? As a child she was often on the point of inquiring, but time passed, and she never did.

> Her name was Connie. She was fifteen and she had a quick nervous giggling habit of craning her neck to glance into mirrors, or checking other people's faces to make sure her own was all right. Her mother, who noticed everything and knew everything and who hadn't much reason any longer to look at

her own face, always scolded Connie about it. "Stop gawking at yourself, who are you? You think you're so pretty?" she would say. . . .

Again, both these examples are in third person, in the realist mode. The example from Connell, however, is told through a limited narrative filter, from the point of view of India Bridge, while the Oates example is a complex amalgam of the limited and omniscient points of view. These include (1) the voice of the external narrator (which describes Connie as having a "quick nervous giggling habit"); (2) Connie's voice (in the description of the mother), as reported by the narrator; and (3) the voice of Connie's mother (in dialogue), filtered through Connie's point of view, as reported by the narrator. The narrative irony in the excerpt from Connell is much more subdued, and the effect of the voice is less layered and more monophonic.

There are other contrasts in the treatment of point of view that affect voice and characterization. India Bridge comes across as middle-aged, somewhat upper-crust, and of a seemingly reticent temper. All this is not only conveyed to us through what she is reportedly thinking, but also through the roundaboutness of the phraseology, the use of the interrogative ("Or were they hoping for another sort of daughter?"), and the genteel and somewhat formal register. The diction of the Oates, by contrast, is much less tony—more middle and working class—and is carefully shaped to convey a sense of both the fifteen-year-old female protagonist and her mother.

Voice and the Use of Detail

As we have seen, the voice of a piece of fiction varies greatly according to the author's handling of detail. Detail can be sparse and understated or meticulously graphic. It can be presented as a seamless surface, as realist fiction attempts to do, or it can be presented as a fragmented, discontinuous surface, as we see in postmodernist fiction.

The attention to spoken idiom has perhaps more obvious impact on the voice of a story than any other kind of detail. First-person narratives, written in persona, and often with an emphasis on idiom, are referred to as voice pieces. It is a mistake, however, to assume that so-called voice pieces have more voice (as seems implied by the term) than other kinds of stories. Every story has a voice—which is not the same as saying that the voice of every story works equally well. And all voices, regardless of whether they are in the dialect of a region, class, working place, or in so-called Standard English, are in some form of idiom. The term merely refers to the manner of using language specific to a place or community.

When I was studying at the State University of New York at Binghamton, Larry Woiwode taught me one of the most important lessons I have ever learned about the use of idiom. I am from Hawaii, where the vernacular is linguistically classified as a kind of "Creole," composed of grammatical and lexical elements from a variety of languages—primarily Hawaiian, Chinese, Portuguese, and, to a lesser extent, other groups who have settled the Islands. While working with Larry, I was struggling with when and how to use the regional idiom to write about regional subjects. At the time, I wasn't interested in writing voice pieces. Nor was I altogether taken with the solution commonly found in third-person narratives—of writing exposition in Standard English and dialogue in the vernacular (usually indicated by some form of altered spelling; in Hawaiian pidgin this would be "bra" for brother, "ass" for ask, and so on). Aside from a dissatisfaction with the existing orthography, I had difficulty calibrating the register difference between the standard and regional idioms to achieve a continuous, whole-cloth effect, which seemed to fit the particular stories I was writing at the time. And, finally, I found that splitting the exposition and dialogue into standard and Hawaiian pidgin seemed to privilege the former. Larry directed me to *Annie John* by Jamaica Kincaid. That is a book, he said, that so fully evokes the story world of its setting that it almost has to be written in regional idiom. However, in going through it, sentence by sentence, one finds that the book accomplishes this effect through a minimal use of dialect; the unique quality of the voice comes, instead, from the careful diction and the use of vivid and concrete sensory detail.

VOICE STILL MYSTIFIED

In the preceding notes, we have breezed, all too quickly, through a large and ambiguous topic. I have raised a number of issues that could not, in the space available, have been discussed as fully as they should. I leave that to you. Last words? Just these: Don't go looking for your voice; write a story.

EXERCISES

1. Write the opening to a story in first person, then in second (or in any two points of view). What changes? If you're inspired, finish the story.

2. Write the description of an *interesting* event you have witnessed. Now, write a fictionalized scene. What changes? If you like, incorporate the scene into a story.

3. Reread a story you particularly enjoy, paying special attention to the voice. What elements are at work? How is the author using detail, language, and stories to create this voice?

Sylvia Watanabe lives in Ohio and Hawaii. Her work has appeared in the O. Henry and Pushcart Prize anthologies and has been recognized by a National Endowment for the Arts Fellowship and an Ohio Arts Council grant. *Talking to the Dead*, her first story collection, was a finalist for the 1992 PEN/Faulkner Award. She teaches in the Creative Writing Program at Oberlin College.

Minimalism and Maximalism: A Question of Style

KAREN SALYER McELMURRAY

By 1970, I'm halfway through my freshman year of high school. I've made strong headway through most of the major rites of passage in a medium-sized high school in central Kentucky—choice of subculture (pseudo hippie, never a class president or a hood), number of late-night back-road drives, number of make-out sessions, and, most important of all, preference for creative writing classes, which give me free reign to express just what I have no satisfaction about, even if I'm not yet sure.

While I am, by 1970, worried about skin care, counterculture paraphernalia, and the revolution in male and female communication, I have become very comfortable with my personal style. For six weeks straight, I wear the same pair of jeans, ones with slits up the leg and triangles of fake leather; I wear them to school, for swimming in the Kentucky river, and to a wild night of revelry I describe to my family as an all-girl slumber party.

At the beginning of fall semester, Mrs. Taylor, my creative writing teacher, reads parts of my story about my grandfather's at-home eastern Kentucky funeral aloud to class. She praises my descriptions, my use of dialogue, the nature of my prose. Mrs. Taylor tells us that creativity is serious business, but not, in fact, a business at all. It is an expression, she says, of mystery. Of what Ralph Waldo Emerson called the Oversoul. I draw doves and ankhs, Egyptian symbols of eternal life, in the margins of my journal.

Mrs. Taylor, who knits tiny shoes while we do in-class exercises, is also visibly pregnant. She lets us know about this; she tells us about her plans for baby, husband, nursery painted lavender and pink. Mid-semester, she bids good-bye to her budding writers, to me, leaving me a special farewell note in my journal. Keep on, she tells me. You're meant for this.

Mrs. Forentos, who replaces Mrs. Taylor, is brown-haired, willowy, wears Nancy Sinatra boots, does fashion modeling on the side. She tells us that stories are a movie in the mind. Show us, she says, lights, camera, action. Make us want to buy popcorn and the next ticket. What she tells me, when I turn in a second story about a mountain woman who is a fortune-teller, is that she doesn't personally like my style. The description, she says, is overblown, if not overwhelming. She uses words like "didactic," "too Romantic," and I do not understand her. I take these attempts at criticism as a personal affront. What, I ask myself, Does Mrs. Forentos know about style, anyway?

MRS. FORENTOS, I MEAN, CAN YOU TELL ME JUST WHAT STYLE IS?

Over twenty-five years later, I teach writing at a small liberal arts college in Virginia. Styles have changed, but not as dramatically as one might at first think. Those wide-legged jeans with the fake leather would now be all the rage.

By this time, I have become a hybrid Mrs. Taylor and Mrs. Forentos, minus lavender nursery and go-go boots and with my own spin on the purpose of writing. Writing, I put at the top of my introductory creative writing syllabus, is what the artist Robert Motherwell said about painting. Far from mere ornamentation, Motherwell says, art is one of the only remaining guardians of the human spirit.

Like Mrs. Forentos, I have encountered students who write stories difficult for me to read, no less respond to. I'm generally against establishing rules disallowing certain kinds of stories, even ride-off-into-the-sunset romances. It's all, I tell my students, how that sun sets at the end of your story, and how the lovers ride off, in a jeep or a Mercedes, and with or without aplomb. It's all a matter of style. It's how you say what you say.

But how to discuss style when the definition of story itself is often a concept too ambiguous for beginners? I have to convince them that "fiction" is a kind of writing distinct from what they might have experienced previously. You are not, I tell my students again and again, going to hand in your first essay on Monday. You are not going to hand in a paper. You are writing a story. You are its possessor, and with it you are free to create any truth, convince us of any version of a nontruth. You are not even to ask what "I (the professor) want" from this assignment.

As we grow more comfortable with the idea of telling stories, I begin to discuss "necessary tools" for the writer, including point of view, setting, description, dialogue, dramatic action. One of the more difficult tools of writing to discuss is style. Just last fall I was talking with a seminar class about particular "styles" that make one work of fiction different from another work of fiction. As examples, I brought in passages from writers as diverse as William Faulkner, Raymond Chandler, Virginia Woolf. Placed side by side, what makes these passages distinct?

> Through the fence, between the curling flower spaces,
> I could see them hitting. They were coming toward
> where the flag was and I went along the fence. Luster
> was hunting in the grass by the flower a tree. They
> took the flag out and they were hitting.
> —Faulkner, *The Sound and the Fury*

> Big John Masters was large, fat, oily. He had
> sleek blue jowls and very thick fingers on which
> the knuckles were dimples. His brown hair was
> combed straight back from his forehead and he
> wore a wine-colored suit with patch pockets,
> a wine-colored tie, a tan silk shirt.
> —Chandler, "Spanish Blood"

> From the oval-shaped flower-bed there rose perhaps
> a hundred stalks spreading into heart-shaped or
> tongue-shaped leaves half-way up and unfurling at
> the tip red or blue or yellow petals marked with
> spots of color raised upon the surface; and from
> the red, blue or yellow gloom of the throat emerged
> a straight bar, rough with gold dust and slightly
> clubbed at the end.
> —Woolf, "Kew Gardens"

As well as the obvious differences in subject matter in these passages, we talk about individual sentences. What words are left out in Faulkner's sentences? Why? What does sentence length contribute, in the Chandler passage, to the "toughness" of his character? What words give one sentence of Woolf's a sense of lushness, a full-to-overflowing quality?

Style is the way words take on an identity on the page. It is a kind of ownership agreement, in which any given writer lays claim, with his or her own identity, to an arrangement of words turned into self-revealing lines, turned into a "work" of fiction, nonfiction, poetry. Just as importantly, however much style can be defined by a nuts-and-bolts examination of words, sentence structure, or sentence arrangement, style is also mysteriously yours alone, inscribed with your unique vision of a sunset, a drive to the Southwest, a journey into the interior world of a character. As Flannery O'Connor says, style is reality deepened by contact with mystery. Choices of words, syntax, endings and beginnings of sentences, punctuation, all meet with a much more intangible "tool" of craft. This element of craft is the unpredictable way words take shape on the page— call it synchronicity, choice beyond reason, or mystery. In *Mystery and Manners*, O'Connor calls it the way in which our day-by-day training in the way language "ought to be" on the page is "intruded upon by the timeless." Call this, if you must, the power of inspiration, the moment in which we simply "know" the way something must be said.

MINIMAL AND MAXIMAL

When such terms as *structure* or *mystery* meet with blank looks from my writers, I offer examples of uses of language that are strikingly different. We examine selected prose in light of its use of tools of craft such as point of view, setting, dramatic action, dialogue. The combination of these elements, in a variety of combinations and intensities of use, like the varieties of line and light and dark in a painting, produces the distinctiveness called style. Then I place, side by side, examples of seemingly opposite forms of style—minimalist and maximalist.

Minimalism

Minimalism was in its inception a literary movement in the 1980s characterized by, as critic Arthur Saltzman says, "flatness of narrative tone . . . sparseness of story . . . a striking restraint in prose style . . . [and a focus on] blue collar workers, misfortunate family relationships, unhealthy lifestyles, and lonely individuals." Spareness in place, descriptive detail, and characterization is balanced by emphasis on dialogue and seemingly dispassionate narrators who experience disconcerting distance from even the most consequential of events. Minimalist writers like Ann Beattie or the late Raymond Carver adhere to what Ernest Hemingway called the "iceberg theory" of fiction—three-fourths of the story, like an iceberg, stays "submerged," and the reader must infer larger meaning. What is left out tells us the most via the tension of implication. Yet, as Carver asserts in an essay called "On Writing," it is the commonplace and precisely, albeit minimally, described object or event that has the ability to summon "startling power."

At first reading of a Carver story like "So Much Water So Close to Home," sparseness would seem to be key to understanding it. We know little about the narrator or her environment. In the first two pages, we know there is a house with lawn chairs and newspaper delivery; we know her husband eats with good appetite. There is also what we don't know in the first pages. Who says what when the narrator answers a telephone call? Who was "dead already"? And why, in two lines of description, do we hear that the narrator stands at the sink, eyes closed, and "sends the dishes to the floor." When, in the next scene, we learn of how the narrator's husband and some buddies went on a fishing trip, only to discover the body of a dead girl in the river, descriptions are also minimal. We know only that she is naked and wedged into some branches of a tree hanging over the river. We know only that the husband and buddies continue to camp and fish, for two days, while the dead girl stays tied to a tree trunk. It's what we don't know, and what we do, that provide the startling awareness of human intent and lack of intention.

We don't ever know, for example, what the girl looks like, or who murdered her. There is no unsolved mystery waiting to be settled satisfactorily. We do know, however, that Gordon Johnson, one of the buddies, fears the "terrible coldness" of the river. We know that Stuart, another buddy, repeats more than once that there is "no shame" involved in a failure to immediately notify authorities about the body of a dead girl. We aren't told, ever, how the narrator feels about her husband, past or present. But we are told what she remembers from the night her husband comes home from the fishing trip, the way she "opened her legs" when he comes to bed. And we are told how she later sits with her husband at a creek and sees her own body in it, "eyes open, face down, staring at the moss on the bottom, dead." And, above all, we are aware, after reading the story, of the precise and random descriptions of bodies in general we have read throughout—the raking of an arm across a drain board, manicured nails, a bare shoulder, a quick look at breasts and legs. While we never "see" any of the characters, we see enough random parts of them to know that, in the end, this could be a story about just how terrible "disembodiment," detachment from how we feel, and what we know, can be.

Maximalism

Responding to minimalism's sparseness, essayist Sanford Pinsker calls for "a revitalized social realism" in prose and commends such writers as Cormac McCarthy and Toni Morrison for writing characterized by profusion. Far from spare, maximalism is about vastness—of space, time, vision. Narratives may occur on more than one level of time, in more than one place. History, in maximalist writing, can become a palpable presence, a ghost of memory visible, as in McCarthy's *All the Pretty Horses*. "Ghost of nation passing," McCarthy writes, "in a soft chorale across that mineral waste to darkness bearing lost to all history and all remembrance like a grail the sum of their secular and transitory and violent lives." Time, in such writing, becomes fluid, not, as photographer and art critic John Berger says, "a question of length, but of depth and density."

Above all, maximalist work is vision, and vision made literal. Unlike in minimalism, the interior world is not implied. It is present in the profusion of language on the page. For example, McCarthy, in *The Crossing*, writes of a sixteen-year-old boy named Billy Parham who captures a marauding wolf and decides to set it free in Mexico. By the end of the first section of the novel, the wolf has been stolen and made a sideshow attraction in a Mexican carnival. Rather than allow its suffering, Billy shoots the wolf and rides toward the mountains with its body.

> He took up her stiff head out of the leaves held it or he reached
> to hold what cannot be held, what already ran among the moun-
> tains at once terrible and of a great beauty, like flowers that feed

on flesh. What blood and bone are made of but can themselves not make on any altar nor by any wound of war. What we may well believe has power to cut and shape and hollow out the dark form of the world surely if wind can, if rain can. But which cannot be held never be held and is no flower but is swift and a huntress and the wind itself is in terror of it and the world cannot lose it.

Far from merely describing a dead wolf, the passage reaches toward spirit in language. In part, McCarthy achieves such spirit by literally using the language of the holy: "took up," "altar." The passage also moves far beyond the point of view of a boy. "We" becomes central character, reader, author, world since the beginning of time. By breaking rules about punctuation and by using a cumulative structure ("and," "and," "and"), McCarthy creates a sense of urgency, an incantatory summoning. Such passages reach deep into world, body, spirit, and unflinchingly describe what is experienced.

BUT HOW TO ACHIEVE SUCH STYLE, ONCE YOU KNOW WHAT IT IS?

Fine to explore the sweeping vistas of maximalism, or the subtler back yards of minimalism. But how to bring those styles to the blank page? When to be a minimalist, when a maximalist? Are such styles mutually exclusive? Are such styles a matter of choice, and how can we know when to choose? The best way to learn style, I have come to believe, is to write stories and discuss them on "macro" and "micro" levels.

Macro

The "macro" approach implies attention to the larger questions of story intent, or the "heart" of the story. My workshop begins with a student summarizing his or her story. This is not a summary of theme, but of plot. Without reviewing the manuscript, that student relates, as he or she remembers it, the chain of events in the draft.

A second student relates what she or he felt the story at hand was "about." For example, one student wrote a story that seemed to be about an angry young man who ends up ripping his parents apart (complete with shreds of flesh in teeth) the moment he realizes he is a vampire. In class, a comment was made that this story is less about the supernatural and more about the difficult relationships between parents and children.

"Why," a student wanted to know, "does this kid feel such hatred for his mother? I mean, I think it's cool and all that he's a vampire, but he plans his mother's death. And the minute that other guy makes him a vampire, that's his first thought. His mother. And how she's kept him down."

Flannery O'Connor, in an essay called "On Suspense in 'A Good Man Is Hard to Find,' " points out that "a story really isn't good unless it successfully resists paraphrase. . . ." So is this business of paraphrasing a story's purpose counterproductive? Does it force us toward easy solutions, and toward easy stories? Many beginning workshop pieces are easily summarized—romances, science fiction, even stories about vampires and werewolves. We can figure out far too easily that a stranger who is just passing through a small town, has engine trouble, and notices that the villagers all have flat blue eyes and suspiciously pointy teeth is in for real trouble of some sort. But the point isn't to show us how well such easy stories work.

Paraphrasing can force us into deeper levels of both story and self. O'Connor also says that a good story "hangs on and expands the mind." How do we get to this point? Can we make a story more about what it might be about? How can images, characterization, plot, setting, all the important elements of fiction, support the most interesting paraphrase of a given story?

Most importantly, as we explore the largeness of stories, their "macro" possibilities, we are forced further into the largeness of our own lives. The "hidden" story, made visible, can be that which is most difficult to confront in our experiences and, at the same time, the story that demands to be told. Beneath one level of story may lie other stories, inaccessible mothers, lost loves, lives we might have led. Beneath the smallest moments of experience may lie vastness, as we find in this moment in Annie Dillard's *Pilgrim at Tinker Creek*.

> . . . one day I was walking along Tinker Creek thinking of nothing at all and I saw the tree with the lights in it. I saw the backyard cedar where the mourning doves roost charged and transfigured, each cell buzzing with flame. I stood on the grass with the lights in it, grass that was wholly fire, utterly focused and utterly dreamed. It was less like seeing than like being for the first time seen, knocked breathless by a powerful glance. The flood of fire abated, but I'm still spending the power.

> Gradually the lights went out in the cedar, the colors died, the
> cells unflamed and disappeared. I was still ringing. I had been
> my whole life a bell, and never knew it until at that moment
> I was lifted and struck.

Follow, as Socrates said, where the question leads. Your story is
about what? And then what? And then?

Micro

On the "micro" level, we begin with the sentence—or smaller than
that—with the word. Say, for example, that sentence one of a story's
draft takes place in a smoky bar where a man has gone for the evening
to escape questions from his girlfriend about their relationship. The
student writes: "It seemed late, the man thought to himself as he
watched the smoke rings rise like wedding bands, reminding him of
Emily, who was now an ice-cold dagger of pain clutching at the heart
in his chest."

The first task, of course, is to eliminate redundancy. Why does it
"seem" late? Is it or isn't it, or is our character experiencing a confusion we'll soon find out about? Don't we always think to ourselves?
Or is the man thinking aloud? Would a wedding band rise? Aren't
hearts usually in chests, or is there a purpose, in this sentence, for
pointing out the location of the one belonging to this character? Has
he not been aware of his heart before? Must pain "clutch" that
heart? What is a better, less clichéd, word? And, while we're at it,
who amongst us has heard, too often, about pain as "an ice-cold
dagger?" The task: Make the story, on its most minimal level, have
a purpose.

And, while we're at it, what about specificity? Is this bar, I ask, in
a fishing village in northeast Maine? Are we talking about a western
swing bar in west Texas? Does the man choose a working-class bar
(when we know that he has a job in an investment bank)? Or does
he choose happy hour at a piano bar on the upper west end? Why,
I ask my students, does a character choose a particular place at a
particular moment? What can a place reveal about motivation, desire, choice, crisis? And, further, how might the specifics of place
contribute to resolution in the story? The man in the working-class
bar smells not just any smoke but a certain blend of Scandinavian
tobacco that makes him think of his father. Thinking of his father

makes him realize, however subtly, that the workings of his own heart are similar to those of his father, who could never completely love his family.

As well as discussing how place contributes to character and theme of story, I want students to choose details that "resound." What kind of smoke? Okay, the bar is dark. What quality of dark? There's music? What pitch? What kind of jukebox? A student wrote of a woman dancing in the far corner of a bar with little tables with felt coasters and a jukebox that played nothing but Ella Fitzgerald. I began to like this bar, and to wonder why the woman was dancing. In that bar, the woman wore dime-store pearls that caught the pink light from neon flamingoes from a restaurant sign across the street. She was slow-dancing with an imaginary partner.

On both the macro and the micro levels of storytelling, the most important thing is attention to how language is used. When is it important to pay attention to "largeness," what a story is about, the scope of what a character thinks or feels? When is it important to zoom in on the minutest details of description or action? And when, after writing and revising, writing and revising, can a beginning writer begin to envision that particular combination of interiority or exteriority, the use of language's lushness or spareness, that comes to be called style?

STYLE AND THE PRESENCE OF MYSTERY

Over twenty-five years after my first high school creative writing class, my own style has changed considerably. My suede-legged jeans have been replaced by skirts called "airy" in the wardrobe of a forty-something woman. One afternoon I find myself watching light on the lawn outside and thinking about what Mrs. Taylor told me, years ago. Writing, Mrs. Taylor said, is mystery. Light and shadows move in the tree branches, up the steps outside the classroom windows. In what way can my students best describe light? When might light be described as a maximalist might see it? And when as a minimalist might? Are these territories of language mutually exclusive?

Cormac McCarthy writes of light in his description, in *The Crossing,* of the dead wolf Billy Parham carries away from a village in Mexico:

> He squatted over the wolf and touched her fur. He touched the
> cold and perfect teeth. The eye turned back to the fire gave back
> no light and he closed it with his thumb and sat by her. . . .

The rest of this passage, as we have seen earlier, rises, with its profusion of language, into the depths and heights of maximalism. But at this particular moment, description is minimal. Dead is dead. In Carver's "So Much Water So Close to Home," a very minimally described moment has vast possibilities of meaning. The central character attends the funeral of the girl found dead on her husband's fishing trip.

> Directly, a nice blond man in a nice dark suit stands and asks
> us to bow our heads. He says a prayer for us, the living, and
> when he finishes he says a prayer for the soul of the departed.
> Along with the others I go past the casket. Then I move out onto
> the front steps and into the afternoon light.

Described in minimalist fashion, there is a nice suit, a nice young man and a casket. But the possibilities, once the central character steps out into the afternoon light, are infinite. This particular death will resound in the consciousness of the reader long after we step forward from the page into the "light" of our own experiences with loss or love or betrayal.

BONE AND BLOOD

In the end, the boundaries between minimalism and maximalism are permeable. One kind of style enhances another, and just as there are no hard-and-fast rules for when to use a particular point of view or a particular plot structure, style itself is a mystery that evolves, as the skills and voices of writers evolve, with practice and experimentation. Style, like voice, as writer Margaret Atwood says, "rises off the page . . . like the singing voice in music." The way style "rises" to the reader, can be taught by examining language itself. We can practice language by copying styles, studying styles, employing specific styles at particular moments in stories. But we must also try to understand the core of what we are "made of" before the style that will eventually be ours can truly evolve. Words, like human beings, are "made of bone and blood," both elemental and unfathomable. This is writing as mystery, unfolding.

EXERCISES

1. Look at excerpts from writers who are either minimalist (Ann Beattie, Raymond Carver) or maximalist (Cormac McCarthy, William Faulkner, Toni Morrison). After reading the selections, create a scenario—a meeting in a restaurant, a trip to the ocean. Write the same scene twice, in imitation of both one of the minimalist passages and one of the maximimalist passages.

2. Put together a bagful of ordinary objects (a paperweight, a letter opener, a photograph). Select an object. Describe the object with as much attention to small details as possible. What does it look like? What unusual markings does it have? What does it smell like? Feel like? Part two of the exercise, which might evolve into a story: Imagine a scene in which the owner of the object is missing. This object is the only way we may know our character.

3. Reread the passage from Annie Dillard quoted in the essay. Write about a particular moment in which you have experienced "the tree with the lights in it," or a moment of enlightenment or realization in the life of a character. The character could be the same one from exercise two.

Karen Salyer McElmurray's novel, *Strange Birds in the Tree of Heaven*, which has received grants from the National Endowment for the Arts, the North Carolina Arts Council, and the Kentucky Foundation for Women, is published by Hill Street Press. At present, she is an assistant professor of English at Lynchburg College in Virginia.

The Conjurer's Art:
The Rules of Magical Realism
and How to Break Them

CARRIE BROWN

In magical realism, extraordinary things are presented as though they are perfectly ordinary. To many minds, this may sound suspiciously like life as usual. After all, we know how peculiar truth itself can be, let alone fiction.

But magical realism does not refer simply to the oddities and eccentricities of human behavior, nor to the sometimes astonishing world of natural causes and events, nor to the surprising acts of coincidence and fate that occasionally appear to be directed by an unseen authority.

To understand how magical realism works in fiction, think instead of radios mysteriously broadcasting the intimate conversations of strangers. Or a door from a café that leads into a mist so thick a man may be supported on its tides; he steps out "into the midst of nothing" and raises a glass of champagne to the companions he leaves behind (from Gloria Naylor's *Bailey's Cafe*.) Or think of lilac bushes blooming wildly and profusely out of season, nourished by a dead man's bones. Think of an island where spring fails to arrive. Think of ghosts. Think of charms to make a man fall in love. Think of talking crows. These are all examples of magical realism.

THE POWER OF MAGIC
I have always been tempted by the form of magical realism. I loved its rococo, exotic details, the richness of language it (often) seems to require, its high-wire risks, and especially the often heartbreaking tension magical realism can maintain between what we know empirically to be impossible and yet believe (or want to believe) with all our hearts. Since childhood, I have been captivated by the heroic promise

of stories in which impossible events happen, and children's literature is rich with a familiar canon of miracles. Stones roll from the mouths of caves. Carpets sail through air. Birds speak in iambic pentameter. A peach as big as a dirigible floats in the sky. Dolls wake up at night to dust the pianoforte. Children fly across the circumference of the moon. Giants flail at the tops of beanstalks. Christly lions vanquish witches. A hedgehog starches the waistcoat of Cock Robin. A girl follows a white rabbit down a famous hole. Such tales allowed the boundaries of what I understood as the real world to balloon thrillingly at the edges, to bulge with portent and possibility, to surprise and horrify and enchant me. The stranger the story, the richer and more inventive its details, the more it seemed to turn the ordinary, domestic world on its head, the more I liked it.

Few can resist magic. The first time a man took a saw to a woman in a wooden box, beads of sweat ran down every forehead in the audience. Think of rabbits pulled from hats, pigeons shaken from handkerchiefs, bouquets of roses extracted from the dirty ears of children. Think of silver dollars erupting from knees and elbows, water that fails to pour from an inverted pitcher, wands transformed into kite strings. We do not believe these things, of course, and yet they hold us captive with an almost religious force.

William Shakespeare, who liked magic and liberally employed ghosts and spirits (think of Hamlet's father, the sprite Ariel, and the magician Prospero) as persuasively and meaningfully as you could wish, understood not just magic's dazzling effects, but also—and this is what's important—the power of its source in the human heart, in human nature in general. We all wish for things with a passion that feels powerful enough to warp matter itself. We fear things we can neither see nor name. We want things we know logically we cannot have (people to come back to life, for instance). And we are all haunted by demons and visited by grace. The power of magic, in fiction as in life, is its ability to draw us near the tempting and sometimes terrifying threshold of possibility, where the real and the imaginary intersect in a tantalizing and significant way.

LINKING MAGIC TO CHARACTER

Consider Shakespeare's *The Winter's Tale.* When the clever and patient Paulina unveils the statue of the living queen Hermione to the king, who believes his beloved wife has been dead for twenty years,

Paulina is not actually performing magic. Hermione has been alive all along, sequestered in a tower. But Paulina understands that King Leontes and all his court *will believe it to be magic* when Hermione steps from her pedestal to embrace her husband. And Paulina arrests Leontes, as he tries to touch Hermione's robe in disbelief, with a theatrical caution that Shakespeare knows full well is an instruction to all readers, too. "It is requir'd you do awake your faith," Paulina says. "Then, all stand still."

"If this be magic," the amazed king cries, "let it be an art lawful as eating." This is Shakespeare playing around not with magical realism, per se, but with the *idea* of magic (and with the ideas of life and literature, too), and it is a wonderful example of perhaps the first and most important rule of magical realism, the one rule that must never be broken. (Though for nearly every other rule in magical realist fiction, there is an equally persuasive example of a writer who did exactly the reverse with splendid results; we'll get to those.)

Why are we so moved by the scene of Leontes staring up into the face of Hermione quickening with life? Because we understand how much this miracle matters to him, its personal implications.

The magic of a magical realist story must never be without emotional or psychological foundation. Special effects are all well and good, and often great fun to write, but the magic elements in any story, if it is going to matter to the reader, must be linked, at an intuitive or psychologically accurate level, to the real lives of the characters. Those elements of magic must be bound in the substantive, emotional worlds of the characters, and therein lies their enchantment. Even the oxymoronic quality of the term is instructive—the magic of the magical realist tale must be so real, so inevitable, so necessary, and so particular to the passions and desires and fears of the characters that you forget it couldn't actually happen.

The "magic" of Hermione brought back to life moves us precisely because we know Leontes has been mourning her for two decades. Otherwise, it would only look like pyrotechnics.

That's the first and most important point to remember about magical realism. As tempting as the lush exoticisms of magical realism can be, ask yourself why you want to tell a story that depends so much, as Paulina says, on "awakened faith"? Answer that question—know your characters, understand their circumstances, their motivations, what they have to risk. But without that understanding, your sleight of hand—your magic—will look hopelessly amateurish: You'll look like the guy who tries to saw the lady in half and suddenly notices blood all over the floor.

I wrote a magical realist novel, *Rose's Garden*, because my main character, a skeptic all his life and a man disinclined to hallucinations, was filled with grief and was prepared to turn away from the world and the privilege of being alive. What could persuade this man—this great doubter—that he was wrong, I wondered? What could persuade him that the world still had power and authority and grandeur? What could force a man who had lost his faith not just to recapture it but to redefine it?

I gave him an angel, but an angel with strings, as it were. An angel who would appear, looking like a rescuer, and then abandon him, sending him on a voyage of discovery in the real world that made everything he thought he understood seem new again.

What happens, I wanted to know, to someone who thinks he cannot be surprised by anything? The answer, of course, was magic.

TO DOUBT OR NOT TO DOUBT

The editors of the anthology *Magical Realist Fiction*, David Young and Keith Hollaman (published in 1984, the volume was the first collection of its kind), say in their introduction that there are generally two types of magical realist fiction (and then a great many variations on the theme).

According to their definition, magical realist stories sometimes begin with a distinctly "magical" event or circumstance and then proceed according to all other laws of realist fiction, with people behaving in psychologically "normal" ways. Or, the stories start off ordinarily enough but gradually become more and more extraordinary.

Many writers of magical realism have chosen to begin right away by establishing the amplified world of their fiction; the advantage is that the reader will understand from the start the dimensions of the fictional universe presented.

Hence Gabriel García Márquez's famous first line from *One Hundred Years of Solitude*: "Many years later, as he faced the firing squad, Colonel Aureliano Buendía was to remember that distant afternoon when his father took him to discover ice." The word "discover" rises out of the sentence like an iceberg in the Sahara.

Alice Hoffman takes a similar approach in her novel, *Practical Magic*: "For more than two hundred years, the Owens women have been blamed for everything that has gone wrong in town." Those two hundred years suddenly distorting the reliable properties of time itself. Consider the opening of William Kennedy's *Ironweed*: "Riding up the winding road of Saint Agnes Cemetery in the back of the rattling old truck, Francis Phelan became aware that the dead, even more than the living, settled down in neighborhoods."

As an aside, these examples possess a sly, difficult literalism that magical realism depends on to be successful. They can be taken both metaphorically, in which case they are perfectly true, or as statements of fact, in which case they become "magical." But most importantly, they admit no chink of light from the so-called real world. Everybody here—the colonel, the neighbors of the Owens women, Francis Phelan—is in on the joke, as it were. What seems strange to us, does not seem strange to them; before long, we feel that we, too, have lived in this universe forever.

But not all magical realism works this way. Characters who are allowed to be surprised by the "magic" around them, even to be skeptical, can sometimes make the magical more persuasive. Just as a character is won over (or worn down), so are we as readers. John Cheever's famous magical realist story "The Enormous Radio" works this way. Jim and Irene Westcott are sitting quietly in their living room, listening to a Chopin prelude on the radio, when suddenly the broadcast is interrupted by the unmistakable sounds of a quarrel taking place between a husband and wife. We sit with the Westcotts in their living room for a moment, alert in the way people become alert when the barometer suddenly falls. We, too, are distinctly troubled, listening in puzzlement alongside the Westcotts.

Finally, Cheever breaks the silence.

> "This is strange," Jim said.
> "Isn't it?" Irene said.

The Westcotts cannot understand what is wrong with their new radio. It seems impossible but yet, listen, there it is—the rough brogue of the Irish nurse singing to the children in a nearby apartment, the hysterical, brittle sounds of a party, the acrimonious, insulting words of a husband and wife tearing each other to bits. Jim Westcott fiddles with the dial. A repairman is summoned. Annoyance is expressed. The Westcotts are baffled. But Irene, almost despite herself, is drawn with a perverse and terrifying force to the radio, where she sits alone, listening to the sound of her own innocence—and that of the world's—being shattered over and over again. And as she falls under its terrible, demoralizing spell, so do we.

Another pair of initial doubters are the sisters in Hoffman's *Practical Magic*. Orphaned at a young age, they are raised by their aunts, the elderly and eccentric Owens sisters, whose neighbors believe them to be witches. Hoffman cleverly allows most of the weight of skepticism in this world to fall not on the neighbors, the outsiders, the exact place where you might expect to see this magic universe assailed. In fact, the neighbors believe wholeheartedly in the Owens sisters' incantations and remedies. It is the main characters themselves, two eminently knowable girls with motives and needs as ordinary and sympathetic as the proverbial girl next door, who shoulder the disbelief that finally gives the novel's magic its most powerful effect.

> "This is so silly," Sally would whisper, watching her aunts mutter spells over the heads of lovesick clients begging for a cure. "It's utter nonsense."

It is commonly thought that doubt and skepticism for the magic in a magical realist novel is a risky business, and perhaps it is, but Hoffman manages it with such virtuosity that a writer feels tempted to try it.

Hoffman is working very hard managing the delicate balance of creating a world in which magic is real—a girl who eats the aunts' offering of a dove's heart to trap a man finds him metaphorically chained to her leg with amorous intention for the rest of her life, and a man so hot with love causes the linoleum of the aunts' kitchen countertops to bubble when he rests his head in his hands in despair—and repeatedly putting her central characters to the test of belief.

"Black cats can do that to some people," Hoffman writes, as if it is all nonsense. "They make them go all shivery and scared and remind them of dark, wicked nights."

But it isn't nonsense, we discover. It all makes perfect sense.

LAYING IT ON, THICK OR THIN

Flannery O'Connor—not a magical realist but certainly interested in the gothic, sometimes thought to be a close cousin—had this to say about specificity in writing.

> The beginning of human knowledge is through the senses, and the fiction writer begins where human perception begins. He appeals through the senses, and you cannot appeal to the senses with abstractions.

All good, convincing writing depends on specificity, of course, and magical realism is no exception. In fact, the lesson is perhaps even more important to get right in magical realism, because you battle the reader's credulity, as well as his general investment in what's going on in your *story*, the minute you introduce something improbable.

The possibilities for specificity in magical realism are particularly fun, as well. When Ulises stabs the abusive whale of a grandmother in García Márquez's story the incredible and sad tale of "Innocent Eréndira and Her Heartless Grandmother," the old woman's blood is marvelously, magically unexpected. It was oily blood, shiny and green, just like mint honey.

In his Pulitzer prize winning novel, *Martin Dressler*, Steven Millhauser describes the Grand Cosmo, a hotel whose amenities exceed all but the wildest imaginations.

> It was therefore possible to say that the Grand Cosmo was never the same from one day to the next, that its variety was, in a sense, limitless . . . the many parks and ponds and gardens, including the Pleasure Park with its artificial moonlight checkering the paths, its mechanical nightingales singing in the branches, its melancholy lagoon and ruined summerhouse; its Haunted Grotto, in which ghosts fluttered toward visitors in a darkness illuminated by lanternlight; the Moorish Bazaar, composed of winding dusty lanes, sales clerks dressed as Arabs and trained in the art of bargaining, and a maze of stalls that sold everything from copper basins to live chickens; the many reconstructions of Hidden New York, including Thieves Alley in Mulberry Bend, an opium den, a foggy street of river dives (the Tub of Blood, Cat Alley, Dirty Johnny's), and bloody fights between the Bowery Boys and the Dead Rabbits, with a nearby shop called Hell-Cat Maggie's in where one could purchase brass fingernails and have one's teeth filed to points. . . .

Millhauser almost overwhelms us with so much specificity that we have no time to step back and question the reasonableness of any of it. With almost manic imaginative effect, he makes the Grand Cosmo real by virtue of his insistent specificity, what the critic George Stade, in a review of an earlier Millhauser novel, *Edwin Mullhouse: The Life and Death of an American Writer, 1943–1954 by Jeffrey Cartwright*, called Millhauser's trademark "rapt march of particulars." Though magical realism seems to require lush, descriptive writing, not all magic must be portrayed in what is commonly thought of as lyrical terms. Some magic, after all, isn't pretty. The Grand Cosmo, of course, is nothing short of horrifying. Moments of magic can be handled plainly, too, and sometimes that style is to their advantage.

Take this moment in Hoffman's *Practical Magic*, for instance. Gillian lay on the window seat in the summer, "so relaxed and languid that moths would land on her, mistaking her for a cushion, and proceed to make tiny holes in her jeans and T-shirt." It's the simplest of moments, strange and yet lucid. The reference to such common articles of clothing as jeans and a T-shirt tether the magic of moths eating away at a lazy teenager directly and convincingly to the real world. Had Gillian been wearing a wedding dress, for instance, or a sari, we might have been less inclined to feel the strange magic of the moment.

Even within single paragraphs, Hoffman walks that fine line between the expected hyperbole of magical realism and the concrete world of real things. Of the two young sisters, she writes, "When they did finally doze off, their arms wrapped around each other, they often had the exact same dreams." Not really, we know. This is magic. But then she goes on, weaving a skillful path back into absolutes that seem much more familiar. "There were times when they could complete each other's sentences; certainly each could close her eyes and guess what the other most desired for dessert on any given day." The effect of this delicate tension maintained between the magical and the real is to give each a kind of heightened clarity and an almost shocking force. Together they achieve a mystical balance in which the real is made rich by the magical, and the magical is made believable by the real.

Either way, whether you lay it on thick or thin, whether you become apoplectic like Millhauser or resolutely ordinary like Hoffman, your objective in describing things that are magical is the same as your objective in describing things that are real. Be specific.

JUST SAY BOO

Ghosts are everywhere in magical realist fiction. They throw pots and surge in and out of walls; they stand at the foot of the bed or appear, tantalizingly, at the end of the garden; they trip up thugs and bear away children, offering benediction and damnation both.

Lois Parkinson Zamora, in her essay "Magical Romance/Magical Realism: Ghosts in U.S. and Latin American Fiction," writes that "ghosts embody the fundamental magic realist sense that reality always exceeds our capacities to describe or understand or prove." If the "function of literature," as she suggests, is "to engage this excessive reality, to honor that which we may grasp intuitively but never fully or finally define," then there is hardly a better steward to position at the door to your magical realist world than a ghost.

What is important to remember, with ghosts as with living characters, is that they are, in fact, characters—and they are only successful if they have histories, if they possess longings and rages, intentions and regrets, the same as the rest of us.

Fun house ghosts, the sort that pop out irrationally to wave giddily back and forth from the walls in the Hall of Horrors at the amusement park, will get you nowhere in fiction; they're cartoonish and easily seen through. But a ghost with a purpose and a past, such as Beloved in Toni Morrison's novel of that name, has as much force in the world as any of her living relatives.

It's not that Morrison doesn't appreciate the cultural familiarity of some ghostly special effects. Here's how the character Paul D first encounters Beloved, for instance.

> [He] tied his shoes together, hung them over his shoulder and followed [Sethe] through the door straight into a pool of red and undulating light that locked him where he stood.
> "You got company?" he whispered, frowning.
> "Off and on," said Sethe.

But Beloved, the ghost of Sethe's murdered two-year-old baby girl, can do a lot more than bend gamma rays.

> It was spiteful. Full of a baby's venom. The women in the house knew it and so did the children. For years each put up with the spite in his own way. But by 1873 Sethe and her daughter Denver were its only victims. The grandmother, Baby Suggs, was dead,

227

and the sons, Howard and Buglar, had run away by the time they were thirteen years old—as soon as merely looking in a mirror shattered it (that was the signal for Buglar); as soon as two tiny hand prints appeared in the cake (that was it for Howard).

It's those "two tiny hand prints," which recall the hands of children everywhere pressed into plaster disks to preserve their shapes and sizes, that wring the heart and raise the hair on the back of the neck, conjuring up the image of a dead baby lost between heaven and hell. By the time Beloved has metamorphosed from a baby to a ghost to a mysterious young woman who walks fully dressed out of a stream one day and comes to find her mother again, to take back what had been rightfully hers and secure a place among the living, we are fully persuaded of Beloved's reality, and as moved by her as much as by any of the characters. Morrison makes sure that we see Beloved in exquisite detail, over and over again, in all her strangeness, from the skin that is "flawless except for three vertical scratches on her forehead so fine and thin they seemed at first like hair, baby hair before it bloomed and roped into the masses of black yam under her hat," to the new, soft skin of her hands and feet, her raspy voice, her face strangely glowing and shiny as the leaves on the strawberry plant.

A ghost, as everyone knows, from Hamlet to William Faulkner's Quentin Compson, is both within us and without, both of this world and the one we can only imagine, a hallucination and a companion both. A ghost is, in short, both magical and real. And as Faulkner wrote about Quentin in *Absalom, Absalom!*,

> His childhood was full of them; his very body was an empty hall echoing with sonorous, defeated names; he was not a being, an entity, he was a commonwealth.

And there it is, the corporeal world suddenly, magically, becomes the universe. That's a trick indeed.

ENDING WITH BEGINNINGS

Still, after all, you are left with the question all writers confront. How do I begin? Leaving aside, for a moment, the question of how to begin any piece of writing, consider the striking way a variety of writers have opened tales of magical realism. Almost all, whether they begin with a sound and light show or not, hold in their prose something that suggests the story to follow will proceed according to different rules than typically adhered to by the "real" world. Sometimes, the implication—and it's only an implication—is that the *story* is old-fashioned in the way that we expect fairy tales to be, where magic is a matter of course. It opens with a bravura show of consciousness about the business at hand—the business of telling stories—and the conventions of fairy tales are all over the prose.

Take the opening scene of *Martin Dressler*, for instance.

> There once lived a man named Martin Dressler, a shopkeeper's son, who rose from modest beginnings to a height of dreamlike good fortune.

Millhauser didn't say "once upon a time," but he might as well have. Here are all the conventions of an old-fashioned tale—a character's humble beginnings, his meteoric rise—and implicitly, helped along by that word "dreamlike," Millhauser suggests the quality of strangeness that will run through the story, sentence by sentence.

Even Cheever's "The Enormous Radio," with its suspicious insistence on the ordinariness of the opening scene, has about it the whiff of old-fashioned storytelling.

> Jim and Irene Westcott were the kind of people who seem to strike that satisfactory average of income, endeavor, and respectability that is reached by the statistical reports in college alumni bulletins. They were the parents of two young children, they had been married nine years, they lived on the twelfth floor of an apartment house near Sutton Place, they went to the theater an average of 10.3 times a year, and they hoped someday to live in Westchester.

Cheever's almost heady summarizing here, the sense that he needs to lay out all the particulars in a no-nonsense manner, also suggests fairy tales, where the stage on which the story will be set is put forth in simple, almost businesslike fashion. Fairy tales always begin at the beginning, and so does Cheever. And right away, precisely because there is nothing in the least surprising about the Westcotts, you know that something strange indeed is likely to follow. Something strange but, oddly, something that will feel familiar, too, something that will feel true to the experience of being human, of being made of flesh and blood. The critic Luis Leal has written that magic realism's aim, "unlike that of magic, is to express emotions, not to evoke them. . . . In magical realism, the writer confronts reality and tries to untangle it, to discover what is mysterious in things, in life, in human acts."

Magic shouldn't ever take the reader out of the world he knows. Make your magic, if you will, of the stuff of life itself. After all, it's the most magical material the world has ever known.

EXERCISES

1. Take an ordinary and domestic scene that you have already written and turn it on its head by inventing a magical event to occur in its midst.

2. Generate a list of ten magical events that could occur in fiction (the resurrection of a dead person, the flight of a witch through the night sky), and then match each event with a character to whom that event would be psychologically meaningful. Choose the best two matches and make them the center of a story.

3. Generate a character sketch for a ghost. What would make the ghost return to life? What unresolved concerns would she wish to resolve? Write several paragraphs of psychological profile. Once you have the psychological profile, write a story in which the central problem is the appearance of that ghost.

Carrie Brown is the author of the novels *Rose's Garden* and *Lamb in Love*, both published by Algonquin Books. The recipient of a Virginia Arts Commission Fellowship and a former journalist, she was a Henry Hoyns fellow at the University of Virginia and now teaches at Sweet Briar College in Virginia. She has three children and is married to the novelist John Gregory Brown.

The Comic Point of View: Putting Humor in Your Fiction

DAVID BOUCHIER

I wasted the second-best years of my life trying to be a serious writer. How else could I communicate my deep insight into the meaning of things, the sadness of the human condition, the fragility of love, and the pain of a sensitive soul doomed to live in a crass materialistic world? Thousands of tedious pages later, it dawned on me that these great truths were already old news in William Shakespeare's time, that I had nothing to add, and that it was time to lighten up.

Shakespeare understood that life is funny at least as often as it is tragic. After every sad scene, he brings in the clowns. Contemporary writers too often *forget* to bring in the clowns, and one sure way to make your fiction more appealing is to add a carefully calculated dose of humor.

"Carefully calculated" is important. Humor *does* sell fiction, but only when it is used sparingly. "Funny books" without cartoons are not a big market. So this essay suggests how to *add* the comic point of view to your fiction without changing its essential themes or qualities.

THE NATURE OF HUMOR

Humor is like sex: Everybody *knows* exactly what it is, but no two people ever agree. College professors have written dozens of books offering philosophical, psychological, sociological, historic, post-structuralist, and even biological theories of humor. They all come to the same conclusion: We don't quite understand humor yet, and we require generous funding for further research.

Therefore, I will ignore the profound intellectual question of what humor *is* and go straight for the trivial but practical question, How does humor work?

It certainly doesn't work on everybody. "Everyone has a sense of humor" is one of those daft clichés, like "Every cloud has a silver lining" and "Every child has a special gift," that vanishes in a puff of smoke the moment we think about it. My father-in-law doesn't have a sense of humor. There are whole nations and whole professions without a sense of humor—think of Serbs, IRS inspectors, and proctologists, for example.

A sense of humor is a special gift. It gives you, as a writer, the magical power to make people laugh, whether they like it or not. Anyone with a sense of humor can *write* humor, although history shows that it helps to be a depressive, an alchoholic, or a drug addict, and preferably all three (think of the roll call of great humorists, and you'll see what I mean). It also helps to forget about your self-esteem, if you are lucky enough to have any. And don't expect it to be easy. Sitting down at a keyboard to *be funny* in cold blood, as it were, takes some practice. There are no guarantees for the humorous writer. Some readers will find your most brilliant strokes of wit as entertaining as the Baltimore telephone directory. The same readers may gag with laughter over your most tragic passages.

The comic point of view is essentially that of the stranger or alien. It captures the amazement and curiosity we all feel when, for example, we travel in strange countries where everything seems odd, and even perverse. It's what social scientists call anthropological distance. All tribes have strange customs, and the writer's job is to become an anthropolgist *to his or her own tribe*. The comic point of view is always the *outsider* point of view—the innocent, the unbeliever, the depressive, the misanthrope, the anarchist, or the Antichrist who sees things as nobody else sees them.

Some writers think this way like breathing. Others have to make a conscious effort to get out of their conventional skin. But the basic operating principles of humor are the same for everyone.

INCONGRUITY

Wit is the unexpected copulation of ideas. Humor can be as complicated as a play by Aristophanes or Tom Stoppard. It can be as simple as a pratfall or a pie in the face. The only quality all humor shares is *the unexpected*—it surprises us by subverting the commonplace. Oscar Wilde was a master of this technique: "If one tells the truth, one is certain sooner or later to be found out" or "The good end happily and the bad unhappily. That is what fiction means."

Incongruity is the basic, and in some sense the only, technique of the humorist. The reader must be surprised by an unexpected event, an unlikely connection, an inappropriate role performance, or a bizarre viewpoint.

There are dozens of ways to do this in storytelling, and it may be useful to distinguish the most common humor devices. In reality, of course, these devices can be mixed and matched in any way the writer chooses.

IRONY

Fiction without irony is like painting without perspective. Irony exposes the incongruities of everyday life—the half-truths, deceptions, and self-deceptions that help us all get through the day. Things are never what they seem, and the essence of ironic humor is the lack of fit between life as it *is*, and life as we imagine it *should* be. We think the world should make sense: It doesn't. We think life should be dignified: It never is. We think life should have a serious purpose, like football or lawn care: But of course the purpose always turns out to be very silly in the end. Irony is the writer's richest and most inexhaustible humor resource.

The genre of the campus novel, from Kingsley Amis to Richard Russo, is a perfect example. Higher education is meant to be a serious business, universities are meant to be serious places. So it's funny when, in Russo's *Straight Man*, the chair of the English Department hides in the ceiling space over the faculty offices to eavesdrop on a meeting between his colleagues.

> It has to be ninety degrees up here among the rafters. I'm sweating profusely, and when I lean forward, a drop of perspiration from the tip of my nose finds the crevice I'm peering down through and lands with an almost audible plink in the center of the long conference table.

Another reason why irony is such a powerful source of humor is that, as Voltaire observed long ago, life is absurd, *but* we try to make sense of it. This doomed effort creates some of the best comedy. One of the funniest books in this century (in my opinion) is Douglas Adams' *The Hitchhiker's Guide to the Galaxy*, which is entirely based on the quest for "The meaning of life, the universe and everything" and comes up with the rather disappointing answer: "forty-two."

John Gay, the author of *The Beggar's Opera*, wrote: "Life is a jest and all things show it; I thought so once and now I know it." This is what the humorist focuses on: that everyday life is a precarious stage show with flimsy scenery and a badly edited script. The show is so fragile that it can always be subverted by the writer who pulls back the curtain and reveals the masquerade.

WORD GAMES AND DIALOGUE

We normally assume that one word means one thing or, in those cases where words have double and triple meanings, that the context will make it clear.

> *When my love swears that she is made of truth*
> *I do believe her, though I know she lies*

Thus begins Shakespeare's 138th sonnet, leading into a hall of mirrors and verbal paradoxes that play with the double meaning of "lie" in Elizabethan English. We laugh, perhaps a little uneasily, when the meanings become unsteady. Millions of ancient jokes rely on this technique.

> A duck walks into a store and says, "Gimme some Chap Stick, and put it on my bill."

Word games are funny, up to a point. But, unless you are the next James Joyce, an extended piece of fiction cannot rest entirely on the dazzling elaboration of language. From the reader's point of view, it becomes tiresome and too much like hard work to figure out a deluge of puns, double entendres, oxymorons, palindromes, and so on.

Smart-talking characters, very facile with language, are a good way of bringing word play into your fiction. Consider this exchange between a mother and her four-year-old daughter, from Mark Leyner's story "Tinker, Tailor, Toddler, Spy."

> "One song and you go to sleep. One. That's it."
> "But Daddy sings me lots of songs."
> "Your father's weak, he's easily manipulated."
> "I know that, Mommy."
> "It's wrong to take advantage."
> "I know; he's so . . . so . . ."

"Acquiescent? Pliable? Docile? Spineless?"

"He's such a . . . such a . . ."

"Doormat? Patsy? Sucker?"

"Yeah. Sucker."

The precocious child, the superior mother, and the idiot father are ancient comedy stereotypes. But we get a wry smile from this exchange, just because the words flow so well.

THE SIMPLE TRUTH IS FUNNY

"If I want to tell a joke, I tell the truth: There's nothing funnier," said Bernard Shaw. And it is possible to get a comic effect simply by writing the plain truth—saying things that everyone has been dying to say but didn't because they might be accused of political incorrectness or bad taste. We have so many sacred cows that if you start shooting you can hardly miss. The language is packed with wimpish euphemisms like "rest room," "correctional facility," "senior citizens," and "downsizing." Because euphemisms are both transparent *and* dishonest, they have great humor potential. Try losing the euphemisms and allowing one or more of your characters to talk in plain words.

Unfortunately, truth hurts, and it's all too easy for the humorist to be blamed for condoning racism, ageism, sexism, weightism, and everything not nice. People write to me every week and say, "How *dare* you make fun of foreign taxi drivers" (or antique collectors, or gardeners, or old people, or joggers, or whatever). I always reply courteously that I *wasn't* making fun but simply pointing out some unwelcome facts. There are so many groups just *waiting* to be offended by the most trivial slight that I despair of finishing the list in my lifetime. Ask yourself, What is usually *not* said? and you probably have an opening for humor.

SATIRE AS A LETHAL WEAPON

Satire is the opposite of truth telling. Satire is a big lie mobilized to get a comic effect. Sometimes the lie is mere exaggeration, sometimes it is a complete invention. Either way, satire is an attack weapon. It inflates the faults and foibles of powerful people or conventional ideas, with the intention of making them look ridiculous. "Humor belongs to the losers," said Garrison Keillor, and that's what satire is about. It's a kind of revenge, often very sweet and always tinged with anger.

Jonathan Swift was the father of modern satire. In scathing books like *A Tale of a Tub*, *The Battle of the Books*, and *Gulliver's Travels*, Swift mocked the pretensions and prejudices of his own time. His technique was quite simple and works as well today as it did in the 1700s. He picked his target, imagined a fantastic metaphor, and exaggerated everything. For example, in *Gulliver*, he created a deadly satire on prejudice with the story of the "Big Endians" and the "Little Endians," two groups locked in eternal battle over which end to open a boiled egg.

Kurt Vonnegut and Joseph Heller crafted marvelous satires on the Second World War, using Swift's tools of exaggeration, fantasy, and aggressive ridicule. But contemporary satire is harder. Politics and popular culture have moved almost beyond the reach of ridicule. It's difficult to come up with something so bizarre that it won't actually happen before your piece appears in print, or even before you find a stamp and mail it. So satire can be risky for a fiction writer, who always risks being upstaged by reality.

DON'T FORGET THE VISUALS

Writing humor for readers is profoundly different from writing for a stage or TV performance. There's nothing to help your words along: no visuals, no funny acting, no sound effects or voice tricks, no reliable audience response. Cartoonist Gary Larson could surprise us into laughter with a simple sketch of cows drinking martinis in a field. Jerry Seinfeld or Jay Leno can reinforce their jokes with facial expressions and body language. But a writer has only words on paper, and has to work twice as hard to get the same effect.

This is the classic case where you must show rather than tell. How do your characters *look*, how do they move, how do they sound, what damage are they doing to their immediate environment? Here's a scene from Michael Bond's mystery novel *Monsieur Pamplemousse on the Spot*. The setting is a very exclusive French restaurant, and Pommes Frites is a bloodhound.

> . . . a large, wet, freshly vaselined nose reappeared on the other side of the window, and pressed itself firmly against a fresh area of glass. Monsieur Pamplemousse gave a sigh. Pommes Frites was being more than a little difficult that evening. He shuddered to think what the outside of the window would be like when it caught the rays of the morning sun.

HOLD THE JOKES

The joke is the primordial form of humor. When we want to be funny in company, we tell jokes, because jokes are economical, easy to remember, and easy to understand. If you like telling jokes, keep them for the next party. They don't work well in fiction. Jokes are a performance art, and joke-telling characters are always a bore.

Instead, create funny characters, who will naturally say funny things.

A FUNNY CHARACTER IS A CARICATURE

Funny characters are unusual, strange, odd, perhaps obnoxious, and always extreme. Your friends and family are *not* funny characters, not even your eccentric Aunt Edna. A truly comic character is a caricature, a creature of the author's imagination.

Consider how Charles Dickens introduces the character of Scrooge in *A Christmas Carol*.

> Oh! But he was a tight-fisted hand at the grindstone, Scrooge!
> A squeezing, wrenching, grasping, scraping, clutching, covetous
> old sinner. Hard and sharp as flint, from which no steel had
> ever struck out generous fire, secret, and self-contained, and
> solitary as an oyster.

No modern author has the luxury of so many adjectives, and this description goes on in the same vein for another three hundred words! But the point is made. Scrooge is extreme in his prejudices and behavior, bizarre in his appearance and daily habits, and has a horrible effect on other people. Once you have met him, you can never forget him. That's the essence of a good caricature.

It helps if your character has a funny name, like Scrooge. The enchanted weaver in Shakespeare's *A Midsummer Night's Dream* is called Bottom. The two leading characters in Bond's successful series of French gastronomic mysteries, quoted previously, are Monsieur Pamplemousse (grapefruit) and his talented dog, Pommes Frites (french fries). It's hard to raise a smile with a character called Jones.

Funny characters are often divided or conflicted. They act one way and think another, play a role badly, or try unsuccessfully to bring two aspects of their personalities together. A character who *wants* to be chaste but can't quite manage it, or who tries and fails to be promiscuous, is always good for a laugh. A funny character is eternally on the edge of the precipice, like James Thurber's everyman, with a precarious grip on reality. The character's struggle to cope with life is funny, because it is doomed to failure.

Cruel as it sounds, humor does come from tormenting your characters with psychological, sexual, social, and financial conflicts. They have to suffer—to be humiliated, confused, worried. Noble and good characters are an unfunny bore. Miguel de Cervantes and Voltaire perfected the type of the naive character who understands nothing that is going on in the world (or pretends not to). James Thurber perfected the character who can never win.

STRANGE SETTINGS AND AWKWARD SITUATIONS

Although humor can be set anywhere, it can be helped into orbit by dropping your characters into a setting that's funny in itself. Look for the off-key, weird, and inappropriate setting, a place where your characters don't quite belong, a setting rife with opportunities for tension, incongruity, disaster, and embarrassment. Dump your characters in places where they don't understand the language or don't know how to behave. In his novel *East Is East*, T. Coraghessan Boyle has his protagonist, a young monoglot Japanese seaman, washed ashore on the coast of Georgia, in an artists' colony surrounded on all sides by rednecks. In Samuel Beckett's *Molloy*, first love happens in a garbage dump.

Even a slight shift in perspective can bring out the humor in a familiar genre. The popular crime stories of Lindsey Davis are set in ancient Rome. Her wisecracking Roman detective, Marcus Didius Falco, knows how to set the scene. Here's the irresistible opening of *A Dying Light in Corduba*.

> Nobody was poisoned at the dinner of the Society of Olive Oil Producers of Baetica—though in retrospect, that was quite a surprise. Had I realized that Anacrites the Chief Spy would be present, I would myself have taken a small vial of toad's blood concealed in my napkin and ready for use. . . . Me first if possible. Rome owed me that.

COMICAL PLOTS AND UNLIKELY CONNECTIONS

Extreme characters in strange situations tend to create funny plots all by themselves. A perfectly straightforward genre plot—romance or mystery—can be full of humor created by character, situation, and dialogue. Jane Austen and Charles Dickens wrote wonderfully funny fictions without ever resorting to crazy plot devices.

But if you can make the plot itself funny, so much the better. Simple twists and reversals on standard plotlines can be enough to bring out their comic possibilities (the hero is the villain, the corpse is not dead, the femme fatale is a transvestite). *The Hitchhiker's Guide to the Galaxy*, mentioned earlier, has an insanely complicated plot that begins with the destruction of the earth and proceeds to trash and satirize every science fiction device ever invented.

Most fiction plots aren't like that. They have serious and funny passages, and the transition between the two can be a challenge. In a play, the scene can change. In a novel, the author can start a new chapter to smooth the bump between funny and serious. The short story writer has a problem, which can best be solved by using *bathos*, the sudden, jolting drop from serious to funny. The reverse transition is almost impossible to manage gracefully in a short piece.

THE HUMOR WRITER'S TOOL KIT

The sources of humor are infinite. Make your own list of the devices that work best for you. But here's a starter tool kit: Reach into it whenever you are stuck for a humor idea. First, the two big ones.

Exaggeration. This is one of the oldest and most reliable humor devices. Take a look at the unlikely memoirs of Baron von Münchhausen as told by Rudolph Erich Raspe, or any of Mark Twain's tall tales. Only a very little exaggeration is necessary. Consider this description of a New York cab ride by Dave Barry.

> . . . the taxi has some kind of problem with the steering, probably dead pedestrians lodged in the mechanism, the result being that there is a delay of eight to 10 seconds between the time the driver turns the wheel and the time the taxi actually changes direction, a handicap that the driver is compensating for by going 175 miles an hour, at which velocity we are able to remain airborne almost to the far rim of some of the smaller potholes.

Understatement. " 'Tis but a scratch," says the Black Knight, in *Monty Python and the Holy Grail*, when both his arms have been cut off. The imperturbable valet Jeeves in the stories of P.G. Wodehouse is never ruffled by any disaster. A narrator or character with the habit of relentless understatement is one of the oldest and most reliable comic devices.

But there are dozens of reliable humor techniques. Here are a few, and your imagination will suggest how to build the list.

- *Intrusion* of the unexpected word, phrase, person, or event.
- *Reversal or substitution* of words, identities, conventional wisdoms, or behaviors.
- *Anachronism*: that particular form of incongruity where *time* is dislocated.
- *Failure and humiliation,* incompetence and embarassment.
- *Miscommunication and misunderstanding.*
- *Absurdity and fantasy*: Nothing is too wild to try!
- *Bathos*: Pride comes before a fall.
- *Insane logical progressions,* the most famous being Joseph Heller's manic explanation of "the catch" in *Catch-22.*
- *Parody*: a tricky technique, because readers must know the original to understand the parody, but worth a try with mainstream culture themes.

HUMOR WRITING IS GOOD WRITING

Great humor writers were and are *good writers* first and foremost. Slow and difficult humor is a contradiction in terms. Humor must be easy to read and transparent. It should announce itself in the first line and move relentlessly forward with something funny in every paragraph.

George Orwell's famous advice in his essay "Politics and the English Language" is doubly true for humor: Use short, simple words, short sentences, the active voice, no clichés, and *if you can cut, then cut.* Shakespeare said it even more pithily: "Brevity is the soul of wit."

EXERCISES

1. You are a junior curator at the Smithsonian Institute in Washington, DC. Crazy people from all over the country send you objects that they have found, or dug up, and that they think may be of historical or archeological interest. You have just received such an object (it can be anything), and your task is to write a letter to the donor explaining *politely* why his great discovery is a useless piece of junk.

2. A man and a woman are in conversation. He is telling her about the problems in his relationship with his auto mechanic. She is telling him about the problems in *their* relationship. Neither realizes that they are not communicating.

3. An American tourist in Turkey has ventured into the remote, nontouristy villages of Anatolia. The tourist (male or female) is tall and handsome, speaks nothing but English, and is uneasy in this strange setting. The inhabitants of a small village decide that the tourist is the long-foretold reincarnation of Alexander the Great (or choose your own historical figure), who has come to lead them to glory and save them from their dismal and boring lives. The tourist very slowly begins to understand what is going on.

David Bouchier is the award-winning weekly essayist for National Public Radio stations WSHU, WSUF, and WMMM and writes a weekly humor column called "Out of Order" for the regional editions of the Sunday *New York Times*. He teaches at the State University of New York at Stony Brook and the New School in New York and has led humor-writing workshops at the Iowa Summer Writing Festival, the Cape Cod Writers' Conference, the Chautauqua Writers' Conference, and many others. His essays and short stories have appeared in many newspapers and magazines in Britain and the United States. The most recent of his four books, *The Accidental Immigrant*, was published in 1996, and his new volume of essays and stories, *Only in America*, is scheduled for publication in 1999.

VI
Revising, Editing, and Marketing

What Stories Teach Their Writers: The Purpose and Practice of Revision

JANE SMILEY

While I was teaching, I devised several elaborate ways to get the students to revise and enjoy it. The graduate students, given their semipro status, were required to come up with four drafts of four stories, sixteen drafts over a semester. The undergraduate students, who had lots of other things to do and hadn't yet committed themselves to fiction writing, were given a series of playful exercises that asked them to look at their material over and over again in new ways, in an effort to spark and enrich their imaginations. The purpose, however, turned out to be the same—to beguile or to require the students to learn to do what every writer has to learn to do—come at each piece of work again and again with as close as he can get to a new mind and a new sense of joy.

While writers most often think they are writing their work—that is, that they have a thought or two that they are putting down on paper and that they're directing these thoughts from beginning to end to communicate something already present in their minds to the reader—writing is more complex than that. Revision has everything to do with learning both what you are writing and how to write it.

TEACHING AND LEARNING

Your first duty, if you want to become a writer, is to become teachable, that is, to become receptive. The desire to be a writer, even the desire to write, does not, per se, make you teachable. In fact, every teacher in every writing class has to spend a fair amount of time, sometimes most of her time, showing the students how to become teachable, that is, how to listen to what others are saying about their stories and how not to resist but how to receive. But you do not need a human teacher. Your own writing can teach you all you need to know, if, once again, you do not resist it.

At first glance, writing appears to be an aggressive act. We come up with some thoughts or a story, take up a pen or sit down at a computer, and put words on the paper or the screen, and the words create something. The thing created is a mental object. It does not exist outside of the mind, the way a painting does or a piece of music does, but it seems to have some of the other qualities of objects. It is self-contained. It is rooted in the world. It makes sense. It is possessable. It belongs, in fact, to the writer, and the writer understandably wants to protect her object. But for the writer at this stage to possess the story to the point of protecting it is to defeat the process of writing itself.

For one thing, writing is not an aggressive act at all. On the contrary, it is a receptive and a responsive act, a process by which the writer assimilates what is seen, heard, touched, and felt—and then responds by molding what's been assimilated into something new. In revising, even the molding becomes a receptive act.

Moreover, if you are observant, receptive, and fluid in your approach, if you understand that your work in progress is not yet an object and not yet ready to be owned by you or anyone else, and if you have faith that what you arrive at will be better than what you began with—that is, more complex, more interesting, and more valuable to you and to the reader—you really do not need an actual human teacher. You have become a learner of writing on your own.

For example, think about waking in the morning and telling a dream. Almost always, when you are telling a dream to someone else, the only thing that interests him about your dream is whether and how he himself appeared in it, and how you felt about that. If he has not appeared, he tends to view the dream as a symptom of some pathology on your part, and he tries to intrude upon your dream with some interpretation of his own. As a *story*, your dream will usually be disjointed, random, and without certain essential connections and facts. In your telling, you may try to plead for the fascination or the importance of the dream, repeatedly drawing your friend's attention to this or that aspect of the dream, but you will readily see that he is unconvinced. Perhaps you will only get a shrug and the response, "Well, that's pretty interesting." But don't lose heart. In unsuccessfully telling your dream, you have learned the first lesson of story writing: that your idea is far more interesting to you than to anyone else, and that you need to work with it, formalize, and understand it before you can communicate it in a way that makes your friend, or any audience, want it for his own.

SOURCES OF STORIES/CONNECTING THE ELEMENTS

Not many stories begin in dreams, but most do begin with something that is idiosyncratic to the writer. For me, gossip is a great inspiration. Little bits of stories about the strange ways that people interact always pique my interest and get me thinking about why such a thing might have happened, what points of view the protagonists brought to the incident, and what the antecedent events might have been. I once wrote a story called "Long Distance" that began in a friend's Christmas visit to her relatives. On Christmas Eve, she heard her sisters-in-law having a *sotto voce* argument about the wrapping of the Christmas presents. Sister-in-law A had wrapped presents for her eight- and ten-year-old children in a certain paper, and sister-in-law B had also used that paper to wrap family presents for her two-year-old. A wanted to preserve the illusion of Santa Claus for her children, and so she wanted B to rewrap the two-year-old's presents in some other paper so that the eight- and ten-year-old wouldn't make the connection between their presents and those of the two-year-old. I have to say that almost every feature of this anecdote seemed outrageous to me, beginning with the fact that the eight- and ten-year-olds still believed in Santa Claus, and ending with the fact that sister-in-law A, the guest, was not offering to rewrap, but asking B, the hostess, who had already put on a series of meals, to do the extra work. Obviously, I did not have the whole story here. Probably there were mitigating circumstances but my sense of the strangeness and outrage of this incident was enough to make me want to do something with this anecdote. It wasn't a story yet, but I thought that later some things might be added to it, or it might draw other ideas to it—and eventually all of the ideas together might reveal some connections not apparent on the surface.

And, in fact, this is exactly what happened. More gossip, more stories, not really related at all except by being present together in my mind, and the whole story of "Long Distance" began to build. I believe this building took several weeks or a month. A certain amount of patient holding of all these things in my mind was required, and patience is one of the first signs that the writer is teachable—teachable by the world, not by a teacher.

On a larger scale, I had a notion of an idea about *King Lear* long before I ever began or even thought of my novel *A Thousand Acres*. Perhaps twenty years passed between the first thoughts that became *A Thousand Acres* and the actual coalescing of the thoughts that I began with when I started to write. Some five or six years went by after I got the idea for *The Greenlanders* before I knew I was ready to write. In fact, I got the first notions of *A Thousand Acres* before I got the first notions of *The Greenlanders*, but I began *The Greenlanders* and finished it before I was ready to write *A Thousand Acres*. This illustrates, I think, one of the benefits of patience, especially patience that doesn't know it is patience, which perhaps should be called faith.

For me, one of the principal fascinations of writing a rough draft is seeing connections and relationships between disparate bits of raw material that have swum into each other's neighborhood. In the story "Long Distance," the disparate elements were the anecdote of the sisters-in-law, a longer anecdote that another friend told me about a phone call he made to Japan, and the very small detail of another friend of mine saying, when told that it was twenty-two below zero, "Refreshing, isn't it?" Added to this were several thoughts I had on my own—when a parent insists that a child should eat something or perform some other bodily function over the opposition of the child, is the parent claiming unfairly to possess the child's body? What does it mean to have your chair and television arranged so that they are facing each other? What does the landscape of north central Iowa look like in the winter? The joy here is feeling these elements, which did not seem to be connected, flow together into a coherent story, and the challenge is, once you have gotten nearly to the end, to find the way they click together in some sort of meaningful whole that the reader can understand.

In *A Thousand Acres*, the disparate elements were the play *King Lear*, farming in the American Midwest, the history of capitalism, the meaning of landscape, environmental degradation, and feminism. "Long Distance" posed an interesting thematic task. *A Thousand Acres* posed a strenuous and sometimes exhausting and dispiriting challenge, but the process was the same with both. I knew all the elements had connections, or they would not have come together in my mind. But I also knew that finding all the connections wouldn't necessarily come easily or instantly.

This is what revision is for.

TYPES OF REVISION

There are several types of revision. What we are taught in high school is essentially polishing—finding the right word, collapsing or expanding some ideas that aren't clear, adding examples. By the time you have decided you are a fiction writer, you have mastered this sort of revision. It isn't always easy, but it's just part of the job.

In a second form of revision, the writer is undecided about where she is going, and keeps adding and deleting parts. Each change causes a major shift in the point the author is making and, I think, shows the writer is quite confused about the focus, the audience, the action, or the facts. Going back to the material may or may not be helpful with this sort of larger problem. For real revision to begin, it is essential for the writer to push all the way to the end of the first draft, no matter how awkward the draft seems, for hidden in the rough draft, as rough as it can possibly be, are all the answers to the writer's questions about the material. But all the questions have to be asked, and they are not asked until the whole arc of the story is complete on the page and in the writer's mind. Some authors, many of them well known, do not hold with this view, and they clean as they go. But they are of a different cast of mind than I am, and perhaps know their stories better than I know mine.

A third form of revision involves a failure to commit to the particular elements of a story or novel, its characters and events. I once had a student who was overflowing with imagination. He would sit down, enter a kind of trance, and stand up four or five hours later with a completed story. The removal of any particular brick, though, would collapse the whole building. He would come to class a week later with what seemed to be an entirely different story, with different characters and different actions, and swear that the two stories were the same, though no one in the class could see it. We had to work hard to teach this student how to focus on what he had already written and fix it, rather than discarding it and hoping to get struck by lightning again.

LISTENING TO THE DRAFT

When writing the first draft, the writer has had to be receptive to the world and the feelings that inspired him; when beginning to revise, he must be receptive to what has already been written, and is there on the page, full of mysteries and clues. The first idea you need to give up when you begin to revise is that you know what this story is about. In reality, you have some memories of what you thought the story was about, and some other memories of things you stuck in that weren't quite right, and, in many cases, no memory at all of some other things you stuck in, and, once in a while, memories of things you thought you stuck in but didn't. All of these memories have now become obsolete. All you have, the best thing that you could have, is what is actually on the paper. Your story is a success, because it is a whole. You can relax now. Your only task is to let what you have talk back to you and teach you what is missing or superfluous or not quite right, and then to suggest what would be better than what you have. It's helpful, and true, also, to think of the draft you have as containing both what it is and what it will be, just as a piece of marble is said to contain the sculpture within it already. All the artist has to do is find it.

What your rough draft contains is the whole system of the story you have been thinking about, the choices you've made and the other possible choices, too. It contains this because you have had more thoughts about the story than you have put down on the paper, and you have also had more thoughts about the story than you have consciously thought. Your mind is larger than your intellect and works in other ways than simply through your intellect. You have had feelings, intuitions, observations, perceptions, and ideas that are not written down but that have been part of your mind while you were working on and around this rough draft. The rough draft as it stands harkens toward these more shadowy parts of the story, and they will be available to you if you can recognize their presence. But since they are shadowy, you have to develop a heightened sensitivity to what is in your rough draft; you have to be receptive to what you have written as if your memories of writing referred to above are not significant. The art of revision lies in not pressing your self upon the story. The story has now made the first step in separating itself from you. It will not live unless it separates itself from you entirely, and it can't do that unless you are receptive to what it is trying to be.

CONNECTING TO LITERATURE

On a basic level, every fiction writer attests to the experience of having a character come to life in an unexpected way. A minor character seems to take over the narrative and be more lively than the major character. Scenes that were meant as filler turn out to be central to the narrative, whereas big set pieces lie dead at the writer's feet. Characters that were meant to last get forgotten. Characters who started out as Joe end up as Bob. Almost all seasoned fiction writers welcome such experiences precisely because when a character takes on a life of his own, he is more interesting to write about and he is making a promise that the story or novel is coming alive. The piece is also separating itself from the dream life of the writer and entering the world of literature.

Every novel or story has dual citizenship. It is an experience and an event in the life of the writer, but it is also an event in the life of the culture. Just as we can see the writer reaching out, assimilating literature, and then producing something, we can also see the history of literature looping through an individual consciousness and pulling something out of it. On one hand, we have a cascading series of lives; on the other, we have a library full of books. Each category is autonomous; I like to think of the writer producing a book, but also of the writer entering into the world of books and being produced, as a writer, by all the books that have come before. It is this, I think, that is your goal. Your rough draft contains a multitude of references to literature, both those that you intended to put there and those that you didn't. Part of your revising process will be to recognize and strengthen your work's connections to other works. This, too, is part of its separation from you, part of the life that it takes on.

A work of fiction connects to literature first through formal story elements. It has characters, plot, theme, style, and setting. As a reader, of course, you recognize these elements in other works of fiction, and now, revising, you become a reader of your own work, who consults her responses to the rough draft in order to understand what is present and what is missing. You must not allow your ego, or your sense of possessing the work, to make special claims for it, but nor must you allow your ego to be unforgiving. You are striving to read your rough draft analytically and diagnostically. It is neither good nor bad. It is simply a work in progress. Judging it is not your job. Understanding it is.

ELEMENTS OF FICTION
Other essays in this book discuss elements of fiction in some detail. But I want to touch briefly on a few here, especially as they relate to revision.

Plot
What is usually missing in works by inexperienced writers is the whole arc of the plot. A plot is a simple, formal, organizational device that

almost always develops some sort of conflict. The conflict may be between two characters or within one character. Some fiction lacks conflict, but successful stories without it are few and far between, and, since a plot is primarily organizational, it is *essential* that you learn how to make one. A plot has four parts: exposition (naming the protagonists, defining the nature of the conflict, giving the protagonists a place to be), rising action (the longest part of the story, which develops the conflict, which in turn reveals more and more about the protagonists and the themes), the climax (the largest and most dramatic piece of the conflict, which sets the protagonists more in opposition to one another, reveals the themes most clearly, and sets up the terms of the resolution of the story), and the denouement (the resolution of the climax, which brings the conflict to a state of equilibrium and suggests the meaning of the conflict, either implicitly or explicitly). When you thoroughly understand these plot elements, you will much more readily and easily diagnose what seems to be wrong with your story.

These are the nuts and bolts of fiction writing, the foundation, the basic ingredients. If you reject them or don't understand them, you will always be more or less in a state of confusion when you rewrite. When you first reread your rough draft, you need to ask yourself: Is it clear who the characters are? Is it clear what the conflict is, and whom it is between? Does the reader have a concrete sense of where the characters are in space and time? Are there enough steps between the exposition and the climax so that the nuances of the conflict are fully developed and the climax is understandable? Is there a climax, or is the climax implied rather than depicted? Is the climax well choreographed and easy for the reader to imagine? Is the meaning of the conflict apparent in the climax? Is the relationship between the protagonist and the antagonist clear in the climax? Is the climax dramatic enough, long enough, weighty enough to balance the length of the rising action? Does the denouement get the reader gracefully and meaningfully out of the climax? Does the denouement bring the story to a state of equilibrium?

In my opinion, all of these questions must be asked and answered for you to understand your story. They seem to dictate a certain traditional type of story, but, in fact, even the most experimental fiction contains answers to these questions.

After you have asked these questions of your rough draft, and your rough draft has answered them, you will know your next step. One of the wonderful things about an organized approach to your rough draft is that you don't have to worry about it. Each step leads logically to the next. There are also close relationships between the parts of the story. What is missing in one part has to do with what is missing in another part, and the parts will talk back and forth through you to each other.

For example, often the ending of a story does not work. You cannot fix this by working on the ending, but only by working on the beginning. The problem with every denouement is in the exposition, and so a bad ending indicates you need to better understand the situation you have set up. A missing climax, also a frequent problem, is not a choice on your part to be nontraditional. It is a confession that you don't know what the conflict is or what it means. The climax is the absolute crux of the story. It is where everything comes together—the characters and what they think of themselves and each other, the meaning of their conflict, the meaning of their lives, the meaning of the action. The climax is where the writer's style rises to its best self, and where the writer's ability to organize is most crucial. It is very tempting to avoid the climax for all of these reasons, but it is the reader's reward. If you avoid it, you have reneged on your contract to provide the reader with something interesting. *You must not stop before the climax or skip over it.*

Problems with the rising action are easier to solve. If you are arriving at the climax too quickly, you simply give yourself an arbitrary number of pages to fill before you allow yourself to get to the climax. If you are meandering, you make yourself cut part of the rising action. Eventually, you will learn the proper balance between rising action and climax and know instinctively when they are out of balance.

Now you have looked at the problems of the rough draft in an organized way and done your first revision. What is in the story already has suggested to you what might still be needed, and even at the stylistic level, words you have already written have suggested what else you might write.

You must keep revising at this level until you have solved your plot problems. Plot problems are so basic that to attach yourself to anything in the story when the plot is still unfinished is to break up the flow of the revision process and unnecessarily protract your work on the story. The good news is that plot problems can always be solved. They are technical in nature. They are about the story being a story, not about you being you.

Characters

While fixing your plot problems, you'll discover that you don't know as much about the characters or the action as you thought you did, but you have learned more about both. Now they interest you more than before. A good revision should involve you more deeply in your work and make you more eager to get at it. As a good reviser, you will gain two boons. First, your work will get better, and so will be more likely to get published. Second, you will like doing it so much that you will care less and less about whether it ever gets published. Your relationship to the work itself and to the process of working will be strengthened.

Your next phase has to do with fleshing out characters, setting, parts of the rising action, that is, supplying more context for the plot. The context of the plot consists of who the characters are, what they say and how they say it, how they fit into the setting, what the setting means to them, how they view the conflict, what their intentions as they enter actions, how the action modifies their intentions, what their backgrounds are. At this stage of revision, you can see what's missing and can enjoy making the necessary changes.

For example, let's say the rising action was truncated in the first draft, and you had to lengthen it to balance with the climax. You discovered that you didn't know enough about your subject, whaling, to write convincingly about the rising action. Solving this problem is easy—do some research. Either you go whaling or you read about it, or you change the whaling to bass fishing, something you know well. When you have done your research to fill out the rising action, you will know much more about the characters, the setting, and what might happen. Or, let's say, your rising action is long and boring and doesn't go anywhere. In cutting several scenes and combining some others, you will make your characters quicker, more lively, and more interesting, even for you.

Style

One of the great rules of fiction writing is that style goes along for the ride. You do not need to work on your style in the sense that you need to use original language. You only need to work on your style in the sense that you need to use precise language. When your understanding of your characters and your plot and your setting is specific enough, your style will be specific, too. Your style reflects your knowledge of the situation and your attitude toward it. If you can't make a plot or develop context, you don't know enough about your piece to fix it

253

stylistically. Style without plot or context is a form of corruption; the originality of style is an attempt to cover ignorance. Fortunately, though, this corruption isn't immoral. It's only boring.

The comic form makes the most stylistic demands, and successful comic novelists, like T. Coraghessan Boyle and Garrison Keillor, are wonderful stylists. Their work bears studying so that you can understand their diction choices and their sense of timing. A wonderful comic style, though, just like any other style, grows out of the fact that the novelist understands more about his material than he is letting on—every word of every sentence communicates, at the very least, what is happening (action) and the author's attitude toward it (tone). It may also communicate the characters' attitudes toward the action, toward each other, and how the reader's attitude toward it all is supposed to differ from the characters'. There may also be references to other works or other aspects of the culture, all collapsed together in a delightful and economical way. An author's style develops—I once edited a book of first short stories of famous writers, and I noticed that most of the stories weren't as interesting stylistically as the authors' later, more mature work.

But I would not say that authors actually have much control over their styles. Your style grows out of who you are. This said, in the last draft of your story, it is both wise and fun to try various word choices, sentence types, and rhythms. Fiddling with the wording is very enlightening, and you should feel no hesitation in owning and using a good thesaurus, but not a dictionary-type thesaurus. A thesaurus that is organized by category into groups of related words is harder to learn to use but helps you expand your vocabulary, and sometimes gives you good stylistic ideas. But even if you use a thesaurus, working on the words will make the story more and more idiosyncratically yours.

KNOWING WHEN YOU'RE FINISHED

You have now finished revising your story. How do you know that? Well, you are rather tired of it. You can't think of what else it needs. It no longer seems flexible to you—if you were to change some large piece of it, it would fall apart. It holds together. You know more about the material than you have put on paper, but if you added something, it would be a little repetitive. There is nothing that you *want* to add. Now you may decide whether you like it or not. Chances are you do like it, because you have invested yourself in it more and more all through the revision process.

In approaching your story in a forgiving and receptive way, you have taken a considerable amount of the tedium and fear out of revising. You have gotten closer to the story and more interested in it; you have come to know it. It is now thoroughly yours and yet thoroughly itself. It is as good as you can make it, which is better than you could have made it (better than you did make it) before you revised it. It is not as good as you will make stories in the future, but you have done what you can with this one. It is time to sell it. Good luck.

EXERCISES

1. Reread a rough draft and ask yourself: Is it clear who the characters are? Is it clear what the conflict is and whom it is between? Does the reader have a concrete sense of where the characters are in space and time? Are there enough steps between the exposition and the climax so that the nuances of the conflict are fully developed and the climax is understandable? Is there a climax, or is the climax implied rather than depicted? Is the climax well choreographed and easy for the reader to imagine? Is the meaning of the conflict apparent in the climax? Is the relationship between the protagonist and the antagonist clear in the climax? Is the climax dramatic enough, long enough, weighty enough to balance the length of the rising action? Does the denouement get the reader gracefully and meaningfully out of the climax? Does the denouement bring the story to a state of equilibrium? Make the necessary adjustments.

2. Examine the ending of a story in progress. Try to solve problems in the ending by revising the beginning.

3. Choose a story or a scene that is in good shape, and edit it for style—word choice, sentence structure, rhythm, and tone. Revise, edit, and polish so that the writing is as good as you can make it.

Jane Smiley, winner of the Pulitzer prize for her novel *A Thousand Acres*, is the author of twelve books, including *Moo* and her most recent, *The All-True Travels and Adventures of Lidie Newton*. She has taught at a variety of universities, including The Iowa Writers Workshop and the Iowa State University in Ames. She currently resides in California.

Eleven Style Considerations You Can't Live Without: Editing and Polishing

ALBERTO RÍOS

Punctuation is power. It's that simple—and that scary. Its power, of course, is an acknowledgment of the strange fact that we take English for at least twelve years, from first grade through high school, and still we say, "I don't know." Dashes and apostrophes and colons continue to make us hesitate: "Where oh where is that style manual?" we might say. Or, we might also say, "style manual?" Oh well, c'est la vie. Or papier-mâché. Or El Niño. Whatever.

Hmm. I could go on with this, of course. In the preceding paragraph, I run through some of the most common punctuation hot spots that, as writers, we know we should know. But perhaps not. (Hey, was that a sentence fragment?) Wait, should there be a period outside those parentheses?

You get the idea.

Well, punctuation is your friend. Punctuation is a set of traffic signals. Or whatever other metaphor you'd like to use. The part we need to understand is that it isn't going away anytime soon, so make up the spare bedroom in your novel and be pleased that commas don't eat much.

The first good question is, Who makes up these rules? Nobody actually makes them up. Usage—something we are all guilty of—finally defines punctuation. Understand, however, that I mean public, historical, ongoing usage, not the casual, uninformed, or individual decision to not worry about an apostrophe. We don't have to like the consensus definitions, but there they are regardless. I have wondered more than once if the writers of style manuals are heavily invested in red lead.

There are a number of style manuals or style sheets, all quite legitimate but protecting their own fields of study. Psychologists have the

APA, or American Psychological Association, publication manual. Journalists use the AP, or Associated Press, guidelines. And so on. Some of us still use the default manual—that is, whatever our high school typing teacher told us to do. If I recall those days correctly, our Gregg typing book told us to—when we were using dashes—leave spaces between them. You're going to hate this, now, but cut that out. That's not the actual rule, no matter how long you've been doing it. Please don't take me off your holiday card list.

The idea here is simple, however. Find—don't simply guess at—the set of rules that most closely reflects the kind of writing you do. And be comforted by knowing that style manuals, including rules about punctuation, agree far more than they disagree.

For writers, there are two good style choices: the *MLA Handbook for Writers of Research Papers* published by the Modern Language Association and *The Chicago Manual of Style*. The MLA guide is often thought to be more closely associated with universities, while *The Chicago Manual of Style* is less associated with any one writing area, but this is a generalization. Either of these will serve you well, but you must find one or the other and look through it with some attention. And know that it is there when you need it. The APA style is also used in many fields, including some kinds of writing.

Abstracting from these style books, let me address the more straightforward punctuation issues raised in the first paragraph by giving you simple, direct advice. And a little more than that where I can't help myself.

THE RULES

1. Apostrophes. If you learn only one thing with authority today, it must be the difference between *its* and *it's*. This is not a true style point; it is simple spelling. But nothing betrays a writer more. The problem is a little like the game of rock-paper-scissors. While a possessive normally takes an apostrophe, a contraction spelled the same way overrules the possessive. So, *it's* is a contraction for "it is," or "it was," or variations thereof. *Its* is the possessive for the pronoun "it." "It's a shame that the dog lost its tail."

2. Dashes. You can look this up. According to the MLA, "[t]o indicate a dash in typing, use two hyphens, with no space before, between, or after." It's amazing but true—like this.

3. Next, acknowledgment. This raises the broader question of English spellings over American spellings, though this is sometimes not a question at all—we simply don't recognize the difference. Perhaps nowhere is this more evident for writers than in the spelling of *acknowledgments*. The British use an extra *e*—*acknowledgements*. The same is true with *gray* and *grey*: The easy way to remember this is that *a* is American, *e* is English.

That's the easy way to remember it, but liking the difference is not easy at all. Many people have an emotional attachment to many of these spellings and will defend them to the death. *Grey* just looks and feels better; the word is more, dare we say it, elegant. In fact, this spelling may represent all the wonderful things some of us might have read growing up if we were good readers, in that so much of our published literary heritage in English is, well, English.

The problem with that of course is self-evident, and leads to some interesting examples. My favorite concerns the American space program. Space travel is the quintessential American accomplishment, and something other than war, real or threatened, that defined the sixties. Space travel was the triumph of the end of the era, making the sixties a truly American decade in so many ways. Now as we see rockets become shuttles in the way that Denmark has become Denmarket, we are moving so fast that we aren't stopping to consider the implications of what we are saying to ourselves. The space shuttle *Endeavour* is a perfect example. *Endeavour*, the British spelling, not *endeavor*, the American spelling. Subtle as this may be, and whatever historical nod the name makes, this takes my breath away. The absolute American achievement gets linguistically handed away. We are still a young country in this regard, with a complicated colonial taste still lingering in our mouths.

The bottom line is that the American spelling is the recommended approach in all style manuals if you are writing American English, and computer grammar checkers, such as Grammatik, will be happy to point this out to you as well. The only real exception is when a British spelling is part of a title or name, as in Ye Olde Shoppe. One of course assumes that this is a British spelling, though it's really more of an affectation, which is the danger in all of this. The sharper edge, of course, is that to a young Chicano, or African-American, or whoever is not included by the implications of such a spelling, such a title suggests, "There is nothing for you inside here." It implies not simply English as a language but as a heritage.

4. Spelling. When you misspell something, or show a glaring lapse in grammar or punctuation usage, or simply don't proofread, I trust you less as a writer. And trust is a crucial thing, a tremendous part of the bargain when you are writing, and considering what you are asking of the reader. You need all the trust you can earn. When you misspell something, and I recognize it, then as a reader I know more than the writer at that moment. This is a needless endangering of your effort.

5. Quotation marks. When I was a student, a teacher once came into my first-year composition classroom and wrote the following on the board, saying afterward only one simple, devastating word: "always."

," / ." / "; / ":

What he meant by this was that quotation marks always go outside a comma or a period, even if the word quoted consists of only one letter, as in "I." Always. Once I was at peace with the word "always," nothing ever helped me more, or more quickly.

6. Colons. A colon normally has a complete thought at the beginning, followed by a fragment that amplifies or clarifies that thought. "When I went to the store, I felt something in the fish section: nausea." The word following the colon here is not capitalized. If, however, a complete thought follows the colon, then the word is usually capitalized. "When I went to the store, I felt something: In the fish section, I felt nausea." That's not a great sentence, but you get the idea.

Also, and this is an emotional one, according to the MLA, "Skip only one space after a colon, never two."

7. Semicolons. Mostly, don't use these. They are completely wonderful marks of punctuation, but beware. A semicolon is normally indicative of more structured writing, such as what you might find in a research paper, and must have a complete thought on both sides. "I was happy; I was also ill." You can also use semicolons when introducing a formal list, especially if that list has commas already in use: "I had green beans, almonds, and carrots; fresh shark steak; and coffee."

8. Marks of punctuation in other languages. They can seem overwhelming. But your computer, and certainly your pen, can make these marks. First, start with respect, and everything will be fine; second, don't be afraid to use them. Otherwise, some interesting things occur. In Spanish, for example, many *niños* may have *ninos*—that is, many children may have godfathers. Not many *años*, however, have *anos*—that is, not many years have anuses. You get the idea.

The problem, however, is further complicated by the varieties of machinery around us, which should be helping us and opening up the world. But much of E-mail, for example, doesn't currently transmit these "foreign" characters. What happens today is that, if one is writing in Spanish, a great lore is developing around how many ways people are finding to avoid saying *ano* in place of *año*—someone might write "I work for twelve months," for example. Besides the humor, in a context such as "I work for an *ano (trabajo por un ano)*," the problem is that the word *ano* might be highly readable as is.

If you are using any of the major word processing programs, you will find different ways to insert these characters if you look. In WordPerfect, for example, if you hold down the ALT key and, on the *numeric* keypad—not the numbers at the top of the keyboard—type 164 (ALT-164), you will get an *n* with a tilde over it—*ñ*. Check with your own program's documentation—it can be done, and there's good reason to do it.

9. Paragraphs. What is your paragraph plan? A paragraph is one thing that distinguishes the form of prose, and fiction particularly, from poetry and other genres. The way that a poet might take care of a line—that thing that distinguishes poetry from other art forms—fiction writers must understand and take care of with the tool of paragraphs. Though there are many uses of the paragraph, if nothing else, a paragraph should be able to take care of itself.

We have all the definitions of good paragraph structure from English classes, of course—that a paragraph should be five to eight sentences long, should have a topic sentence, and should dress warmly. These are all good ideas, but in prose writing, you must listen just as much to what your story is telling you, and even requiring of you as a writer. A good paragraph is normally the place for making one thing clear. When you have another thing to say or another person starts to speak, move us. Changing to a new paragraph can and should make a reader feel the difference, the movement, the change.

This is a good tool but often overlooked. At minimum, short paragraphs mean *fast, move, hurry*. Longer paragraphs might mean the opposite. Whatever ethic you establish, be consistent and let the paragraphs help you tell the story. Let the reader, however unconsciously, feel the rhythms and music of the plot.

10. Dialect. Here's where you pursue the moment, and maybe break all the rules. To genuinely create character, here's where you must create your own punctuation and spelling, if that's what your writerly heart tells you. By dialect, I don't so much mean extreme speech; I mean just as well the exceptionally small nuances of a character's vocabulary and rhythms and sparks. All speech is dialect: That's what makes your characters come alive. Writing dialogue is where you can take your biggest chances. Once you use those quotation marks, it's not you the writer talking. It's you the writer listening.

11. Ignore everything I've said. Absolutely. Ignore it all as long as you have something equal or better to offer your page in exchange. And remember that you do not get to follow your story around. It must take care of itself in the world. The one real question that must be clearly answered is whether or not your usage is—or seems to be—based on intent or error. If you give it a tie for a belt and a hat for a shoe, you may or may not have done something new and interesting. Your amusement, however, is its life. Be wise.

BELIEVABILITY

Fiction's cruel burden is that it must be more believable than real life. Fiction writers need all the believability they can get. Correct punctuation, spelling, and grammar—in the right place—are at the very least familiar, which sometimes serves as believability.

Punctuation and the larger issues of grammar give us common ground, even in the middle of what is otherwise fiction. The surrealists themselves, attempting all the while to subvert traditional views, when writing their "prose" nevertheless used standard grammar and punctuation. They recognized the power of connecting the reader to the idea, no matter how briefly. Sometimes called universal grammar or deep structure, the power of so many languages is that when a noun is put where a noun goes, and a verb where a verb goes, and so on, despite what the words actually mean, they will make a kind of sense. This is the gift given to us as writers.

What this all boils down to is that, if you are reading this and have gotten this far, the big lessons are over. You can read, and spell. You know how to write. Writing *well*, however is a separate enterprise altogether. Writing well consists of very small lessons, and every one counts now. It's the small things that will make you great. A comma may seem altogether insignificant to you in a given moment, hardly worth the trouble. If you find that is so, stop right away and smack yourself on the back of the head.

There are two points to remember. As a reader, you can take me anywhere, into any universe, but you can't let go of my hand, and you can't bore me. Not letting go of my hand is what I've been talking about here. Not boring me, that's up to you.

EXERCISE

Here is a small dinner mint of an exercise. Don't look back at the beginning, but you'll recognize this as the very first paragraph of the essay. See if, with some authority, you can spot the problems.

> Punctuation is power. Its that simple—and that scary. It's power, of course, is an acknowledgement of the strange fact that we take English for at least twelve years, from first grade through high school, and still we say "I don't know". Dashes and apostrophes and colons continue to make us hesitate: where oh where is that style manual, we might say. Or, we might also say: Style manual? Oh well, cest la vie. Or paper mache. Or el nino. Whatever.

Alberto Ríos is the author of *The Iguana Killer: Twelve Stories of the Heart*, *The Lime Orchard Woman: Poems*, *Teodoro Luna's Two Kisses*, *Whispering to Fool the Wind*, *Five Indiscretions*, and *Pig Cookies and Other Stories*. He teaches in the Creative Writing Program at the University of Arizona in Tucson.

On Sending Out and Getting Back: Publishing Fiction

STEPHEN DIXON

There are few rules in sending out stories to magazines but many words of advice. My first advice is about readiness. You know you're ready to send your work when you can't improve the piece and when everything you're continuing to do is hurting it. You've worked and you've worked on it, and it's as good as it can be at this particular time.

WHERE TO SEND

Then how do you determine where to send it? You make up a list of where you want to send your work, and you put the magazines you want to be published in most at the top and the magazines you want to be published in least at the bottom, and everything else, in graduating degrees, in the middle. To make the list, you look at a magazine's importance, what it pays, how well and widely it's distributed, how influential a magazine it is, how it looks, whether it takes some pride in its design. You find these magazines by looking at the major annual anthologies like *The Best American Short Stories*, which lists where they got their stories from, and from trade books that deal exclusively with or have sections about magazines. You also find these magazines by browsing through magazine racks of bookstores. But remember, no matter what, sometimes your top choice on the list isn't right for the particular story you have ready, so you go on to the next choice, and so on, till you find, working down the ladder, the one that is best for that story.

Does it help to read the magazine you're sending to? Of course— because if it only publishes stories by writers who live on the West Coast, and you don't, then you're wasting your time. Or your story might not fit the magazine's themes for the next few issues, or the magazine doesn't take stories with curse words, and so on. Also, it helps to subscribe to a magazine you'd like to be in, especially the literary journals and quarterlies. Subscribing insures, to a degree, that magazine's existence, making it possible for you to send to it in the future. (It also makes that magazine feel it exists not just to have writers try to place stories in it.)

But, no matter what you read or subscribe to, you shouldn't try just to write to fit into a particular magazine's format. Even if fifteen pages is the ideal length for the majority of magazines, it's not the length one should aim for just to increase the chances of being accepted. Each story determines its own length. You should also only send to magazines that you want to be in, that have published writers you've liked or stories by unknown writers you've admired. You also don't want to send to a magazine that endorses a philosophy or style of living that you abhor. It's important, though, to take a chance sometimes. Once, I sent a story to a poetry magazine, saying, "You think you'd be interested in a story every now and then?" and the magazine took it. I had sent the story because I had liked the looks of the magazine and wanted to be in it.

HOW TO SEND

Always send an SASE (self-addressed, stamped envelope) and a short, informal cover letter with your story. A good cover letter won't get you published, but it will increase your chances of getting your story read.

When I first started submitting, the letter would explain who I was and have something in it about my previous publications. I'd thank the editors for looking at my work and let them know there was an SASE in the envelope, just in case they only took out the story. When I started to submit my stories and had nothing or just one or two stories published, I'd say that in the letter. Many magazines like to be the first to publish you or the magazine to publish you in what its editors think will be a distinguished career. (I'm sure I've disappointed many of these magazines that might have thought that of me.)

It can, by the way, sometimes help to have someone else send your work to a magazine for you, with maybe something in a cover letter about how that person appreciates the story. My first published story was sent by a co-worker who happened to be a friend of a magazine editor. I was working for CBS News in New York; Hughs Rudd, a fiction writer, was on the same show with me. He'd heard I also wrote stories and asked to see some, and because he thought a couple of them were more ready to send out than I did, he dispatched them to George Plimpton of the *Paris Review*. Of course, Mr. Plimpton would have to have liked one to take it, but it certainly didn't hurt to have someone he knew and admired screen the story for him.

Some practical advice: If you have a number of stories to send at a time, get a hundred-count box of nine-by-twelve envelopes and lots of stamps. And send "Fourth Class, Manuscript Rates" or "Standard Rates," as it's called today. My experience has been that nine times out of ten, first class is no faster than manuscript rate.

And don't forget to book-keep. When manuscripts are out, keep a list of the magazines you've sent to, what you've sent them, when you sent, the editors' names and addresses, and the titles of your stories, of course. Once a story has been returned, I usually put parentheses around the story's title and the magazine's name. Then, when a story is accepted, I put the name of the magazine and the story's title under a third listing, "Stories Accepted."

WHAT NEXT?

What should you expect when you're expecting? Expect a long wait, for most magazines. Expect the story to be rejected. Expect nothing, but hope for the best. The chances are small (but they're there) of a story being accepted, unless you're one of the few writers with name recognition like John Updike, Cynthia Ozick, Philip Roth, Robert Stone, and John Barth.

But how long should you wait? For major magazines, a month, since they have larger staffs. For small magazines—journals, quarterlies—two months. Some magazines can take up to six months.

My strategy for dealing with the length of time (and this may only work for an established writer) is that I generally give a magazine about six weeks to consider my story before I begin pestering it politely ("If you haven't received my story—title—which I sent six weeks ago, or you've received it and are still considering it, or you rejected it some time ago and sent it back, could you please let me know?"). And I always include a self-addressed postcard for response. I also say that I'm not asking for the story back; I'm just concerned about its whereabouts ("If you are still considering it, please take your time doing so"). Then I'll send the magazine another polite letter three weeks later.

I give a magazine a three-month maximum before I tell it the story should no longer be considered for publication and that I'm submitting elsewhere. (By this time, I probably already have. See below.)

But I don't send nasty notes to editors who have had my work an egregiously long time (or who have rejected me insultingly). It makes no sense to feel that way. Your work is accepted for the right reasons as well as the wrong reasons, and a story can be rejected for the right reasons as well as the wrong ones, too. Just take a hint, though: Three or four straight rejections via form rejection slip, or with comments that indicate the editor or editorial staff doesn't think much of your work, and you should stop sending to that magazine.

I also don't phone magazines asking about my story, where it is and so forth. Nor do I ever want to meet the editor. Best that you know an editor solely through correspondence (if you happen to meet an editor at a party, that's a different story) and that you keep your correspondence thoughtful, civil, informative, and short.

MULTIPLE SUBMISSIONS

Not everyone in the business will agree with me, but I recommend multiple submissions.

My reasoning is, if a magazine takes six months to look at your story, why not send it to another magazine, of comparable worth, at the same time, or two or three other magazines?

You should only multiply submit to magazines of comparable worth, though, since if one accepts it while it's still out at another magazine, you won't feel you've lost anything. But if a low-tier magazine accepts your story while it's still being reviewed by a better magazine, you might feel you've made the wrong decision in letting the lower-tier magazine look at it before the better magazine has had a chance to reject or accept it.

I've been "caught" a few times, in my multiple submissions, or let's say "reprimanded," and that's over thirty-five years, and we're speaking here of thousands of submissions. The first magazine's editors said, "You wasted our precious editorial time. We have a small staff with thousands of manuscripts to read, so we can't be reading stories that are simultaneously submitted elsewhere. Don't bother sending to us again." (I did send them a story, though, after a waiting period of two years so they could cool off and maybe change editors, and they accepted it.)

In another case, a magazine's editor, from whom I had retracted a story that had been accepted elsewhere, said, "Great. Though we wanted to publish it, and I was just sitting down to write you an acceptance letter, it's much better for you as a writer to have the story in *Harper's*—greater distribution, attention and money. Try us again soon." (I did, and that magazine took my stuff.)

I now don't multiply submit to magazines whose editors I have a written relationship with or who have accepted my work in the past. (After a while, I get to know what stories of mine certain editors prefer, and I send those editors those kinds of stories—certain page limits, topics, language.)

MORE ON THE "TIER METHOD"

It used to take me twenty submissions to place a story; now it takes about five. To increase my chances of getting accepted, I send to what I consider the four or five best magazines in this country (*The New Yorker*, *Harper's*, *The Atlantic Monthly*, *Esquire*, and, in the old days, *Playboy*). I send to them, as I said before, because of their circulation and reputation and because they pay well—enough money, when one of them took just one story of mine, to keep me solvent for half a year. Not to mention that the chances of getting a story included in a major anthology are better if the story's been in a major magazine.

But the truth is, out of the more than four hundred stories I've published, I've managed to sell about twelve stories to major magazines. So, after the first four or five big guys reject my story, the odds of placing it start increasing, because I then send to what I consider the very best literary magazines: again, the ones that have the greatest circulation, reputation, and that pay the most.

If the story's rejected by one of these—there are actually about ten top literary magazines—then I go a tier below: magazines that pay less, have a small circulation, but a reputation as good as the top literary magazines, and so on. Tier by tier I drop, until I'm on the fifth or sixth tier—magazines that pay nothing and have almost no circulation or reputation and from which a story was never taken by a literary anthology.

By this time, I just want my story placed. Sometimes I have to send to five or ten of these lower-tier magazines before one takes my story. And usually I really just want to get my story in a magazine before it comes out in a book-length story collection, which, after two or three years of having a story rejected, is pretty close.

HOW MANY STORIES?

How many stories should you send to a given magazine at once? Most writers send one story at a time, but here are two anecdotes to help you decide.

The first time I submitted a story to a magazine, *The Atlantic Monthly*, I sent five; this was in 1964. The three other Stegner fellows at Stanford University, where I was writing at the time, said I was crazy to send so many, and Mr. Stegner himself said a writer should sent out two at the max, but preferably one. His point was that you reduce your chances of getting a story accepted by sending out so many because an editor will react against such a potential reading load, and to the writer's inability to weed out the wrong stories for that magazine, and reject all the stories summarily. But, at that time, I'd already written about twenty publishable stories and thought, *Why not give the editor a wide range of my work*? After all, how did I know what he'd like? In the end, the editor took one for an "Atlantic First," returned three, and said he was holding the fifth for future consideration as a regular *Atlantic* story, though he eventually sent that last one back.

I once sent the *South Carolina Review* three stories, and it took all three and published them in the same issue along with an editor's forward to the stories, making it a bigger deal than it would have been if the journal had only published one.

OTHER WAYS THAT STORIES GET TAKEN

Stories are taken in all sorts of ways, some of them unconventional.

Twice after a reading, a magazine editor asked me if a story I'd read was unpublished, and because it was, he took it. Another time, I met the editor of *American Review* at a literary cocktail party, the first I'd ever gone to (I'd avoided them until I was dragged to this one: "You might meet someone who'll do some good for your work"). At the party, the editor approached me and said, "You look like a writer," and we talked, and he said to send my stories to his magazine. I told him I had sent several times already and had been rejected in the oddest of ways: One story had been returned to me in an SASE that wasn't mine; another time, I didn't get my stories back but I *did* get, not in my SASE but in a

Jiffy bag, the galleys to *The Gay American Cookbook*. The third time, I told him, I got my own SASE back, but it was empty.

So the editor, hearing this, said, "Oh, send to me directly," and I said I had, but I left that party and did as he said and he took my story in a week. (So I'm saying it probably helps to go to literary cocktail parties or the equivalent thereof—conferences, readings—and perhaps even come to know someone at a magazine or know someone who knows that person, and that can sometimes expedite the reading of your submitted work.)

Sometimes stories get taken quite by accident. I have sent, by mistake (my list system, see page 263, isn't infallible), the same unchanged story to the same editor of a magazine a year or two after it was rejected there, and it was then accepted, with the editor not even suggesting that he'd previously seen it. Maybe it had been rejected by an editorial assistant the first time, but I wasn't naive enough to ask the editor that once it had been taken.

Sometimes, the editorship of a high-tier magazine might change, and I'll send a story to them that's already been sent to a low-tier magazine. It's worked a couple of times. A couple of times, though, I also had to write that low-tier magazine a note saying a story should no longer be considered for publication because it's been accepted by *Harper's* or *The New Yorker*.

GETTING IN, GETTING CLOSE
Actually, that latter citing would be a lie. I've never had a story in *The New Yorker*, though I have had about 150 stories rejected by them in the last thirty-four years. In fact, there was a story of mine I didn't like much, "Ann from the Street." I thought it was the weakest story I'd ever written and didn't destroy. So I sent it to *The New Yorker*, feeling, they've rejected every other kind of story of mine, maybe this one is a story they'd like for some reason I don't know about. They wrote back the most favorable rejection I'd ever received from them, even up until today. *We almost took it*, they wrote. *The story was as well received here as anything you've sent us. It was very close. Very close.*

STICKING WITH IT
Above all, don't fret rejection. What's the alternative, giving up? If we're talking of just the act of writing, why would you give it up if you love to write and there's an inner urgency to write? Rejections of

your manuscript shouldn't kill your writing. What should probably kill it, because I don't think good writing comes from writers who don't like to write or are only in it for the fame, success, and money, is that the act of writing no longer gives you any pleasure, or there isn't, you feel, any need to write anymore and you won't feel the loss if you stop writing.

But if we're talking about submitting your work to editors and judges, why not continue to submit it if you think the work is good enough to be accepted and published? How is the work going to help you as a writer if it just sits in your desk drawer or on your WP disk? Nobody's been rejected more than I have, and probably not many writers have had as many serious literary stories accepted as I have had. Rejections and acceptances usually go hand in hand. And I have to admit that I did give myself a couple of six-months-or-else ultimatums about getting a piece published, but those deadlines came and went and I continued writing with the same enthusiasm and love of the craft and at the same feverish pace as I always had, even though editors didn't meet the publishing deadlines I had set for myself. It turned out that the deadlines were just tactics on my part to write even harder and to put even more of myself into what I was writing. After all, nobody plays tricks on themselves more than writers.

And look at it this way, too. The odds may be twenty to one to get a story of yours published, but think of the satisfaction you get when that story is finally accepted. It means you're not the only person in the world to think your work's worth publishing.

And think of it this way, too. Little magazines pay. It might be fifty bucks and it might be a grand. One magazine, a literary one, just sent me a check for $775. Hey, I can use it; I've got expenses, and not just the money it takes to get my typewriter cleaned twice a year. In a good year, you may, if you send out as often as I do, earn three thousand dollars from sales to literary magazines.

And the story might be picked up by a major anthology, like *The Best American Short Stories* or *Prize Stories: The O. Henry Awards*, adding another $500-plus to your annual income.

And an agent might see the story, because she reads that particular literary magazine or annual anthology, and she'll want to represent your longer or collected works.

And before you know it—oh, it might take thirty years—small magazines will be requesting stories from you, though probably no more than two or three times a year.

No, you never want to give up if you have something to write and you feel the urgency to write and there are good, solid, serious magazines and publishers out there that might want your work.

And *you* only know if they do or don't want it, by sending the work.

Don't get discouraged. It only stops you from doing what you, I hope, most love to do, as if anything could stop it for very long.

EXERCISES

1. A man or a woman is sitting on an outside window. Do something with it.

2. A vehicle your character is on is running out of control. The vehicle could be a plane, car, boat, roller skates, bike, skateboard, motorcycle, soapbox cart, you name it. Do something with it.

3. Someone comes up behind your character and grabs him around the neck. Do something with it.

Stephen Dixon has published nineteen books of fiction. His last, *Gould*, a novel, was published by Henry Holt. His last story collection, *Man on Stage: Play Stories*, was published by Hi Jinx Press of Davis, California. He has three books coming out: *Tisch*, a novel (his first completed novel, never before published) from Red Hen Press in California; a story collection—*Sleep* from Coffee House Press; and—*30*—, a novel and a sequel to *Gould*, from Henry Holt. He's been teaching at the Johns Hopkins Writing Seminars since 1980 and has published, although he's stopped counting, around 450 short stories.

ADDITIONAL WRITING EXERCISES

The Truth, the Half-Truth, and Anything but the Truth

Write three sentences about yourself. The first sentence must be true. The second sentence should be partly true. The third sentence should be utterly false. If you want, you can add sentences at the end. Example: "My name is Peter Gadol, and I grew up in Westfield, New Jersey. Westfield is where Charles Addams lived for a time, and where, one sultry August afternoon, I found him sketching our steep and weathered Victorian house. He was hot, so I invited him inside for some lemonade and introduced him to my rather hirsute cousin and my wax-bald uncle. I'll never forget the queer smile that broke across the cartoonist's face." Now reverse the order and write three more sentences about yourself. The first sentence must be completely false. The second sentence should carry some truth. The third sentence should be fact. Which was easier, telling the truth first and winding toward imagined lines, or the other way around?

— *Peter Gadol, California Institute of the Arts*

First Lines

Steal the first sentence of a published story you haven't read. Write the first page or so. Example: "It was the best of times. But how could anyone live up to Cindy's hair color . . . ?"

— *Kyle Torke, Elon College*

Writing What You Know

Recall a moment in your childhood when you discovered a secret or realized something momentous about yourself or an important figure in your life. Describe the events of that day. What triggered the discovery?

— *R.A. Sasaki, author of* The Loan and Other Stories

Writing the Recurring Dream

Recall a recurring dream. (If you can't remember any, start keeping a notebook and pen by your bed, and record dreams when you waken.

After a while, you'll notice that certain settings, characters, and/or plots recur.) Try to write the recurring dream, making details as vivid and precise as possible—you may choose to write it as a story, or a poem, or a sketch, or as unstructured prose.

— *Susan Hubbard, University of Central Florida*

Fantasy and Invention

Write several short paragraphs describing various fantasies of yours, ones you've had in the past or ones you give yourself as you write. Allow the fantasies to be as wild as they are in your imagination. Write at least one fantasy in each of the following categories: (1) heroic, (2) erotic, (3) revenge, (4) wish fulfillment. Now invent several episodes in the same categories, but make them seem realistic—that is, make everything up, but pretend as if you are writing about something personal, intimate, and autobiographical, and try to convince the reader that these are *most certainly not* fantasies. Use dialogue, action, and thought. Avoid conventional or hackneyed situations.

— *Joe David Bellamy, St. Lawrence University*

Sketches and Portraits

Do three portraits and seven sketches of people you know well, or barely at all. The difference between a portrait and a sketch is mostly one of intensity and speed.

— *Liz Rosenberg, State University of New York at Binghamton*

Working From Photographs

Take a photograph (maybe from a family album but, even better, of a stranger from a collection in the library) or a painting that's always fascinated you, and write the story of that photograph's or painting's protagonist, making sure to develop a fully rounded character capable of surprising us in the process.

— *Lance Olsen, University of Idaho*

Naming

In naming your character, you are making a fairly large decision about his or her identity because many names come prepackaged with assumptions. As a writer, your challenge is to work against such stereotypes and associations attached to certain names. Write a character sketch for each of the following names: Cody, Boris, and Brittany.

You definitely do not want Cody to be a cowboy type, for instance. (Make Cody a woman, for starters.) In your sketch, describe at least the following attributes and preferences: body type/size, coloring (eyes, hair, skin), favorite footwear, kind of vehicle he or she owns (could be a bicycle, in-line skates), kind of vehicle he or she would like to own, occupation, hobby, one passionate habit (cigarette smoking is most obvious), one gesture (for example, rubs one elbow when anxious).

— *Ron Tanner, Loyola College, Baltimore*

Questioning Your Character

You've dreamed up a character about whom you need to know more. Do a ten-minute brainstorming exercise in which you inventory the contents of this character's nightstand or top dresser drawer. Think of the drawer as one of those private catchall spaces in which a person puts miscellany that is too important to throw away but not easily categorized. In other words, you don't want to be listing socks, undies, and T-shirts, but rather the flotsam and jetsam of a life, ranging from a ticket stub to a single earring. Give microhistories of the items as you list them. Does a particular object crop up that has such associative or totemic power that it suggests a whole story? Write it.

— *Suzanne Matson, Boston College*

Motivation

Create a character around this sentence: "Nobody has ever loved me as much I have loved them." Do not use this sentence in the fragment of fiction you write. The sentence comes from Guy Davenport's aunt, Mary Elizabeth Davenport Morrow, via his essay "On Reading" in *The Hunter Gracchus*.

— *Brian Kiteley, University of Denver*

Borrowing Characters

Take a favorite TV or movie character and place him or her in a context completely outside that of the television show or movie. Use what you know about the character to be consistent with the original context but also to develop the character within this new situation.

— *James Reed, The Nebraska Review*

Inventing a Life

Select one of the personals ads from a local newspaper or magazine and construct a life for that person: background, family, personality traits, hobbies, phobias, etc. Although you may choose to write it out, you may also do this in a bulleted list, rather than paragraphs.

— *James Plath, Illinois Wesleyan University*

Show Don't Tell

Take the following character "descriptions," and convert each into a paragraph containing only action. Put the character in an everyday situation. Let the way your character rips apart lettuce for the salad he is making, or the way she gets her cup of tea, show us what these sentences are trying to tell us:

- Maureen was not the kind of girl you would want to marry.
- Ed was crazy, in a good way.
- Ed was crazy, in a bad way.
- Laureline was on the brink of leaving him.

— *Dinty Moore, Penn State Altoona*

Animals as Characters

Animals can serve as useful characters. Think of the importuning Siamese cat sliding between a potentially amorous couple on a couch. Write a scene—involving two or more people—in which an animal asserts/inserts itself. Through this interaction, we should see each personality revealed. Example: Mary's pet iguana, Ted, eats raw hamburger from a bowl under her dining room table while Mary reviews fund-raising plans with her business partner. . . .

— *Ron Tanner, Loyola College, Baltimore*

Disaster Scene

This one is just for fun. Write a disaster scene set at a restaurant. Any sort of disaster will do, but those of a personal/psychological nature tend to be more intriguing—or at least more subtle—than the *Pulp Fiction* kind.

— *Susan Hubbard, University of Central Florida*

Indirection

Imagine a seemingly peaceful family of four—mother, father, daughter, son—sitting at the dinner table. One of them has a confession to make to the family, but is afraid to reveal it. Through the subtleties of body language and dropped hints, the confession is divulged, though it is never explicitly expressed. Who has the confession to make? What is it? How is it divulged? What is the family's reaction? What is the confessor's reaction to the family?

— *Tom DeMarchi, Florida International University, Miami*

Sudden Fiction

Write a sudden fiction of an event that in real time would take five or ten seconds to occur—a death, a fall, a dazzling realization— that takes five pages in your fictive slo-mo.

— *Lance Olsen, University of Idaho*

Short-Shorts

Take a "finished" piece of more than 1,500 words and cut it to 250 words. Don't just cut sentences and paragraphs: Weigh each phrase, image, and word with a view to creating the tightest kernel of a story you can. The point? To find and polish the central point while cutting the unnecessary, the verbose, the carelessly expressed.

— *Robin Sterns, Millikin University*

The Exquisite Corpse (for a Group)

"The Exquisite Corpse" is a popular group exercise for poets, but it works for fiction writers as well. The first writer is responsible for plot point A in the list below. He writes his idea in sentence form, then passes the paper to the second writer, who concocts plot point B, and so on. The resultant seven-sentence stories, of course, are short, strained, and inelegant. But they break away, quite often, from pre-dictability and the "familiar" plots.

1. Write first sentence, introducing one character.
2. Introduce second character and establish conflict.
3. Problem grows more complex.
4. First character speaks.
5. Second character speaks.
6. Climax.
7. Resolution.

— *Dinty Moore, Penn State Altoona*

The Unexpected Point of View

Take a story you might be tempted to write—say, the experience of suffering at the hands of a bully and the way that conflict was resolved, or any other commonplace story—and invert it, presenting the story from the unexpected point of view (in my example, the bully's).

—*Ewing Campbell, Texas A&M University*

Binary Vision

Write a story—in first person—from the point of view of the victim and then from the viewpoint of the perpetrator of a crime.

—*Cynn Chadwick, University of North Carolina at Asheville*

Foreground/Background

Write three to five pages in which you move back and forth (every few paragraphs) between two "fields of action." Have two things going on simultaneously—one on "front stage" with the character(s), and one in the background, for example, with the weather, or what's playing on TV or the radio, or what's going on at the edges of the room, or next door, or down the street.

For instance, two characters are talking and trying to decide what to do about a third person (this is the front-stage action); meanwhile, a big, black thunderstorm is blowing down from Canada and turning over people's garbage cans along the street outside (background action). You'd have a few exchanges of dialogue, then a paragraph or two of description about what's happening out there with the weather. And back and forth like that. Keep going. Don't make connections between these two fields of action for the reader. Just let them exist side by side. Let them make their own sparks. Advice: You may want to write a couple pages of just one field of action first, say the front-stage action, and then write a couple pages of the background action. You can interweave them in the next draft. But definitely try the interweaving. You'll probably discover some interesting echoes.

—*Nance Van Winckel, Eastern Washington University*

Questioning Your Character

Interview your narrator or protagonist. If you ask the right questions, these people will have plenty to say to you.

—*Lucy Ferriss, Hamilton College*

Word Choice

Choose an eclectic batch of nouns, verbs, and adjectives from the dictionary or from memory (or use the following list: *vicuña, arrears, nymph, cholera, tut-tut, beanstalk, undulate,* and *wolfman*); then dream up a minor character who would use all of these words (not necessarily correctly) in a single short paragraph. Write the paragraph.

    —Julie Schumacher, University of Minnesota, Twin Cities

Eavesdropping

Go to a public place, and record a conversation as best you can. After you have a page or so, use the dialogue to create a new scene. Transplant the speakers to an entirely new setting, and imagine their thoughts, their actions, their gestures during the conversation, and use these thoughts, actions, and gestures, along with sense details, to flesh out the scene. Make it as interesting as you can, and if there is not already some tension in the dialogue, try to create some in the characters' actions or in the way they interact with their environment.

    —John Fleming, Saint Mary's College of California

Fast Paced Dialogue

Write a fast-paced three-page dialogue between two characters in which neither allows the other to say more than ten consecutive words. Encounters like the following are permitted.

> "And?"
> "And."
> "And so what?"
> "So what then?"
> "I don't think so."
> "Really. Well, you wouldn't."

The guarantee on this one: Eventually, the voices will begin to distinguish themselves one from the other.

    — Lucy Ferriss, Hamilton College

Learning From Film

Select a small section of a fine film. Start the film. Do not look at the screen. Listen to the dialogue and any other sounds. Replay the same section of film this time with the sound off. Note carefully what you see—where the camera focuses. Now replay that scene watching and listening. Then go to a scene you've written and see how the experience might give you new choices in cutting and adding.

— *Carol Lee Lorenzo, Emory University*

Fight Scene

Make a list of crisis fights you've engaged in (in real life) or battles you've watched people play out before your very eyes. Loud, talky argument fights. Conversations that dissolve into screaming matches. Your sister and her crazy kids at the supermarket, your dad in the backyard shouting at your brother's friends, your apartment mate on the phone with his girlfriend Joy, the one he doesn't much seem to like. Start a story by doing the following: Write a sentence of description to set the scene; focus on the lighting, the place, the atmosphere, the background—where are we? The next ten sentences are dialogue, exclusively, crafted from the fight scene you witnessed. What do you change? What do you leave verbatim? Let the voices escalate, then move back to description, bodies, gestures, and so on. Continue this story by letting this fight lead to even worse trouble for these characters, and conclude it by having them engage in a completely different kind of conversation (perhaps a return to the scene of the original crime?), one that catches them in a different mood, a different light altogether.

— *Heather Sellers, Hope College*

Using Silence

Experience making silence real. Set a scene in twilight; establish its specific conditions in sensory, quickly. Keep it active, changing throughout the scene. Use atmosphere/description in tiny brush-strokes, small amounts of realistic detail, in between dialogue and action. Think of it as making silence tangible. Think of it in the way white space is used in a painting or like the rest sign is used in music. How does dialogue sound when dropped into the silence of twilight? Use the conditions of twilight as the pressure and texture between characters, moving around and between what they say.

— *Carol Lee Lorenzo, Emory University*

Dialect

Choose a way of speaking unique to a character, not just dialect from a part of the country but region combined with class, race, individual experience, and age. (Need help? Take a quick look at *A Confederacy of Dunces* by John Kennedy Toole, *Dolores Claiborne* by Stephen King, or *Push* by Sapphire.) Write a first-person scene so vivid with that speech pattern that your reader can hear the character speak.

— *Robin Sterns, Millikin University*

Now and Then

Write a four-page story in which the plot proceeds in chronological order. Now, rewrite it so that it moves backward in time, from the most recent to the most distant moment. Rewrite it a final time, in which the sequence is out of order entirely, making connections by association and memory rather than by the clock.

— *David Baker, Denison University*

Revisiting Plot

Take a story you like very much, make a photocopy, and cut it into incidents or episodes. Now play with them. See how the story might have worked if the parts were arranged differently. Make an alternate arrangement that you think works. Consider the choices you and the author made.

— *Karen Blomain, Kutztown University of Pennsylvania*

The Absence of Plot

In his book *Making Shapely Fiction*, the late great Jerome Stern includes a section about the kinds of stories you don't want to write, one of which is The Bathtub Story, the story in which nothing really happens: Someone, for instance, sits in a bathtub and thinks about things. But he also includes at the end of the section the charge to break the rules, to ignore all he has said about what not to do, as "great art is formed from the broken rule." Write a scene in which someone is sitting in a bathtub, and write what he or she is thinking. Link five thoughts and their associations back at least ten years. Couple those thoughts with the growing cold of the water or the way the afternoon light through the bathroom window fades—with time passing in the here and now. If you're lucky, you'll know this person's life by the time you're through, and never have left the tub.

— *Bret Lott, College of Charleston and Vermont College*

Playing God

Ernest Hemingway tried thirty-nine different endings for *A Farewell to Arms* before settling on one that he thought worked well enough. For a story you've written, come up with three different endings that are largely external/descriptive, and think about how each ending changes the way the story is read. One should try to end with a line of dialogue, one with a description of a character's action or inaction, and the third with narrative summary.

— *James Plath, Illinois Wesleyan University*

The Use of Things

Make a list of ten common objects you might encounter in a day. For instance: backpack, jar of spaghetti sauce, beat-up tennis shoe, telephone book, carton of eggs, bike tire, father's war medals. Now select one that interests you. Then think of three actions that could include this object. For example: (1) In the grocery store one quiet Sunday afternoon, subject steals a jar of Prego spaghetti sauce. (2) Subject is hurriedly unloading a large bag of groceries from shopping cart to station wagon, jar of Ragú falls through bottom of bag and splatters all over parking lot and several cars. (3) Subject, lying down, reaches under the bed and grabs a jar of Contadina and opens it and sticks his finger in the sauce and eats greedily. Now, take the action you like best and make the character real, begin a story, and see where it takes you.

— *Karen Blomain, Kutztown University of Pennsylvania*

Generating Symbols

Get a fortune cookie or a piece of Bazooka bubble gum—anything that contains a random fortune—and conjure up a symbol (defined as something that stands for something else), then write a short story making the fortune and symbol central to its conflict. Do not alter any words of your fortune, and make sure the title of your story metaphorically reflects the symbol as well.

— *Ricardo Cortez Cruz, Southern Illinois University at Carbondale and Illinois State University*

Gadgets

Research the history of a common device or gadget, paying particular attention to the compelling social and historical elements that moti-

vated its invention. Have a character use this trivial knowledge, perhaps as an anecdote that informs or illumines an activity the character is performing while speaking of or thinking about the device. A character, say, narrates the history of the zipper while making love.
— *Michael Martone, The University of Alabama*

Making Simple Actions Symbolic

Attempt to narrate or describe simple actions (the turning on of a light switch, say) to find, in the difficulty of such simple rendering, the possibilities in the things we take for granted.
— *Michael Martone, The University of Alabama*

The Failed Story

Begin with a failed short story. It must be a story you still care about, one you still believe in on some level. Write three brand-new openings for it, each at least two paragraphs in length. In each new opening, begin the story from a different moment in the action. Don't merely reshuffle already written paragraphs, but generate new material. How does starting your story from a new point create previously unanticipated possibilities for your characters? What happens if you "begin" the story from where your original version left off?
— *Suzanne Matson, Boston College*

Improving Language

Take a scene you have been having trouble with; it can be a few paragraphs or a couple of pages. Highlight all the modifiers. Then, using a second color, go through and highlight only the verbs. Include words like "violated," "shattered," "ran." Now, looking only at the highlighted language, try to see the theme or tone that is implied. Try controlling the pitch of the scene by changing the undertone of those words. If your scene is full of hot modifiers, try using cold words instead. Change "stewing" to "unresponsive," or "faithful" to "exact." If the scene is set out-of-doors, try using modifiers and verbs that convey a sense of containment and repression. Try changing these words to favor one character over another. For example, if Sarah is a potter and Bob is a chemist, write the scene first using words like "cool," "slipped," "molded," and then rewrite it using "precise," "measured," and "reacted."
— *A. Carey-Zúñiga, FIDM College*

INDEX